The Brainwashing of the American Investor

The Book that Wall Street does not want YOU to read!

Written by

Steven R. Selengut

1stBooks - rev. 03/25/02

TABLE OF CONTENTS

PREFACE

This is an "action" book designed to provide a viable, safe(r) and more realistic approach to the Stock Market and to investing in general. It describes a strategy and shows you how to implement it using a strict set of rules. It is different and definitely not mainstream Wall Street propaganda! In fact, we will take every opportunity to explain precisely how it differs from what Wall Street wants you to do or to think. It is also a "work in process", simply because there are always things to learn, questions to raise, and fine-tuning adjustments to consider. Owners of the book are encouraged to join a "forum" where the author's regular releases to clients are published, and where they can raise their own questions as well. Every attempt will be made to define terms and explain concepts throughout the book, but if you are unsure about the meaning of something, raise your question in the Investment Management Forum. (Excerpts from The Forum are included throughout.)

There are places in this book where questions are raised and no answers are provided immediately. This is the plan, not an omission. Readers are expected to think! Too often in the field of investing, formulas are provided, tricks for success are proposed, and gimmicks are sold to the public as though they are "Investment Messiahs". It Just Ain't So! They aren't. Many of the points and opinions raised in this book are repeated for emphasis. The more you hear about something, the more important it is. There is no for sure way to prosper out there. This is one of the things you need to learn. (The Management of Ignorance is discussed in Chapter 6.)

This is an "interactive" book! If you wish to comment upon, raise questions about, or discuss anything that is put forth below, please contact Sanco Services, Inc. We plan to plug any "holes" in the content in as timely a fashion as possible, through The Investment Management Forum, a free discussion list that can be linked to through our Web Site at sancoservices.com. You're input will be helpful.

When you digest the content of this book, *you will realize that it is more than just about discipline; it is a discipline!*

*　　*　　*　　*　　*　　*

The author (through Sanco Services, Inc.) is an Independent Investment Adviser and is registered in several states. All figures, security names, etc. are historical data and should in no way be regarded as a prediction of future events or results.

INTRODUCTION: THE PREMISE

Power! With the possible exception of Washington, D. C., "Wall Street" exerts more power and influence (certainly per square mile) than any other place in the world! Although our government (through the SEC, FTC, FCC, & several other "alphabet soup" entities) tries to regulate and control "the beast", it cannot possibly succeed! Why? "The Street" has grown so powerful (with an assist from a spoon-fed media) that its incredible influence on Washington has become a "special interest group" of mammoth proportions. Additionally, it is so quick to change the appearance of its many enterprises, that the feeble efforts of legislators and regulators are always "too little too late"! The beast rules, there is no doubt about it!

Someone once made the point that: "power corrupts", and "absolute power corrupts, absolutely"! In order to protect the investing/speculating public from being manipulated and abused by this smiling, red-suspendered, "beast" in pinstripes, we probably need volumes of better regulations and an encyclopedia of less self-serving rules of behavior. But, as unlikely as it is that meaningful change will happen any time soon, we need to educate the investing public about how they should interact with those who are conspiring to separate them from their money! It is this conspiracy that really makes Wall Street "tick".

Slaughter On 10th Avenue.com

Once upon a time, a new kid with great potential came to town. **It was speculated that he had communications skills and powers that were light years ahead of the present technology and that all one had to do was sign up, log on, and invest money to become a millionaire!** Thousands of "techies", recognizing the potential of the new kid, wrote tens of thousands of business plans, raised billions of dollars in "seed money", spent small country GNPs on marketing, and ran to their downtown underwriting friends to sell their "dot-coms" to the public.

Now in the land of huge salaries, pinstripes and suspenders that is known with some respect (if not awe) as "Wall Street", there are Financial "INSTITUTIONS" that are charged with many responsibilities, not the least of which is to protect the weak, the ignorant, the uninformed, and the uninitiated from investments, investment plans, ideas, and products that are "UNSUITABLE". These institutions go to enormous lengths to gather information about their customers so that their "Financial Advisors" know exactly the types of investments a person should or should not be making. Thus, they just never let their clients make an investment mistake! Right?

WRONG! **They collect the information to protect themselves from lawsuits, knowing full well that the very structure of the industry** (from the separation of Underwriting and Retail, right down the line to broker commission schedules) **has absolutely nothing to do with what is in the best interests of the client!**

Arm in arm with their "expert" associates in the financial media, the institutions launched their dot-com invasion on an unsuspecting public. Wisdom from the Oracle at Wall Street: buy everything with "dot-com", technology, or tele-anything in its name or product mix. **Beg** (your broker to get you some of that new issue at any price), **borrow** (all the money you can on margin in all of your accounts), **steal** (from your children's educational funds), **and sell all of those boring high quality securities with old-fashioned products and concepts** (food, shelter, clothing, etc.), including your treasury securities, municipal and corporate bonds. THE FUTURE IS NOW. DON'T GET LEFT BEHIND; THIS IS THE NEW FINANCIAL PLAN, an investing utopia where prices only go up and everybody wins! Damn the torpedoes, full speed ahead!

Far away, in the land of Washington, a wizened economic guru cautioned Wall Street and its armies of smooth talking, opinion-for-hire analysts, that their "irrational exuberance" was out of control and that eventually reality would just happen! But no one heeded his sage warnings or those of other (far less well known but equally responsible) professional investors as they continued to caution the public that the speculative fire in the NASDAQ Market was certain to be extinguished, painfully for all involved!

But **the Institutional "Hydra"** continued to produce more "product" to whet the insatiable appetites of "professional financial advisors" everywhere and their ever more greedy "squeezes" (clients). They knowingly continued to pave the road to disaster with their promotions, predictions, and irresponsible marketing of just-about-anything-you-can-conceive-of.com, knowing that they were playing to an unlimited audience of avaricious speculators. A Herculean Rock was needed to stop the immortal beast! None would be found!

The record is unclear as to the forces that initiated what I am about to relate to you, but filtering down through generations of expert opinion (testimony?), is a rumor of a high level meeting that took place between many of the elite institutional CEOs late one evening, **just after their millennium hoax had played itself out**. Sitting around an impressive mahogany conference table amidst magnums of champagne, tins of caviar, and other pretentious symbols of their great status and power, they developed a wealth enhancement scheme whose brilliance is lauded throughout Leavenworth to this very day! No one really knows who is responsible, but Financial Institution CEOs have no shortage of MBAs from whom they can freely borrow ideas to call their own. Here is how this one played out as the "chiefs" engineered the latest move from greed to fear:

Engineering The Move From Greed To Fear

The Chairperson speaks: "As you all know, our institutional money machine is transaction driven. It doesn't matter what the client does, or with whom, so long as he does something! So let's start to move some of our own trading account dollars back into securities with some real value. We'll take our profits in the technology sector slowly so nobody notices right away. Then, we'll start to talk about those old-fashioned "Asset Allocation" ideas, and start to promote our "Quality Mutual Funds" that have been such dogs for two years."

"Now one of our high priced law firms has suggested that we could have some very serious class action suits if NASDAQ crashes, so we have to create an "illusion of innocence"! It has to appear as though our clients were properly advised to put all their money into (those ridiculously speculative) NASDAQ securities. The problem has to be something totally out of our hands, so we're going to create the perception of an economic downturn. First, we'll play up a few "surprise" dot-com failures. (No one seems to care that 95% of all restaurant start-ups fail, but then we've never tried hard enough to take them public. Maybe next year!) Next, we'll lay off some "pinstripes", and create some negative figures in a few technology areas. Ever since we banded together to exploit this news hungry media, "self fulfilling prophecies" like this one are a piece of cake to get rolling!"

"It won't take long for the media sharks to dive into the water and create a panic of about the same proportion as the one we created with that ingenious computer loop back in '87. We'll "double dip" big time on this one. Money will be flying all over the place as the fools (Wall Street jargon meaning "the clients") sell everything we just convinced them to buy, and begin buying the new stuff we just purchased for our own accounts. I bet we can even get the FED to start lowering interest rates! Then we'll be able to sell fixed income securities again. Hmmm, I never could understand why people like bonds better at lower yields than at higher ones! I don't know about you guys, but I've always appreciated those invisible 3% mark ups a lot more than commissions! This is just too easy! I can see the headlines: **May Day! May Day! NASDAQ Flight 1999 has crashed and burned; the Body Count is High; there are Few Survivors!"**

"I guess that's about it for the overall plan. **Now, whose turn is it to have an analyst that predicted this crash?** This is a "biggie" so let's go with someone who's pretty well established; none of us needs another million-dollar salary to support. Right? Make sure you get all of your people to push the same story about the economy. Then, if my interview on CNBC goes the way it should, we should be "in the clear" again. Just brilliant! We'll discuss the duration of this new "rally" in the Quality and Value Sector at our next meeting. That one's in Rio, isn't it?"

Brain Washing The American Investor

Wall Street firms spend billions of dollars annually to make people transact; to move their money from one financial product to another; to change direction. One firm's recent advertising campaign headline is: "Move Your Money!" Most investors (people who have money to invest) are unqualified to make investment decisions. Most of the brokers and financial planners from whom they buy "Investment Products" are equally unqualified, if not intellectually, at least motivationally!

People are encouraged to be speculative by the media, by the brokerage firms, and by their peer groups. If you were to take a poll, you would find that the majority of people wouldn't be able to distinguish between investing and speculating. They aren't trained to think in those terms. Risk, what's that? There are hundreds of thousands of people out there who couldn't begin to tell you anything about the structure of a mutual fund! It's your responsibility to either know what you're doing, or to hire someone who does. **Why do you think Wall Street wants you to think that you know what you are doing? So that you will transact, and "move your money "!**

You are expected to believe that Wall Street has your best interests at heart, and that they are not at all responsible when one of their recommendations goes bad. They may lead you down the speculative path to destruction but you are ultimately responsible.

Wall Street sells to a "Get Rich Quick" mentality. If you get caught up in that approach, you can count on failure in the long run. You'll find yourself crying about your bad luck or the dismal economy. But it's totally your own fault for trying to do part-time what Wall Street professionals fail to do full time.

Wall Street sells its products as cost effectively as it can through its least experienced, and hungriest employees. It is more than likely that these are the people you will be in contact with unless you do something about it. Why would you take advice from anyone who has no investments of his or her own? If the idea fails, was it yours, his, or one of those "we thinks" that Wall Street know-nothings promote so ardently? It's your money at risk and it's your fault. It's your fault for listening to "wet behind the ears", self-proclaimed experts with little or no experience, other than canvassing the telephone book for suckers. It's your fault for accepting simple sales propaganda as "research material" just because it comes from a high salaried MBA at a prestigious Wall Street firm. AND, if you do it the "new fashioned" way, it's your own fault for fantasizing that minimal or zero commissions and ON-LINE TRADING CAPABILITIES make you a "savvy investor"!

Stop the crying and learn from your mistakes. Yes, you blew it all by yourself through your own greed or fear. **Try to keep in mind that Wall Street is the single most powerful sales entity in the world and it will always make a fool of you if you allow it to. Every firm is the same! EVERY ONE, PERIOD! No one out there has even the slightest respect for your intelligence, and why should they?** You gleefully allow yourself to be manipulated all the time. Do you have a strategy? Does your Financial Advisor? Just what is the difference between Financial Planners and Financial Advisors, Investment Advisors and Investment Managers? (This is covered in some detail at the end of Chapter One.) Most people have no clue as to investment strategy, but establishing a viable operating plan is a huge step in assuring that an investment program will work. Employee "Financial Advisors" and commission driven "Financial Planners" can neither afford to have a strategy of their own nor can they be expected to make you operate within yours! Why? Because it requires an ability to say "No, Mr. Client, I won't do that for you, its not going to help you meet your objectives", or something to that effect. YOU DON'T WANT A "YES MAN" AS AN ADVISOR!

Just as a test, ask your guy to do something that you know is wrong for you and see what happens. Better yet, tell him you're going to receive a $50,000 windfall and see, not only what is recommended but, more importantly, what questions are asked before the recommendations are made.

Find yourself a method of identifying reality! Find statistics you can look to that mean something and that are not controlled or manipulated by Wall Street. For example: why after 100 years without an over-the-counter stock in the Dow Jones Industrial Average, were two added in 2000? Are the indices designed to report the performance of the stock market or that of the economy? Why do stronger "performers" constantly replace weaker ones in the DJIA and S & P average? Because the averages and indices are in competition with one another...it doesn't matter what they actually mean! And just what is performance anyway? (See Chapter Five.)

The Dow Jones Industrial Average was originally designed to be an indicator of the direction of the overall economy. Over the years it was changed only to reflect major changes in the structure of the economy, such as the growth of the services sector, etc. As an economy moves from agrarian, to industrial, to service, such changes are appropriate. Companies that either went out of business or changed industries through divestiture or acquisition were replaced with ones that were more in tune with the present. BUT, they were always well known New York Stock Exchange Companies, and the objective of the exercise was to provide a useful "leading indicator" of the economy. A tool. The S & P 500 average (I believe) had a similar "modus operendi" until recently.

Now we simply have a horse race between the two averages. "What can we do to make the DOW more reflective of what's going on in the stock market?" How can we keep these averages climbing? These are totally new questions, and the "answers" to them have totally changed the meaning and usefulness of these once well-respected numbers. They are just a few more instruments in the "Wall Street" orchestra; subject to whatever "beat" the power "conductor" wants to "go on" in the new "Wall Street" season.

Further complicating this whole scenario (How much money it must have taken to sneak this one by the regulators boggles the mind!) are the new and improved index funds! Have a huge, but dying "Bull Mastiff" in your firm's trading account? Just get it placed in one of the averages and, "abra-kadabra"; it instantly becomes the best performer on The Street for the week! A thousand puppet-like account managers must run out and buy the correct "weighting" of the stock for their portfolios, regardless of the investment merits of the company! Now tell me, does this sound anything like investing to you? The index funds were a huge mistake that will be painful to correct.

Wall Street is always selling something, and they always try to follow the path of least resistance. The person you are speaking to and relying upon is someone's employee, and it is not likely that he is allowed to be an independent thinker. You can also bet that he or she will do (buy, sell, borrow, short) absolutely anything you ask. Keep looking until you find someone who has the backbone to say "NO"!

Whatever Wall Street is pushing, under analysis, will turn out to be better for them than it is for you. They just don't try to make less money! It's your money and your responsibility to find out what's going on. WHAT ARE THEY SELLING NOW? Is it really a bad economy and a correcting stock market? GET REAL! Forget the averages, they've been manipulated too long and are no longer valid. Avoid "snake oil" salesmen in pinstripes and suspenders. Establish a plan. Adopt a strategy.

The brainwashing of the American investor is certainly nothing new, nor is it something that is going to go away any time soon. And the purpose of this book is not to complain or to cry about it either. In fact, I absolutely love it! **The purpose of this book is to teach you how to use the process to your advantage; how to keep one step ahead of this manipulative beast; to use "them" as surely as "they" try to use you.** You can make money in the markets with a minimum of risk through the proper use of simple tools (but, not the ones you hear being advertised) and information. Managing your assets is the same as any other form of management. You must establish reasonable GOALS and OBJECTIVES. If you don't PLAN, ORGANIZE, CONTROL and DIRECT what is going on; if you don't establish RULES, GUIDELINES, STRATEGIES, and PROCEDURES; you will fail.

In the chapters that follow, you will learn one of two things. You will EITHER learn how to manage your assets safely and productively toward the achievement of clearly stated objectives OR you will come to the important conclusion that you need to find someone to manage your assets for you. Not everyone is equipped emotionally or intellectually (too smart is not a good thing here) to be a successful investor. Analysis of the incredible amount of information out there can become paralytic. **You will also learn a whole lot about the investment minefield we lovingly call Wall Street, and that education starts right now!**

Shooting From the Hip (Contributed by a Wall Street Source Called "Deep Pockets")

"Deep Pockets" is a real live person and a top producer at a major brokerage firm. His "claim to fame" is that he has been successful as a broker while maintaining his integrity. He does what his clients ask him to do, but not without stating his opinion. So, you say, what's the big deal? You'll learn. This is the first of a series of contributions from **"Deep Pockets"**:

*   *   *   *   *   *   *

"What a snowstorm! I awoke to eighteen inches of fresh snow that January morning (The blizzard of '77). As a resident of Northwest New Jersey who loved to ski and to snowmobile, it would have been a welcome sight on any other day, but not this day! That day I had an interview with a major Wall Street Wire House (brokerage firm)! A father of one with a schoolteacher wife and graduation from Business School only a few months away, I needed a job! The radio had announced the closing of the New York Stock Exchange for the day, but maybe someone in the Personnel Department of this Wall Street giant was waiting to interview me."

"I took a chance and drove to the train station. This was the start of an incredible journey! Not the one to New York City that day, but the one to a twenty-five year career on Wall Street that has seen it all, taken some bruises, and taught some valuable lessons."

"The first day back from training class was filled with optimism. A new career, passing the Series Seven exam, and a $1,000 a month training salary...life just couldn't get much better. In my wildest dreams I couldn't have imagined what was lying just ahead. We were called "Account Executives", the first of many titles to follow and replacing that of "Customers' Man". **Each week we had a sales meeting where we learned the name of the new "Stock of the Week".** Wall Street had few products back then. There were stocks and there were bonds, and perhaps a fixed income unit trust. Forget Mutual Funds! People were still reeling from their losses in the big bear market of the early seventies."

"Each week we "cold called" name after name in the phone book; thousands of calls. I reviewed all of the key points about the stock of the week, but there were few, and I mean very few buyers. People didn't want to hear the word "equities" and, having been burned in the wake of one of the greatest secular bull markets in history, people hated Stockbrokers. Once again the "buy at any price" mentality burned the masses. Buy and sell disciplines had been thrown out the window as P/E (price divided by earnings) ratios went from single digits to one hundred and two hundred times earnings. As valuations adjusted from their unreasonable levels, the correction of the early seventies brought great pain to investors. People couldn't get enough at two hundred times earnings, yet no one wanted the same issues when they were cheap. The "stock of the week" never seemed to work out too well either. They moved up a point or two (at a time when that was a big move) that week, only to move back down as they became a source of funds for the next "stock of the week". So it went month after month. Few of the trainees survived!"

"Eventually the correction was over and people warmed up to equities once again. It started with gaming stocks (Atlantic City) and spread to the oils, through the banks, on to the Blue Chips, then into technology and on to the "net". The markets have boomed and busted through the eighties, the nineties, and into the new millennium. **The Wire Houses have managed people's money until it has disappeared.** One scam after another: Partnerships that sold everything from oil and gas to horse semen; Mutual Fund after Mutual Fund (now over 6,000), all designed to make you (the investor) rich, "loaded" and "no-load", chock full of fees, each taking its turn in the limelight and then becoming just another fund."

"New launches were always timed to the current hot sector, always buying in at the top and always marketed based on the past, or most recent performance. And so it goes, the cheap funds (sectors out of favor) get sold and the most expensive funds (hot sectors) get bought. The cycle goes on and on: "Buy High, Sell Low", over and over again! The markets (powered by our great economy) over time move higher and higher. The brokers move from firm to firm (for the front money), and the investors try to get even. A few investors have a plan and the discipline to follow it. The masses fall into the cycle. The smart ones hire someone who knows what they are doing, someone who brings reason to the investment process and keeps emotion out."

"I started doing business with an Investment Manager some twenty years ago. I have watched his investment process bring accounts to new high levels through all of the market cycles just described. There a few items that set his investment style apart from the Wall Street crowd":

"Buy Low, Sell High! What a great idea. No, he didn't invent it, but he put it into practice on a disciplined basis. He buys stocks when they are cheap, letting someone else be the hero who has paid the all time high price for a given company."

"Stock analysts make recommendations for many reasons. All too few of those reasons are designed to provide you with timely investment advice. Think about this: over 90 percent of all Wall Street recommendations are on the buy side. Less than 5% are on the sell side! Why? Sometimes a firm has a lucrative investment banking (underwriting) relationship with a company and a strong rating is a reward for doing business with the firm. Can a Wire House (and those in the syndicate) bring a billion dollar deal to investors and then rate the stock a sell? I don't think so. When other analysts on the street collectively see only good things for a stock, it takes a lot of guts to go against the tide and offer a negative rating individually. If you're wrong your career may be over. Why all of these recommendations anyway? Commissions! Typically a lower rating follows bad news and a large drop in the price of the stock. Too late!"

*   *   *   *   *   *   *

The Learning Curve: Not Just a Box of Chocolates

You are about to embark on a learning experience just as revealing as the one "Deep Pockets" began more than twenty-five years ago. Open your mind! New ideas are coming at you that could permanently change the way you look at things financial. You will begin to question what "Wall Street" experts put out there for you to believe. You will start to question the index numbers, averages, and analytical garbage that pollute the airwaves. You will become free of the "drugs" Wall Street uses to manipulate your every financial move!

Listed below (in no particular order) is a selection of thoughts, concepts, and considerations that you will probably not agree with or even thoroughly understand. A few chapters from now, you will!

"In thirty years of investing, I've been unable to find a correlation between a calendar 'year' and any meaningful investment, economic, business, market, or interest rate cycle."

"We won't hesitate to caution you now that **paper profits increase nothing but hat size. Control your greed with some profit taking.**"

"One of the advantages of dealing with individual stocks is that you can selectively take profits on 'winners' and reinvest the proceeds either in undervalued issues, or income producers. **Thus, you are never 'out' of the market and, more importantly, never caught without cash when a correction (inevitably) happens.** By the way, corrections only become visible when it's too late to prepare for them."

"Ultimately, **the income generated by your assets is more important than their current market value.** Realized income pays the bills!"

"Stop analyzing, charting, predicting, reading, reviewing, classifying, and crying. It's time for action"

"The best way to reduce your taxes is with your vote. It is never smart to lose a dollar (on a fundamentally sound investment) to pay 30 cents less in taxes."

"Trading absolutely always produces more growth in capital, more growth in income, and more inflation insurance than any other strategy."

"Portfolio management is the effort to achieve personal goals and objectives using a stable strategy. Speculation, on the other hand, is a 'lotteryesque' approach that seeks a shortcut to the objective while introducing excessive risk into the process. **99% of all speculators think of themselves as 'investors'.**

"Averages and Indices are investment tools designed to provide investors with a sense of direction, but not of a particular portfolio! **There is no clear relationship between any of these tools and the actual performance of any properly diversified portfolio.**"

"Profit taking is a management or business decision. It is not an attempt at 'timing' or an effort to predict the future. **Profit taking throttles greed and protects wealth.** The problem with most investment strategies is that they are based on the premise that the future direction of the market is predictable. It isn't."

"**To benefit from a correction, you must take action during the rally.** Trading eliminates dangerous positions in overpriced securities and replaces them with safer ones in 'undervalued' issues. We think of it as correction insurance.

"**Working Capital is expected to rise every year, even if the market crashes and interest rates rise.** It's a totally new and different kind of analytical tool."

"**Aggressive trading of quality issues is a winning strategy**, period. Aggressive selection of high-risk securities without a 'sell' discipline is not."

"**Most market gurus will advise you too late to unload** last year's favorites and, unfortunately, they don't have the courage to recommend new names until significant moves to the upside have been made."

"Anything that goes up in price for an extended period of time becomes vulnerable, particularly when the pace of the rise has been fast. For the Mutual Fund investor, the similarity to a chain letter is very real. **Someone is going to be left holding a bag full of securities purchased at the highest prices in the history of mankind.**"

"Investors look for opportunities which fall within particular pre-defined guidelines. **Speculators look for good 'bets' based on biased research they receive from paid analysts, and commissioned sales persons.** The point is that plain vanilla management guidelines can get you through the whole investment exercise with less expense, less frustration, and more success than all the Wall Street 'wisdom' combined."

*   *   *   *

<u>IN THE BEGINNING, THERE WAS MONEY!</u>

*   *   *   *

CHAPTER ONE: INVESTMENTS 101

Most of us come out of high school and even college with absolutely no knowledge of securities, investing, retirement planning, etc. "Investments 101" is rarely listed in any non-business curriculum; and, even if it were, how much attention would be given to the subject by a group of people so unlikely to have any funds available for investment? Most people go out into the business world barely able to balance their own checkbook!

If you're lucky, Mom and Dad had some money and took the time to explain some of the basics to you (if they really understood them themselves). They may even have developed a personal or IRA portfolio for you over the years to get you started more comfortably. Still, it's likely that your first experience with investing (without parental assistance) was with a Stock Broker, an Insurance Agent, a Banker, an Employee Benefits person, or some other form of Financial Planner. **With the possible exception of the Employee Benefits Person, all of these individuals (even the banker) feed their families with the commissions or other financial incentives they receive for placing your money in various forms of** *"Investment Products".*

Investment Products

Could you hear the disdain in my keystrokes as I typed the words "Investment Products"? The reason for this is that I belong to the old fashioned school of investing that considers portfolio design, development, and management a very personal exercise. How can a packaged product be right for thousands, even millions of people? How does one know what he owns, etc? Believe it or not, investment products are relatively new on the investment scene.

In the 1970's there were very few Mutual Funds of any kind, and public participation Money Market Funds didn't exist at all. Today there are more Mutual Funds than there are common stocks listed on the New York Stock Exchange! It's just incredible how these "products" have become so popular and it's more incredible still how Wall Street has made the investing public love them so well. Most people would tell you that they are "safer than the stock market"! Many don't even realize that their Mutual Funds are Common Stock Portfolios!

So clever is Wall Street, particularly when it comes to their seduction of the media, that one often hears statements on the radio that, to a professional investor, sound like the screech of something metallic on a grammar school chalk board. So "news-thirsty" is the media that they will publish any and all analyst predictions just to sell papers, gain market share, woo listeners from other stations, and so on. The newscaster, commentator, or analyst will explain things matter-of-factly in terms that he fully expects everyone not only to understand, BUT TO ACCEPT as the proper way of doing things in the investment world! For example, the other day a radio commentator was analyzing the impact of a court ruling that would allow a well-known company to remain intact. "Well", he speculated, "you can expect a spike in the stock price because portfolio managers will load up on the stock *so that their quarterly reports show how smart they were to have held a large position in it"*. How smart they were indeed! How stupid do they think the Mutual Fund buying public really is? You don't need to hear the answer, BUT the point is that this media "expert" (that people rely on, at the least for factual information and at the most for solid advice) didn't go on to offer any cautionary remarks about the validity of those quarterly reports or about the morality of the practice. Is the Mutual Fund performance statistics "con game" an "institution" in and of itself? Do you really want to be there?

Similarly, a few weeks earlier, a commentator was explaining how fund managers are compensated, evaluated by their bosses, and rated by analysts. The performance of the funds they manage is compared with the performance of other funds managed by other managers in the same or different investment houses.

Superficially this could even sound fair. But isn't what is advertised as "most important" (i.e., the interests of the client) missing? If they are awful its ok because everyone else was pretty bad too! The only way they could all be bad at the same time, as they generally are, is if they all invest in the same securities and take the same amounts of risk! What does that tell you? Is this the result of what the investor wants or what the speculators insist upon? Probably neither, it's what the culture (see below) demands.

In any event, some investment products are an easy and acceptable method of investing for people who are just getting their portfolios started. The larger the asset base, the less need for this type of investing. As the asset base gets larger, so does the commission prize for product salespersons. **The Insurance Industry is easily in first place when it comes to concealing the risks of the stock market within products that were originally designed to preserve estates and provide retirement income!** It took many years for company lobbyists to pressure State Insurance Departments into allowing them to attach mutual funds to Insurance and Annuity Contracts. Most owners of these contracts have no idea of the dangers involved! Mutual Funds, contrary to what the public has been led to believe, were once considered so risky that they were not acceptable securities for satisfying margin borrowing requirements, and that was when those requirements were pretty lax anyway! Neither were the vast majority of over-the-counter (OTC) stocks traded in the NASDAQ market acceptable as collateral! **Many funds and OTC stocks remain in the "unacceptable" category today!**

I totally believe in the concept that Life Insurance is an essential element of most personal financial plans, as a provider of valuable protection. I'm not even opposed to the idea that whole life insurance is important to force younger people to save. BUT, I seriously question the wisdom of using a cumbersome, committee orientated, entity like an insurance company to manage one's investments. It is totally irresponsible for the insurance industry to attach equity mutual funds of questionable quality to such

3

important contracts. It is nothing short of shocking to think that the present administration in Washington is considering releasing a portion of Social Security Trust Funds to individuals! Have they totally lost their minds? Or, has "The Street" injected so much false wisdom into the minds of Americans that they actually believe that the man in the (other) street can succeed in the investment world.

WHO WILL BE THE WINNERS? AND THE LOSERS?

Similarly, I feel very strongly in favor of the use of a deferred annuity contract to develop a cash pool that can either be "annuitized" (converted into a guaranteed lifetime series of monthly payments) or liquidated to become a part of a larger managed retirement portfolio. BUT, annuities are not for the wealthy! They are self-liquidating entities designed specifically for the protection of people with limited assets (i.e., those who have less than enough capital to generate the income needed for retirement). Variable Annuities should be outlawed entirely. Neither the buying public nor insurance company sales people are sophisticated enough to appreciate the risks involved! (See Chapter Seven)

As a stock market investor, you should not be interested in the vast majority of "investment products" anyway. If you understood them better, you wouldn't be. There is no doubt that individually managed portfolios do better in the long run (compared with the averages) than Mutual Funds, no matter how creative the fund managers "Model Record Keeping" happens to be. However, investment management needs to be done more frequently than evenings and weekends. You have to decide how serious you are about running your own portfolio. Delegating the management to a personally unknown Mutual Fund Manager is (to me) a pretty scary idea!

Finally, don't think for a minute that Mutual Funds are cheaper than individually managed portfolios. If Wall Street made little or no money from them, why would they push them so hard? Think about it, and then see what "Deep Pockets" has to say in Chapter Seven.

"Wall Street" Corporate Culture

Raise your right hand if you've ever had a boss. Keep that hand in the air if you've worked in a large company in either a supervisory or managerial position. If your hand is up, you know about "corporate culture". This is one of those wonderful euphemisms for describing the amount of independent expression that is allowed within an organizational structure. Can you speak your mind? Does your boss really want your input? How much interest do your superiors have in your advancement? How do your peer level managers spend their day? Remember "the Peter Principle" of organizations: "people in organizations tend to rise to their levels of incompetence"! Truer words were never spoken and, consequently, more time is spent in trying to impress the boss, in forming alliances, and in seeking higher salary levels than is spent in doing the work of the organization. Having lunch or after work activities with the "right" people is the way to get ahead in large organizations. **Independence, honesty, integrity, long hours, and hard work are just not "the right stuff".**

Wall Street is no different. **The most important thing to the drones, the analysts, the money managers, the investment committee members, and everyone else is their own career and the amount of money they will make.** When a BMW Salesman gets restless, and has learned to stretch his nose high enough in the air, off he goes to Mercedes, but only for a signing bonus, benefits, etc. Funny how the "BMW growth fund" he was managing/analyzing/selling is no longer better than the "Mercedes fund" he owes his allegiance to now. And what will be "best" next month? The job is to advance the career. The method used is the same in large organizations of all varieties and in all industries: "kissin' up" moves the career along. That's what it's all about.

You will not get a whole lot of independent thought and advice from your contacts in big companies. They sell what their superiors want them to sell and they tell what they are told to tell. Your interests are secondary, at best. Never lose sight of this! Go one step further. When a Wall Street analyst does "original research" at my.new.mousetrap.com, do you honestly think that he's going to receive an honest appraisal of the company's prospects? If one of your employees told the press how bad your products are selling, what would you do?

The balance of this section is devoted to basic investment concepts that must be understood. Don't breeze through it. In fact, come back often.

Money in Motion

Wealth is power. Few would dispute this tenet but fewer still understand how the wealthy are able to remain so (i.e., wealthy and powerful) while having a significant presence in many different investment arenas. Simply, they keep their money moving between a seemingly endless supply of investment opportunities. When they lose (and everybody loses occasionally), the losses are not devastating. **The principles that allow "the rich" to seem so smart are easily assimilated into any size investment portfolio (even one that doesn't include movie studios, professional sports franchises and the like).** These principles are Quality, Diversification, and Income, three simple concepts that help to minimize both risk and greed. Wealthy people understand risk; they became (and stayed) wealthy by managing it!

Wealth is knowledge. Getting rich in the stock market is not as easy as many on Wall Street would like you to believe. If all those salespeople and gurus were so good at investing, why are they still selling and soothsaying? This book contains the knowledge of the market, of human nature, and of wealth accumulation that has come from 30 years of experience. *You will have to wade through the knowledge to have any hope of executing the strategy.*

I used to advertise on a financial talk show that aired on a major New York radio station. I was initially impressed with the host of the program because I was "interviewed to determine if my product was within the realm of sound investment advise and practice". I was accepted, and assured that I would be the only "Investment Manager" recommended to the audience.

As the show's popularity grew, more and more speculative ventures, funds, boutique products, commodity programs, etc. began to advertise on the show, and the host started to do paid "Investment Seminars" with all of us. Interviews were no longer necessary. Appearance fees replaced them! Eventually, the integrity of the show succumbed to the pressure of the bucks that were to be made by endorsing every conceivable product out there. The relationship could not be sustained because the show had become a Wall Street sideshow with no direction and no message.

As self-righteous as the Media is about their role in preserving our constitutional rights of free speech and expression, you better believe that the almighty dollar is worshipped just as fervently!

Every profession has its teachers, critics, sales people, and practitioners. Monday morning quarterbacking has become as much an art form in the investment world as it has always been in the world of sports. But, just as you wouldn't hire a respected sportscaster to manage your NFL franchise, neither should you rely on a product salesperson, a professor, or a radio talk show host/news analyst to manage your investment portfolio. There is book learning; there is concept, theory, and analysis; AND THERE IS PRACTICE. Who's going to perform your heart surgery, the head of Columbia Presbyterian Hospital's Cardiac Surgery Unit or the Professor of Surgical Procedure at Columbia University?

There is theory and there is practice. It has been said that: "what most investors know about investing could fit upon the head of a pin"! This holds true for the majority of employee and/or commissioned "Financial Advisors" as well. Answer this question before you act on anyone's advice. **How much sense does it make to take investment advice from any person who has not made himself or herself wealthy through the process of investing?** How many brokers do you think have a portfolio of their own with a value of $50,000, $100,000, or a million dollars? What percentages of brokers even make it into their fifth year? Here are two others that you really should find the answer to: "How many years of experience does the average Mutual Fund Manager have? How many Mutual Funds have a ten year track record (in their original design)?

You may not be able to find an advisor who is an "investments only millionaire", but you must find one who is at least an experienced investor! There are hundreds of Investment Managers out there, and thousands of advisors. Be selective. Understand the motivations. Find an honest person!

In spite of these obviously poor qualifications, most of you will run right out and do whatever these "Financial Advisors" tell you to do, and without question in some cases! Worse yet, you'll buy something "hot" from a cold caller. One of the goals of this book is to expand the head of your (investment knowledge) "pin" by opening your eyes to the realities of the investment world. **Knowledge is power! Experience is knowledge in practice!**

Buy and Hold vs. Trading

The conservative "Buy and Hold" investment strategy resulted when three major (and ancient) force fields converged sometime early in the last century. **Equity investing was a noble pursuit reserved for the rich and famous** in which they provided the financing for, and participated in the growth of, the "bubbling" new American economy. "Trading" was left to the companies they owned. Historical records proved unequivocally that an investment portfolio "un-managed" in this way would grow along with the overall economy **in the long run (which at the time was believed to be upwards of ten years).** As a bonus, the markets would remain stable. In most circles, stability is still thought of as a "good" thing.

Bolstering the commitment to this uniquely un-businesslike strategy (businesses buy and sell, or die) were two lesser but growing forces:(a) a desire to avoid the Robin Hood like confiscation tactics of the Federal Government, and (b) a reluctance to pay a fee for periodically changing one's portfolio.

But the growth of the U. S. economy accelerated so quickly and so broadly that equity ownership became the right of the masses. The early "Captains of Industry" recognized that they could no longer control the equity markets directly, so in a major change of direction, they took over and now control the primary distribution channels of the securities markets! You got it; they are the Wall Street Institutions, the "Masters of the Universe"!

In a world without tax codes and commissions, few would argue that a trading approach to stock market investing makes more sense than the traditional "Buy and Hold". Trading is viewed unfavorably, more for tax and commission reasons than for purely economic ones! We're going to attempt to change that! The Buy and Hold approach was developed in an era where the DJIA didn't move more than a few hundred points per year, a 100,000 share day was huge volume, Mutual Funds weren't even a twinkle in a young man's eye, and frankly Scarlet, no one really gave a damn!

"Buy and Hold" is an investment dinosaur, although it makes a modicum of sense in very small start up portfolios comprised of closed end mutual funds! (What are they? See Chapter Seven.) An examination of very few charts (try Kimberly Clark, Pfizer, and Morgan Stanley/Dean Witter for starters) is all that is needed to see that it is easy to make serious multiples on your money simply by buying and selling the same stocks over and over again. Few people take the time to figure this out. Most tend to fall head over heals in love with a stock whose price goes up, and up, and up.

They will even buy more at ever-higher prices until their position (from a diversification standpoint) becomes far too large. Wall Street loves you! Most of you, just as surely, will watch the stock price go back down, and down, and down. "My accountant says that I don't "need" any more income this year so I'll just kiss off this bonanza and pay less in taxes". Sound familiar?

Why sell, they say with wonder at your stupidity in their eyes? My [- - - - -] (fill in the blank with the name of the last stock(s) you rode all the way up AND all the way back down) will never go down in price, The Street says it's going to $167 per share before it splits, and what about the tax consequences? Just as a point of reference, Lucent today (July 26, 2001) is trading at less than 50% of what it was worth when it originally became a public company in 1996! (How many splits ago?)

In today's investment world, we can do away with immediate tax consequences in many investment portfolios (IRAs and 401-Ks, for example). We are now able to minimize commission rates to the point where they are hardly a concern. (This writer would argue that they are of little concern anyway, but no one really wants to hear about that. Have you ever wondered why Charles Schwab is always grinning?) This genius (Schwab, and I sincerely mean genius) created a huge industry out of a concept that is really of very little investment significance! Wall Street is exceptionally smart (in giving you what you want whether its good for you or not), and it is particularly good at profiting from human frailties and addictions (kind of like a drug dealer)! **Speculating in the stock market is just as real an addiction as slot machines and roulette wheels.** Don't do it: it's bad for your financial health!

The fact that we can do something more cheaply does not mean that we will be able to do it better. Variable costs are not as important to control as fixed costs. Consult any management textbook. If my cost for something is "X" and I sell it for a 10% gain, my gross dollar profit is actually higher if the "X" is larger! And a 10% profit after commissions is, after all, a 10% profit. In a perfect world, all commissions would be equal and we could focus on more important matters!

Isn't it ironic that the very same people, who will do what ever it takes to slice the last pennies off of a commission, will blindly pay the huge mark-up included in a new issue or dollars more per share by using market orders?

Wouldn't it be nice to construct a world where we could also eliminate the need for Financial Planners, Accountants, and Lawyers? No Financial Planners because we all would be educated in finance and it would be simple to understand how things relate to one another. No Accountants, because there would be no complicated tax code, and no Lawyers (on general principals) because that would solve most of the world's problems. A simple flat tax (none at all either on corporate income or on capital gains) and no confiscation of assets from our heirs would solve the problem nicely. (We've all got our pet political issues. See Chapter Seven.)

Trading just makes you more money than buy and hold, with or without commissions and taxes AND, you will wind up actually being able to use more of your retirement "nest egg" because the taxes will have been paid during the asset accumulation stage!

Heed the voice of experience! I once had a client who had inherited a million dollar estate that had been poorly managed by a Bank Trust Department for generations. It was badly managed, not for lack of growth in value, but for lack of foresight! Somehow, my client received the stock portfolio (amazingly, in certificate form) AT HIS GRANDFATHER'S COST BASIS! WOW! Not quite as bad as a gift of a Great Dane puppy, but there are similarities. (It's great to have assets, so long as you can afford the upkeep!) Imagine shares of $60 Exxon with a $.15 cost basis. He had similar holdings in many other good companies (General Electric, A T & T, etc.) (Yes, AT&T. See how things change!) Actually, the managers must have been forbidden to sell anything, because the allocation of the positions was way out of proportion, especially the 70% or more that remained in Exxon!

So what's the problem? Simply this. The man had a reasonable income, but no other assets. There were things he wanted to do to diversify his new portfolio (and to improve his lifestyle), but he couldn't afford to pay the taxes (even at long term capital gain rates) on the profits! Without changes, he wouldn't be able to significantly increase his income. **In developing wealth, don't lose sight of one important long-term objective: a comfortable retirement, paid for by the income from your investment portfolio.** Try to position yourself on the way there, instead of waiting for the last minute. **$1,000,000 worth of Microsoft stock generates how much retirement income?**

Speaking of Microsoft, which has a "cult following" of shareholders who think of themselves as invincible. Does anyone remember what happened to Occidental Petroleum when Armand Hammer died from natural causes years ago? It tanked, and just hasn't been nearly as exciting since. Wal-Mart, on the other hand, recovered nicely after the unexpected death of Sam Walton.

How do you think investors would have reacted had it been Bill Gates instead of Payne Stewart in that runaway jet? Chew on that one! What would you have done? Be honest. Now put a paper clip on this page and come back to answer this question again after I'm done with you.

Sometimes The Tail Wags The Dog

Why do people bother investing at all? If you buy securities you have to pay someone a commission. If you're fortunate enough to make some profits (and you decide to realize them), you have to give some of those profits away in the form of taxes.

Let's consider another scenario. When you buy your morning coffee and newspaper, do you resent the money the deli owner is making on the deal? Or, would you try to negotiate with the newspaper company to whittle down their profit per paper. And what about the middlemen who sold the deli owner the coffee beans, paper cups, lids, sugar, "sweet and low", and cream? Aren't these "extra costs" the same as commissions? Should the government make deli owners disclose their markups?

What about those taxes! Why not storm into your boss's office and demand a CUT IN SALARY so you can move into a lower tax bracket? Ridiculous? No more ridiculous than your Accountant's advice that you should lose money on some investments to offset profits you've made elsewhere. Sure there are times when that is a good strategy (when a company has become worthless, not just unpopular), but your Accountant is probably not qualified to determine which securities should be sold, or when. Why is this strategy only implemented at the end of the year? Three questions come to mind. Would he suggest the sale of all or part of a Mutual Fund, particularly if he sold it to you? Would he mind if you only paid half of his bill to help him reduce his own tax bite? Is he suggesting another security that you should buy?

The Voice of Experience (again, sorry): Tune-in your "way back" machine to the early 80's when oil prices skyrocketed, interest rates went into the high double digits, and prices of Oil Company Shares went through the roof. One phone call cost a client of mine thousands of dollars when he insisted that I defer taking profits on his oil company shares until the following year. Prices plunged before year-end, erasing nearly all of his gains.

Never lose sight of the "dog". **Income and Profits are the "Holy Grail" of investing. Nothing else really matters.** Stick with the plan and take profits when your targets are reached. Sit Brutus; good Dog!

Contrarian Trading

Contrarian trading is different from Contrarian thinking. Contrarian thinking is based on the premise that we should do the opposite of whatever the popular trend seems to be, with no other rules or parameters entering into the decision making process. This is not really a viable investment strategy because it has neither management nor investment principles at its foundation. The opposite of speculating in one thing could be speculating in another. Contrarian Trading, on the other hand, takes place within a very well defined set of rules and procedures. It is a strictly disciplined and totally managed approach that doesn't allow much divergence from classic textbook investment principles. Sticking to the basic principles of investing is often, in and of itself, Contrarian!

Unlike "Day Trading", which is commented upon a bit later, this style of trading applies management and investment disciplines to such Wall Street realities as: the "group mentality" in price movements, predictable over-reactions to both good news and bad, portfolio window dressing, etc.

The November Syndrome (an example of Contrarian Trading)

Every fall, good year in the market or not (Who makes this determination anyway, the institutions, the media?), I explain to my clients why year-end is always a special time in the stock market. Investors are encouraged to lose capital in order to pay less in taxes. A related misconception is that it is better to wait until next year to take profits (refer to the lesson above). Here is a message you will absolutely not receive from your Wall Street "Financial Advisor":

"Unless a security has lost its fundamental quality, and unless you have some form of guarantee that your profits will still be there in January, I intend to realize each and every profit as soon as the sell target has been reached, IRRESPECTIVE OF THE TAX IMPLICATIONS."

[By the way, only banks, insurance companies, and the Federal Government can issue securities that are "guaranteed" as to principal or interest. If you ever hear it with regard to future market value performance of any security, plan, program, fund, etc., call 9-1-1!]

Another year-end phenomenon (which plays out to a lesser degree at the end of each calendar quarter) is "Institutional Window Dressing", a euphemism for consumer fraud. This is a process that will be examined in more detail later, but you need to understand its impact. **Remember always that Wall Street Institutions have little or no respect for your intelligence.** They cannot publish quarterly or annual reports either that show holdings in unpopular securities, or that are missing the names of stocks and groups that have become "hot"!

You may not even see these reports until they are several quarters out of date. However, the big corporate clients' Employee Benefits Committees do meet with their Investment Company "Money Managers" regularly, and there is just no way the fund managers are going to jeopardize their careers by appearing stupid! They will always, and without conscience or question, Sell Low and Buy High to give the appearance of brilliance. **Hey! Get angry! It's your money they're playing with!**

These Year-End strategies generally add to the weakness of securities that have been weak throughout the year (You should buy more of them!) and to the strength of those that have been

15

more popular (You must take profits on these!) If you were to selectively buy (high quality) names from the list of New York Stock Exchange 12 month lows in November, you would (more than likely) be able to sell these very same companies profitably within a very few months. I GUARANTEE IT! (That was just a test. Your left eyebrow should have moved up and you should have been looking around for the telephone when you heard the "G" word.)

The basic point is that the stock market functions outside the realm of the tax code, the calendar, the basic principles of investing, and even the law! Don't take unnecessary losses that just deplete capital. You must never accept this practice as "appropriate" or "necessary" behavior. **If you have an emotional problem with paying taxes on your gains, send me the money. I'll be happy to pay more taxes.**

Make decisions based on sound investment principles, and in a time continuum that has no artificial constraints. AND, most importantly, recognize that Wall Street will not. **The November Syndrome creates tremendous misinformation as well as incredible opportunity. A few months later, Wall Street will begin talking about the mysterious "January Effect".** This is when those incredibly intelligent pinstripes sell the overpriced securities they just purchased so that they can go pay more for the ones that they just sold!

Interesting place Wall Street!

A Store Filled with Symbols

Let's take a trip to the local hardware store (HD or LOW). We see shelves filled with merchandise. Paint (SHW), Plywood (GP), Water Softener Salt (MII), Light Bulbs (PHG), Tools (SWK, BDK), etc. Hundreds of products produced by hundreds of manufacturers. How did they get there? Who were they purchased from? How much did they cost? What's the point of having so many products on the shelf? Is the objective to increase the value of the inventory? How much will you have to pay to buy something?

They may have been purchased directly from the manufacturers, but many were certainly delivered through layers of middlemen (brokers) who added a little profit for themselves to the final cost of the merchandise (commissions). Many of the "commodity", or raw material type products may have been purchased during weaknesses in paper or copper prices, for example, to actually **TAKE ADVANTAGE of lower prices.** What a concept, buy low anyone!

But they got to the merchant's shelves for one purpose and one purpose alone! They are to be sold for a profit as quickly and as effortlessly as possible. And yes, if we can get the consumer to come into our shop to pick up the merchandise and carry it home himself, we'll keep our delivery costs down and spend as little on customer service as possible. But how do we fix a price to charge for those kitchen cabinets, chain saws, carpets, hinges, nails, clothespins, bags of fertilizer and so forth? **What is a reasonable profit objective?**

Does any real world enterprise (products, not commodities) "Buy and Hold"! Of course they don't, they trade. Commodity based firms "deplete their inventory". Retailers buy the highest quality product they can get their hands on (even competing brands). They then determine what a reasonable markup is, over and above their "cost basis". And, then, when you come into the store, they actually sell the thing to you for the price they had "stamped" on the merchandise well beforehand. What a concept: this trading. What were the very first (global) businessmen called? Buy and Holders, or was it TRADERS? Did Columbus come to the Americas to obtain and to hoard spices? Trading runs the world because trading works. America would never have been discovered in a "Buy and Hold" world.

Investing must be handled in the same manner as the management of a retail enterprise. Love profits, not increasing inventory value. Worship turnover! Sell as many burgers as you can. Let's see: is it easier to sell a hundred items at a ten percent profit or 10 items at a 100% profit? Every equity position (AND all fixed income positions) is for sale. The key is to set a "reasonable target price". It's easy to get all caught up in Wall Street analyst hype and hold on until that "$80 stock" actually gets there. But, it's easier to set a more attainable target that can be reached quickly, and count on rapid inventory turnover to produce big profits. Go down any newspaper listing, particularly NASDAQ, and see if you make it through the "A"s before you count ten companies with a twelve-month high above $60 and a current price below ten!

"If we start the year with 25 different quality products (equities) on our shelves, and we can sell 75% of them at a reasonable profit throughout the year, we'll be able to stay in business. If, however, we can turn over our inventory several times each year, we can make a lot of money!"
[Courtesy of R. McDonald, December 1992]

A Tale of Two Strategies

Your General Store (Reasonable Objectives)

Item	Cost Basis	Mark Up	Selling Price	Turnover Goal	Total Gain	Return	Success %
Lamp Shades	$10	10%	$11	24 x yr	$24	240%	95%
Chain Saws	$100	10%	$110	6 x yr	$60	60%	95%
Televisions	$400	10%	$440	4 x yr	$160	40%	95%

Your Stock Portfolio (On "Street" Drugs)

Item	Cost Basis	Mark Up	Selling Price	Turnover Goal	Total Gain	Return	Success %
Lampshades, Inc	$10	210%	$31	Once, after 12 months	$21	210%	30%
Saws.com	$100	150%	$250	Once	$150	150%	40%
TV's 'R' Us	$400	75%	$700	Once	$300	75%	50%

There's no reason not to manage your stock portfolio in the same manner you would run your General Store!

Your Stock Portfolio (Off Drugs)

Item	Cost Basis	Mark Up	Selling Price	Turnover Goal	Total Gain	Return	Success %
100 LOW	$4,000	10%	$4,400	2 x yr	$800	20%	90%
100 CLX	$3,500	10%	$3,850	2 x yr	$700	20%	90%
100 BMY	$6,000	10%	$6,600	2 x yr	$1,200	20%	90%

I Once Had a Client...

I once had a client who insisted that I avoid buying two or more competing companies. This was many years ago when there were a whole lot more oil companies than there are today, and a guy named Pickens was going to do all he could to change that. Most of my clients had positions in two or three of the oils, and celebrated with me repeatedly as one after the other was taken over. The other client did well with his Exxon, but nothing big ever happened.

The lesson here is that **the "market" moves in groups of many different shapes and sizes,** particularly when it comes to the popularity or disapproval of specific industries. It pays big time to own several different positions within the same industry while staying within the boundaries of PROPER DIVERSIFICATION AND QUALITY STANDARDS. I sent my son a framed picture of Mr. Pickens to put over his fireplace. My message to him was: "Every now and then you should thank this man for paying your way through college!"

Types of groups include more than just industrial classifications. Wall Street will popularize such things as "big cap" "mid-cap" and "small cap", or emphasize "value" or "growth" as the place to be right now. It makes a whole lot more investment sense to watch groups with names (i.e., "drugs", "retailers", "oils", etc.) than to watch "buzz word" groups. Hmmm! A small cap stock might just be last year's big cap company that failed to meet analyst expectations. Now, some analyst has been told to report to the world that the company is about to come out of bankruptcy. Just what distinguishes a growth stock from a value stock anyway? Will the definitions or criteria change either from institution to institution or from month to month? **Different buzzwords will develop from time to time, giving rise to tremendous low risk opportunities in the group or groups that are currently OUT OF FAVOR.** Such changes will also continue to produce hundreds of new specialty mutual funds, all of which will be statistically proven "best in class", just like automobiles, expensive restaurants, and New York radio stations! Ever wonder about that?

Keep in mind that Wall Street knows (is certain about) only one thing. It can market absolutely anything (even companies that don't exist) to the speculating public. Did I say speculating? You bet I did! **Maybe "they" live in the land of certainty after all!**

Fixed and Variable Costs

Any viable enterprise studies its costs very carefully to determine just how much of a "mark up" is needed for profitability. Just what do I have to spend to keep this business producing the units I want to sell? Certain costs (labor, rent, utilities, insurances, etc) are, for the most part, fixed. You have to pay them whether or not you sell even one widget, muffler, topcoat, sled, lawn chair, or staple gun. Managements go gray trying to manage their fixed costs. The PROFITS from your product sales have to pay these costs and more for the enterprise to stay in business.

Smart managers pay their top sales people big commission bucks to keep them motivated. (Ever seen the AMWAY yacht?) Expense accounts are fine. Entertainment of clients is encouraged. Advertising and Marketing budget numbers boggle the mind. Why? Because they lead to increases in sales, and sales produce profits. You don't ever want to restrict your (investment) variable costs artificially. They are the seed money that grows your profits.

Fortunately, investing involves very few fixed costs. Some brokerage firms have the audacity (like most banks) to charge you for the privilege of using some of their more sophisticated account statements (For instance, those that allow check writing, automatically categorize expenses for tax purposes, and provide a Visa Card.), sending checks to third parties, wire transfers, etc. Many firms charge a maintenance fee for inactive accounts. Even the old fashioned cost of a Safe Deposit box has been eliminated by the maturity of coupon bonds ("Those were the days my friends, we thought they'd never end...) and electronic, "Street Name", record keeping.

The bigger your relationship with the brokerage firm and the more commissions you generate through trading, the more likely it is that your "Account Executive" will be able to "waive" these onerous and insulting fees. (By the way, banks will also waive fees for good customers.) What do on-line brokers do? I would guess that they charge for anything other than "bare bones" services.

For the most part though, you can drop your bucks into a brokerage account Money Market Fund for free and never spend another cent! But why would you want to do such a thing?

Commissions (Taxes) Are Variable Costs

Commissions are variable costs, but ONLY when they are paid in a "buy" or a "sell" transaction. Paid in any other form, they are as much a fixed cost as your car payment. (And by the way, unless you are in the business of buying and selling them, neither fine automobiles, houses, nor show horses are "investment portfolio" assets!) If I pay a lot of commissions (in the form of an annual fee) because I bought a lot of securities and held on to them, I have probably acted foolishly. If I paid a lot of commissions because I traded a lot of different positions profitably, I have probably made a lot of money. You want to do all you can to hold fixed costs in line, but variable costs are generally the result of some action that is intended to produce a financial gain. You have to spend money to make money!

Taxes are variable costs too, and as much as we hate to pay them, they are a very good thing because of what they represent, i.e., the realization of PROFITS. If I have made a lot of money (even after making every legal effort to "shelter" that income), I will certainly pay a lot in taxes. But what is better: $70,000 net after taxes on $100,000 in profits, or nothing at all?

Invasion of the Business Snatchers

Over the past several years Wall Street has moved into the Investment Management Business in a big way through various forms of "Wrap Fee" arrangements. **This is primarily a "product" offered by the full service variety of brokerage firm, and they sell it as a way for clients "to obtain personal**

professional portfolio management with positively no commissions. You just pay a small annual fee".

I think I mentioned before that investors should be suspicious of anything that Wall Street recommends. Remember, no matter how they try to disguise it, they will absolutely never do anything that will reduce their revenues or profits. Yours yes, theirs no! Institutional brokerage firms like the Investment Management Business because they can reduce their fixed overhead expenses (salary and commission), and because they can develop a captive, dependent market (the money management firms they hire) for other products that their huge empires produce. They also can collect huge dollars in fees for doing absolutely nothing!

The cost of this type of arrangement for most investors is going to be 3% per year or a bit less, dependent upon portfolio size alone. The "managed" portfolios are available in all the standard Mutual Fund flavors (growth/income, value, mid-cap, emerging markets, you name it). The idea seems simple. The management fee replaces all charges to the client and never again is there a discussion about commissions, exchange fees or "churning". If I call a commission a management fee, is it really no longer a commission? Just what is it that the brokerage firms are asking their clients to do, and just how personally managed are these programs? And do you really believe that your "Financial Advisor" is not getting a cut?

They Do It With Mirrors

Let's say that you have $100,000 (probably the minimum allowed) and you agree to pay the 3% annual fee to enter a "Wrap Account" arrangement. You have just added $3,000 to the fixed costs of running your portfolio. Assume further that there are 25 trades during the year, that the average gain per trade is 10% (for a total profit of $10,000), and that the portfolio generates an additional 2% in dividends and interest. **What is "THE KEEP"?** Is it a 12% (+ or -) growth in Working Capital? Right? Nope!

Amount Invested .... $ 100,000
Minus Total Fees Paid   - $ 3,000
Net Amount Invested   = $ 97,000
Plus Capital Gains   + $ 10,000
Plus Dividends & Interest   + $ 2,000

Total Working Capital = $109,000 (approx.)

First of all, your fixed costs are deducted quarterly in advance, and they are calculated on the value of the portfolio, not the investment that you made. In the illustration above, your year-end market value would not be $112,000 as you would like it to be. You would wind up with less than $109,000 or a growth rate of approximately 9%! What if there were no capital gains? (The underlying assumption is that the value of each security held at year-end is equal to its purchase price.)

Now let's look at the full commission scenario with less of an increase in fixed costs. The account is managed in the same way: a 10% average gain per trade for a total of $10,000 in profits + a 2% interest and dividend "kicker", and the same year-end market value assumption. There are the same 25 trades, but now the commissions are paid in the normal manner and are thus included in the stock's "cost basis". They are not deducted from the 10% profit. You are the Manager of the portfolio so there are no fixed overhead charges at all! It's obvious that you have to sell at a slightly higher price to realize the target of 10% net/net. Let's further assume that commissions and charges were a whopping $100 per trade! The result? **You Keep $112,000 in Working Capital and enjoy a growth rate of more than 12% because your gains are after commissions which have become what they should always be, after all, a variable cost!**

Amount Invested .... $ 100,000
Minus Total Fees Paid   - $ -0-
Net Amount Invested   = $ 100,000

Plus Capital Gains	+ $ 10,000
Plus Dividends & Interest	+ $ 2,000

Total Working Capital = $112,000 (approx.)

"WOW", you say, "just think how much I would make at a discount broker if I paid just $250 dollars in commissions instead of $2,500"! Guess again, the results are precisely the same. $10,000 in profits + $2,000 in other income, $-0- in Management Fees = $12,000 or 12%. **So much for that industry!** Plug the figures in above to make this crystal clear. Your trades would not be more profitable because the manager is still shooting at a target of 10% above your cost basis. Your dollar gain would actually be less! Comprendez?

Note: I have managed hundreds of accounts through dozens of brokerage firms and with every conceivable type of WRAP account or discounted commission arrangement. **There is absolutely no correlation between the amount of commissions paid and the long-term rate of capital growth in the portfolio.** Take a look at the trading results illustrated in Table Three, at the end of Chapter Two. Can you determine if this was a Wrap Account arrangement or a regular "pay as you trade" account? Only Your Manager (you) Knows For Sure!

Is Bigger Really Better?

Now let's examine the process undertaken by Wall Street to determine just who is "qualified" to be an "Approved WRAP ACCOUNT Portfolio Manager" for the big institutional brokers. Requirement number one is size. No manager with under $100,000,000 in managed assets need apply! No manager without "subordinate" decision makers is eligible. Don't bother either, if you don't have a variety of "products" to offer. What does this sound like to you? Got it! A Mutual Fund Store with a new wrinkle: monthly or quarterly personalized account statements, and **that is the limit of the "personal investment management" you will receive from your investment manager!**

Not only will you never meet the person that is managing your investment portfolio, you will never even have a conversation with him! It is likely that the management firm will not even know your name! Would that kind of a relationship be acceptable in any other profession? Your "Financial Advisor" will act as the middleman throughout the entire process of selecting an appropriate manager, reviewing the objectives of the program (actually, the Mutual Fund), and analyzing the manager's investment performance. If he's an honest person, he'll tell you that he has never met or had a conversation with the investment manager either! Just for kicks, ask him how he gets paid on the sale of this kind of arrangement. He absolutely does get paid, but it's not called a "commission". I know that you've seen those TV ads that imply that you will meet with the "Manager". Sorry, the meetings will only be with your "Financial Advisor. Please, give us a break!

Had enough? There's more, further adding to the wool that is slowly being drawn down over your eyes. Your $100,000 will be invested in exactly the same stocks as those who signed up yesterday, last month, and last year! You'll have odd lots of up to 100 different issues; some at their all time highest levels and very few that are in a "buy low" position. You have just purchased another mutual fund. **I understand that you can even get a WRAP Account where the "Investment Manager" actually puts the money into a selection of Mutual Funds! It's hard to believe that even the super salespersons of Wall Street could find buyers for that one!** There is no individuality, no personal attention, and no real chance of meeting your financial objectives.

This is a "one size fits all program". How many different managers would you need to run a diversified portfolio, certainly no less than two? Who coordinates and re-allocates? I guess you are really still the manager, huh?

Want more? The Investment Management Company must run its trades through your brokerage firm and, believe me when I tell you that they don't provide the service for free. Additionally, because of the size of the total fund relationship, the fund manager receives the low end of his billing schedule (probably .50% or less), allowing the brokerage firm to keep the lion's share of the up front management fees you are paying. Not quite greedy enough for you yet? For directing this traffic to the manager, the brokerage firm steals (oops, I'm sorry, collects) an additional 10% of the management fee for its sales efforts!

Registered Investment Advisors (RIAs) are required to disclose to their clients precisely how they are compensated for what they do and sell. Was any of this information shared with you when you started up your Wrap Account? You don't have to ask, you must be told! Feel abused? You should.

Still, most Investment Managers would kill for this kind of business because it is an endless source of new clients, and a relationship that they will do practically anything to continue. Integrity anyone? If ever there was a blatant conflict of interest (like an Accountant selling mutual funds and collecting commissions), this is the place.

Fact or Fiction, you decide: Approved Wrap Account Investment Managers obtain thousands of clients and millions of fee dollars from the major brokerage firms every year. There is no way they can generate the dollars, achieve the recognition, and become popular with the media without this type of business! The CEO of XYZ Brokers recognizes this dependency, and suggests that the "management company" form an alliance with his firm's underwriting department, thus assuring a captive market for new issues being brought public. Wouldn't it also be nice if the manager removed stocks from "our" managed portfolios if we lower our opinion and added those that we are pushing?

Why do you think Congress cuts the SEC's budget practically every year? Less money, fewer investigations of Institutional practices like these! (See Chapter Seven.)

A Word About Day Trading

"Day Trading" has become a very popular way for Wall Street to separate unsuspecting investors from their "hard earned". Because it has no foundation in the basic principals of Investing (i.e., Quality, Diversification, and Income), it is a speculation of the same type as Options, Futures, IPOs, Commodities, and Roulette. Basically, if the deal is that "you will get rich quicker and easier", it's just another type of gambling, and not true investing at all. Plus, think of the commissions it generates!

Recently, business news radio stations have been carrying advertisements for computer software that can spot "hot movers" that can be turned over rapidly to let you make big bucks even more quickly. It just can't fail; we're led to believe! Really, who is doing the programming?

If you are fortunate enough to buy a stock that meets all of your investment criteria (quality, diversification, and income), and that achieves your target price within twenty-four hours, that's just great, and it may just happen. Most day trading schemes are based on large numbers of shares and very small price movements, and are inherently risky ventures, with no recognition at all of the Principles of Investing, which are covered in depth below.

A Personalized Set of Rules

Every investor is different from every other investor. Risk tolerance varies with age, financial position, and/or experience. There are optimists and pessimists out there, making dissimilar decisions in similar environments. Each of us has our own investment equation and it is important that we make an effort to understand who we are and how we act in times either of stress or of elation. This needs to be done before we develop our personal investment plans and strategies. Knowing who we are, what we are trying to accomplish, and how we deal with the very emotional thing called "money" is an important foundation for an investment program.

Wealthy people, successful businessmen and women, work within a personalized set of rules and procedures developed over time to help them achieve a defined set of objectives. Each of us has to come up with a plan, appropriate rules and procedures, and so forth, if we expect our investment program to produce results. We have to be able to establish an investment plan, organize our portfolios in a manner that will help achieve our objectives, and focus on the plan in a DISCIPLINED DECISION MAKING ENVIRONMENT. We must establish a plan and implement it over an extended period of time, with only occasional and minor fine-tuning adjustments allowed.

Investing absolutely involves RISK. If there is no risk of any kind (market or price movement, interest rate, deadline expiration, etc.), there is no investment. A CD (Certificate of Deposit) or a Money Market Fund, by definition, is not an investment, but the interest rates available from either are useful tools in performance evaluation. **In looking at performance, "beat the bank" is a worthy investment "benchmark" because: if you can't beat the bank, why even bother to assume the risk?** Investors deal with risk through the hierarchy of INVESTMENT RULES that they set for themselves. Investment rules can and will be different at varying times in a persons' investment life, but **THERE ARE REALLY JUST THREE BASIC PRINCIPLES OF INVESTING** that need to be mastered. Interestingly, each of them deals essentially with risk minimization.

A discussion of these principles (Quality, Diversification, and Income) will follow, but first it's important to deal with another "Wall Streetism" that you will find more and more insidious as you gain knowledge and experience. The "Street" has established itself as an

Icon whose knowledge of all that has and will ever "happen" is unquestionable. On a daily basis, radio news or CNBC commentary will quote a Wall Street analyst who will explain away the events of the day, the week, or the quarter as reactions in (either!) direction to heightened or lessened "uncertainty" in the marketplace! Well sure, that makes a lot of sense. But does it really?

What is certainty, and does it exist at all in the Stock Market? Wall Street firms want you to believe that they know what is going to happen in the future! Their analysts (We're going to put Wall Street analysts under a microscope at the end of Chapter Three.) are so smart that they can predict the future. As far as I "know", the last crystal ball lost its power centuries ago. *We can be "certain" of only one thing in the investment world, and that one thing is that we will always function within an environment of "uncertainty".* A little later on, during the same show, you might here another opinion that tells you that Money Managers are "placing their bets" on something. Is this the statement of an omniscient entity or an admission of ignorance on the part of an institution with too many mouths to muzzle?

Have we progressed so far backwards that it is acceptable for Professional Investment Managers to be compared to blackjack players? (You're right; these guys would be playing baccarat.) Is the Media being irresponsible (for insinuating that investing is, after all, just gambling) or altruistic (for warning us that serious risk of loss is involved)? Maybe they are just being realistic, recognizing that the bulk of their drooling audience is just looking for a "play" anyway. Maybe they are just more ignorant than we (or they) would like to believe! In any event, if you're looking for a game you should try one that's a bit less expensive when you lose.

Standards of Quality

Each of us deals with investing differently and there certainly are many perfectly acceptable ways of doing so. I suspect that there are some ways to speculate that I would find more acceptable than others, but the important thing is to know which of the two (investing or speculating) you are doing! In the long run (Anything less than five years is not the long-run!), the inherent quality of the securities we buy will ultimately determine how successful our investment program becomes. Obviously, the higher the quality of the stocks we own, the lower the risk of loss in the portfolio. But how does one go about measuring the "quality" of a Home Depot, an Amazon.com, or a General Motors?

One of the basic relationships that we deal with in investing is the one between "risk" and "reward" The higher the potential reward, the greater the risk. If the reward seems high, and the risk isn't up front and personal, right in your face, keep looking. It's in there! If you can't afford to lose the amount you invest, you should not allow yourself to accept the risk. **This element of control is totally your very own personal responsibility. YOU HAVE THE POWER TO DECIDE! "You da man"!**

Some people will "do their own research" and either be wrong more often than they'll admit out of love for their own analytical ability, or do nothing more than sheepishly (sic) follow the advice of some self proclaimed guru or "Wire House" "suit". (A Wire House is simply a brokerage firm. The term comes from the use of an employee called a "wire operator", whose job is to send orders to the floor of the exchange over the "wire".) Neither of these approaches will work consistently because of their basic premise: "A really smart, tuned-in, human can predict the future movement of individual stock prices, but only if he or she has impressive degrees, and is paid some ridiculous salary by a "Wall Street" Institution". That just isn't so either. Good managers rely upon others to do the grunt work (research) and upon meaningful (fundamental) numbers to judge the viability of companies they choose to invest in.

"Fundamental" analysis and "technical" analysis are the two main disciplines used by Wall Street analysts to gather data in support of their guesswork (or purchased opinions). Fundamental numbers include "profits", "debt to equity ratios", "P/E ratios", etc., and are used to describe the present corporate financial reality. Technical analysis involves the use of trend numbers, averages, lines, graphs, and tea leaves, in an effort to predict the future movements of stock prices.

Predictions of the future are most often wrong, particularly those that are based upon input from (drum roll please) those Masters of Hindsight, those Monuments to Meaningless Numerical Trivia, "Wall Street's" Answer to David Copperfield, the Technical Analysts. **My personal feeling is that research is "the intellectual rationalization of the speculator" (and those who prey on speculators), just shined up a bit for public consumption via the media.**

There are many services that provide all the fundamental analysis anyone could ever need to make well-informed investment decisions. Pick one. Understand the information it is providing, and set your own Quality Standards! I use the very simplistic information provided in the monthly Stock Guide published by Standard & Poor's International. Then, of course, there is the Value Line Investment Survey. Could you imagine trying to carry that around in your briefcase? There are many similar services but most are mouthpieces of the mythical "Wall Street Knows All" monster, and are naturally biased and self serving. After what you've read so far, I'm "certain" that you'll never look at another "Wire House" research report. If I'm wrong, return to the beginning of the book and start over!

Analyze This: Most of you have received confirmation notices with notations on them that ***"XYZ Brokerage Makes a Market in This Security"*** or you've heard investment commentary with regard to brokerage firms "trading their own account". The Wall Street "Hydra" has many heads. Each time regulators lop one off, two new ones appear! Slow as they are, corporations are quicker than governments. I suppose it's easier to direct high priced in-house council to develop new semi-legal products than it is to get a government over-run by Attorneys turned Politician to agree on how to regulate the beast (or on anything at all, for that matter)!

The S & P Stock Guide, which your full service broker will be glad to send to you, rates the financial viability and relative quality of companies from as low as "D" (for a dog in reorganization?) to as high as A+. (Standard & Poor's doesn't even know that I exist and I get nothing at all for this endorsement or any others that appear in this document. Pity!)

Ratings of B+ through A+ are considered "INVESTMENT GRADE" or lower risk companies. **These are not rankings of possible market performance a la a Value Line or the latest brokerage house recommended list. They are analyses of survival statistics like "current" and "p/e" ratios.** You would be surprised at the ratings of some companies, particularly those that comprise the closely watched Dow Jones Industrial Average (DJIA). The majority of investors believe that all of those "Blue Chip" companies carry the highest possible ratings. Isn't that what blue chip is supposed to mean? Would you bet on it? Check it out now and think about it for a while before reading further.

THE THIRTY STOCKS IN THE DOW JONES INDUSTRIAL AVERAGE

Symbol	S&P Rating	Dividend Paying	Blue Chip	Symbol	S&P Rating	Dividend Paying	Blue Chip
T	B	Yes	No	HON	B+	Yes	No
AA	B+	Yes	No	IBM	B	Yes	No
AXP	A-	Yes	Yes	INTC	A	Yes	Yes
BA	B	Yes	No	IP	B-	Yes	No
CAT	B+	Yes	No	JNJ	A+	Yes	Yes
C	A	Yes	Yes	JPM	B+	Yes	No
KO	A-	Yes	Yes	MCD	A+	Yes	Yes
DIS	B+	Yes	No	MRK	A+	Yes	Yes
DD	B+	Yes	No	MSFT	B+	No	No

EK	B+	Yes	No	MMM	A	Yes	Yes
XOM	A-	Yes	Yes	MO	A	Yes	Yes
GE	A+	Yes	Yes	PG	A	Yes	Yes
GM	B	Yes	No	SBC	A-	Yes	Yes
HWP	A+	Yes	Yes	UT	B+	Yes	No
HD	A+	Yes	Yes	WMT	A+	Yes	Yes

Although most are "Investment Grade" Securities, 47% are B+ or lower. Only seven are in the elite A+ category! The term "blue chip" has an ironic twist. Here's a type of gaming chip being used to describe what is defined as "a high-priced, value security with good earnings and a stable price".

You'll find that most millionaires focus on stocks that fall within the "Investment Grade" classifications. This is because they understand the concept of risk and how to go about the important task of "risk minimization". **Eliminating risk is impossible; managing/minimizing risk is essential!** You'll also find that most professional investors (not investment company employees) would hold the personal opinion that Wall Street Strategists "can't even figure out where we are, much less determine where it is that we are heading!" Do they really even care? Aren't they really just saying what there employers are telling them to say?

You must keep in mind that all employees have very personal agendas that absolutely influence the opinions and predictions they publicize. Wall Street propaganda is designed to fill consumers (**consumers buy products; investors buy securities**) with confidence in the products and concepts that they are selling. **If you pool all the expert analytical opinion, all you will have is a very expensive bowl of intellectual bull chowder.**

Only The Best Liars Succeed!

Here's a "Wall Street" buzzword you're probably unfamiliar with. "Coverage"! I'm not exactly sure what "coverage" is, but I get several cold calls a week from representatives of research firms, bond houses, and well known brokerage firms who want to make sure that I have "coverage" with or by them. (Thank goodness for a good secretary!) Sometimes they break through "the screen" and I have the time to play along to see what they are selling. I always ask them why I would want their *"coverage"*. Naturally they are all the very best at what they do, be it research, bond pricing, or stock picking. **However, they all start to mumble when I ask how much of the security they own personally, or what special risks are associated with the 12% bond that they want me to buy for my clients in a 6% environment.**

Then it really starts to "fly" when I ask them how they managed to get through my secretary who is an expert at keeping these people away from me. (Of course I already know that it was some kind of story: returning my call, met me at a conference, referred by a friend, etc.) **The next question I ask is:** "do you really think I would do business with you or believe anything you or your firm has to say when you've already proven to me that you are a liar?" **The next question you should ask is:** where do the successful liars wind up in these prestigious Wall Street organizations?

Elements of Diversification

Several years ago, I was speaking at an IAFP (International Association of Financial Planners) meeting somewhere in Florida on many of the basic principals that you'll be reading about here. **(Note that I am not a "Financial Planner".)** It was around the time that Wall Street was touting "Junk Bond" funds as a great new investment idea. These securities were safe because they were a "diversified" group of bonds that surely (the marketers hoped) would not all default! How many savvy investors do you think fell for this proposition? If I own 20 different pieces of junk in my portfolio, does it in some way make the portfolio "un-junk"? Really. Still, greedy investors stood in line to buy the things in spite of the incredible risk involved!

I was the first speaker that day, and my presentation was intended to be a disembowelment of the Junk Bond product, **"perhaps the biggest scam orchestrated by 'Wall Street', ever!" were the words I used.** The next speaker (a representative of a major Wall Street bond firm) was late, missing my entire presentation. It was a bit tense in the room when he got into his spiel on the "outstanding investment merits" of his firm's brand new junk bond funds"!

Years later, a similar product based on foreign government debt became even more popular than the junk bonds. The interest rate on these wonderful instruments was about twice the going rate in the USA, and was guaranteed by "the full faith and credit" of Columbia, Peru, or Madagascar, for example. *The fine print pointed out innocently enough that it was the return of principal that was not (guaranteed).* "But don't worry Mr. Client, all you have to do is hold on for eight or nine years and you'll be sure to break even!" Is that a good thing?

Diversification is not just the presence of many different names, products, categories, countries, and industries. Rather, it is a manageable portfolio of purpose-directed investments, each of which can stand on its own merits as a profitable venture. Every investor must establish his own diversification rules on several levels.

Diversification formulas are also very personal, and they should be reviewed from time to time to determine if they are still suitable for the goals and objectives outlined in your latest investment plan. One of the few things I would agree with in the behavior of Life Insurance Salespeople is their constant review of a person's circumstances to see if their current plan remains sound. Of course their motivation is to sell more product! Mine would be to see if any "fine tuning" adjustment to the mix of securities is necessary.

<u>Fine Tuning is an important concept</u>. It is not something that people who live on commissions are generally comfortable with for a few understandable reasons. First of all, they could be talking to you at your own initiation because you are either unhappy with or confused about your present investment plan. Or they could have initiated the contact themselves, planted seeds of discontent about your present program, and now need to implement their own plan while you're hot to make a break from the past. Fine-tuning doesn't generate enough commissionable change.

It is very unlikely that your present plan (assuming that it is actually a plan) is so terrible that nothing you own deserves to be kept! Still, most "Financial Planners" and "Investment Advisors" will recommend that everything be sold! Remember to question the motivation of any advisor who benefits directly from his advice. Be wary of a recommendation that includes the immediate sale of your holdings and/or purchase of annuities and Mutual Funds. These two products occupy the highest rungs on the commission ladder.

Have a look at the new guy's personal investment portfolio before you trust him to design your own! You deserve an experienced person. **It's not your responsibility to train the new and the hungry, even if they happen to be related to you!**

You won't believe how often this scenario unfolds; try not to let it happen to you!

GIRL MEETS BOY

A young widow is living off of the income from her portfolio. Girl meets "Financial Advisor" boy and falls in love. Girl accepts boy's "advanced" financial advice. NASDAQ crashes, portfolio is gone, and income too. Boy gets laid off...

The Financial Industry is very large and growing larger every day, creating excellent career opportunities for people who just might be (or become) a part of your life. Your "gut" will tell you to help your loved ones' progress by letting them handle your investment program.

Of course your [Insert child, fiancé, nephew, or lover, etc.] is the best and the brightest! **If so they will survive and prosper without your product or securities purchases.** Don't become the main character in one of these horror stories! Remember that the survival rate in the securities business is about the same as in the restaurant business. **If you want to help, just write a check when they need to pay the rent. Don't let them blow their own inheritance while you still need to use it!**

Diversification Level One: Fixed Income vs. Equity

No matter how complicated we have been brainwashed into thinking the investment world is, there are really only two classes of investment securities: Fixed Income and Equity. Dependent primarily on your age and your plans for retirement, your portfolio should consciously be allocated between that class of securities whose primary role is income production (the former), and the other class, whose primary purpose is to generate growth in capital. **Regardless of age and salary level, any six-figure investment portfolio should have a portion allocated toward income production.**

The PURPOSE of "fixed income" securities [which include such things as Corporate and Municipal Bonds, many different types of Government Securities, Preferred Stocks, REITs (Real Estate Investment Trusts), and QUIDs, QUIPS, and a myriad of other acronyms that have been developed to describe the new breed of debenture-like preferred shares, etc.] **is simply to produce a safe and constant flow of income.** Any "growth in capital" is simply gravy, resulting from a willingness to take advantage of changes in the perceived direction of interest rates. Surprisingly, this concept is difficult to grasp for many investors. But the wealthy person's portfolio is always well stocked with income producers (especially municipal bonds). **It's like an insurance policy for the "growth" portion of the portfolio (i.e., if the market value of your securities falls by 7% but you have generated 8% in dividends, interest, and capital gains, you will show a net gain for the period). Right?**

Why aren't Fixed Income Securities popular with investors, commissioned Financial Advisors, or the Wall Street media? Probably because of the "horse race" mentality that Wall Street nourishes so successfully. Fixed Income is not nearly as exciting at the personal portfolio level as it is among professional institutional bond traders where the figures and the pressures for "performance" are incredible. Fixed income filters down to the investing public either in the form of "odd lot" individual bonds (I think $50,000 or $100,000 is considered a round lot compared with 100 shares of a common or preferred stock.), or "investment products" called closed-end and open-end bond funds, and various types of "Unit Trusts". (See Chapter Seven.)

This is an area where Investment Products really do play a valuable role in portfolio development and management, but they too are not something you hear a whole lot about. Other than for professional bond traders, they are just plain boring! Prices don't jump around as they do with other securities. There is little chance for exponential growth, and thus, there is less likelihood of media attention.

Wall Street wants action! It's a lot like Las Vegas, isn't it? The Casinos don't care if you win or lose. They want your action: the hours played and the average amount wagered. Losers get the same "comps" and benefits as winners. The croupiers just get tips! Eventually "Wall Street" will be even smarter!

Commissioned sales people have little use for "fixed income" Investment Products because they are traded very infrequently. Most people are reluctant to trade them at all. Thus, the commissions per dollar of investment (over the life of a 30-year bond) are very low compared with the same amount of money invested in equities. But I have had many experiences where Financial Advisors use the public's ignorance of Fixed Income Security behavior to encourage unnecessary transactions. "Your bond fund isn't doing very well (What is it supposed to be doing?). I want you to sell it and buy this bond fund which has "performed" much better (according to the marketing of the Mutual Fund company)."

The only thing a bond fund is "supposed to do" is to generate a regular stream of income. That's it. At any point in time, bonds of the same quality and duration will produce similar interest rates. Switching from one bond fund to another generates nothing but penalties for the investor and commissions for the salesperson. The same is true of fixed annuities. Unless you are totally changing your financial plan, be careful about drastic changes in your fixed income portfolio.

The market price of a fixed income security varies inversely with the perceived direction of short-term interest rates. (Prices go up when lower rates are expected and down when higher rates seem to be on the horizon.) Investors don't like fixed income securities because they know so little about them, and because of their price movements. Prices of "safe(r)" securities just aren't supposed to fluctuate; it's not fair! **Actually, if you invest in the right types of fixed income securities, interest rate movements, in either direction, will be your friend. If you (or your financial advisor) have no "tradable" fixed income securities in your portfolio, you are letting an outstanding long-term growth opportunity pass you by!**

There is Magic in Your Municipal Bond portfolio! Many people of means fail to recognize the usefulness of a well diversified, income producing fixed income portfolio! Once you have one, never let it go. Here's a real life example. I'm building a house in South Carolina and I needed to raise a significant sum of money to buy the property and to get the infrastructure started. Financing possibilities were endless; partial portfolio liquidation must be the last possible choice. The cost of the money had to be minimized.

If we can borrow money for less than what we make with our assets, and if it is a short term proposition, why not? The problem with using equities within this line of reasoning is simply that you cannot be sure of your income level. Using your bonds as collateral for a short-term "margin loan" to avoid the liquidation of an important asset can provide extremely cheap financing!

My Municipal Bonds produce around 7%, or $42,000 tax-free per year. My margin rate is about 8% at the moment. Are your gears starting to mesh? It gets better. The interest paid is deductible from my taxable portfolio income, making my actual cost of money a (theoretically) negative number, with an actual negative cash flow of only 1%! One more thing, the loan is self-liquidating because the monthly cash flow is greater than the monthly interest charges. **You are never too young to develop a Municipal Bond Portfolio! FIRE ANYONE WHO ADVISES YOU TO LIQUIDATE IT!** One other point you need to know about this particular financing method. You must own the bonds first. **The IRS frowns on borrowing to purchase a tax-exempt cash flow, and deducting the interest on the loan.**

Trading Fixed Income Securities profitably is a bonus. If you are managing your Asset Allocation properly, you will be purchasing fixed income securities periodically at whatever prevailing interest rates happen to be. (This is a real life example of "compounding", regardless of the interest rate received.) In a falling interest rate environment, you will discover that some of your Preferred Stocks or closed-end (municipal) bond funds have moved up in price to the point where a considerable (10% or more) profit can be realized. *If you can find a reinvestment* *opportunity with a higher current yield, take the profit and increase your cash flow!*

The **PURPOSE** of "equity" securities [which include Common Stocks, closed-end stock funds, and equity mutual funds] **is to produce capital gains income.** Any other income (dividends) is simply gravy, and is the direct result of a firm belief that dividend-paying securities are safer than those that pay nothing, and a conservative portfolio management rule that insists upon cash flow from every security.

In order to pay regular quarterly dividends, several important "fundamentals" must be solidly in place. First of all there must be sufficient cash flow to pay out the money. Secondly, the firm must be operating profitably in order to support the payments for any length of time. Both are signs of strength and stability in a company, and add to the inherent safety of the stock.

At the personal level, if you ever start up your own business, you'll know that a certain amount of financial strength and steady cash flow is needed before you even think of paying yourself a salary. (It was six or seven years before I felt comfortable doing so in my little start-up business.)

Now doesn't this simple little explanation point to something else? Is it anything short of crazy to bet on unknown new companies? And what about those "growth" companies and their "plowing back earnings into the company rhetoric"? What they are doing is plowing back earnings into executive salaries (check the public records) while their debt continues to rise. It pays to stick with companies that boast sound "fundamentals". Paying a regular dividend is one of them.

Here's a research project for you. Check out the executive salaries of any "growth" company that says it is operating profitably but doesn't pay a dividend.

The Equity portion of the portfolio can be as high as 100% for the young person just starting out. As the size of the portfolio and/or the age of the investor increases, the proportion at risk must be reduced (no matter how solid the equities are, they are still more risky than high quality fixed income securities). There were many investors, particularly in the "hot" NASDAQ stock market of the late '90s, who felt that their growing portfolio market values allowed them the luxury of undertaking greater risks. *On the contrary, it is the wise investor who understands that real wealth has been secured when you no longer have to put serious dollars at risk!*

Most of the remainder of this book will deal with the development and management of a working equity portfolio.

Diversification Level Two: The Size of Individual Positions

A perfectly diversified portfolio will have no more than 5% of its assets in any one individual security, either Fixed Income or Equity! This determination is based upon the amount actually invested in the security, not the current market value. (This is one tenet of The Working Capital Model, explained in Chapter Five.) The 5% figure is certainly just a guideline, but it is of vital importance to never let the amount invested in any one security get out of line. Disasters must be avoided, and this is the easiest way to keep the risk associated with any one investment under control. The operative question should be an easy one to answer: If the market value of this security goes to zero, will the level of portfolio pain be acceptable? Yes or No!

This could be the most difficult aspect of diversification strategy to manage because of the outside influences that heap pressure upon the investor! More often than not, the "buy" decision is the result either of some brainstorm concocted by a hungry "Financial Advisor", or the result of a Media story that has pushed the person's "greed button". To manage money successfully, you must be disciplined. You must develop a good filtering system!

Some investment theorists would say that a controlled percentage allocation to speculation is acceptable. My contention is that speculation is as addictive as nicotine or heroine, and must be stopped "cold turkey" even before it begins. The worst thing that can happen is for the investor to get lucky and make some money. I've seen the speculative portion of a portfolio grow and grow, until it takes over the program. I've seen clients finance their addiction by liquidating the income producing assets they had taken years to accumulate.

Recognize speculation as a cancer in an investment portfolio and you will magnify your chances for a successful experience. Any idea that sounds like a sure thing, or that is predicated upon knowledge of the future, is a speculation. A listing of speculative securities that will absolutely endanger your financial health would include: options, indexes, and futures of any kind, commodities, and IPOs (Initial Public Offerings).

Where did the "5% in speculation is OK" idea come from? Just who is selling these speculations anyway? Wall Street and its down-line cronies have got to push these high-risk ventures some how, so they try to make you believe that some speculation is OK. It's a lot like the junk bond scenario described earlier. If I go to the racetrack and place equal bets on all the horses, I'm going to win! Get the idea?

Any time you are tempted to "bet the farm" on a hot tip, remember WHOOPS, or IBM at $40, W. T. Grant at $0.00, or First Jersey Securities. [For those of you who are unfamiliar with these names or prices, they are classic stories of: (1) a AAA Municipal Bond failure; (2) the saga of IBM going from an A+ to a B rating (where it remains today); (3) a bankruptcy in a major retailer; (4) a big (discount) Securities Firm that (allegedly) succeeded for years selling fraudulent "story" stocks to unsuspecting investors.]

The WHOOPS fiasco is perhaps the best example of the lot! These AAA (The highest possible quality rating.) bonds were brought to the public by all of the major Wire Houses and were instantly gobbled up by investors. I believe that the eventual default had something to do with Nuclear Power Plant development or operations. However, the point is that some slick Attorneys were able to get the Washington Public Power Supply Authority off the hook for the interest and most of the principal! Neither the bank trustees, nor the Wall Street Institutions were able to save the investors from major losses! It never really seemed like they tried very hard either. Basic contract law was tossed out the window. Politics? No one is talking. Investors eventually received just pennies on the dollar; the lawyers did better!

One of my relatives was just receiving a significant insurance settlement from a near fatal accident around the time of the offering. His unsuspecting and inexperienced investor father placed the entire sum in WHOOPS bonds. Ouch! But that's not as "globally" sad as the fact that some supposedly experienced "Financial Professional" allowed (even encouraged) him to do so. Now there was a justifiable lawsuit that never happened!

Diversification Level Three: Industry Representation

I've pointed out before that the market is a "groupie" kind of place, in the sense that one group or another is always falling from grace for whatever (contrived?) reason Wall Street comes up with. Rarely will you hear the big guys identify a flight from "the financials", "drug stocks", or "the tech sector" simply as profit taking by investors who are switching to under-priced bargains somewhere else. When "The Street" pans one sector or group,

45

they normally will find a reason to play up another. (Coincidentally, they'll have plenty of the new favorites in their trading accounts**.) Once you have implemented your trading strategy, you will appreciate the help! You will already have taken your profits in some previous "hot" group, and should have plenty of "smart cash" available for investment in the new pariah.**

Wall Street never encourages the purchase of stocks that are going down. Ninety per cent of Wall Street analysts' recommendations are "buys"! They only want you to buy stocks that are "strong" because "they probably will go up forever", and because you'll feel stupid if you don't own them. This "chain letter" mentality sinks a lot of IRAs and 401k programs every year because it just doesn't work that way. Professionals take their profits and move on to other opportunities. The new opportunities are generally in the group(s) we all hated last year and into which those rich guys put their money before their puppet "Wire Houses" gave you the ok to follow suit!

The "Circle of Gold" (a chain letter, from the Seventies)

Read the first paragraph and then answer this question: When did this article appear in the Investment Management Forum?

"The DJIA has put together a 2.75-year hot streak…doubling in value! This is far more impressive than the rally that preceded the market "break" which occurred [xx] years ago next week. I don't see much similarity between the economic environments that existed then and now…but investor attitudes are identical: GREED, INVULNERABILITY, RECKLESSNESS, and CERTAINTY…"

"Over the last few months we've seen periods of significant weakness and a shift of dollars into ever more speculative investments. It's unusual...to find such large numbers of quality investments [good companies down in price] at such high market levels!"

"This is probably a good time to remind you that **paper profits do little to produce productive wealth and...even less to prepare you for (the inevitable) correction.** Anything that goes up in price for an extended period of time becomes vulnerable, particularly when the pace of the rise has been fast. **For the Mutual Fund investor, the similarity to a chain letter is very real. Someone is going to be left holding a bag full of securities purchased at the highest price in the history of mankind!"**

"It's natural to want to milk the last dollar out of a rally, but it's foolish to leave all your chips on the table indefinitely. Mutual Fund results are "uncorrected" numbers; an illusion of brilliance that fades with each downturn. **These managers cannot take profits in the face of (Unit Holder) GREED, and are unable to buy bargains when the greed becomes PANIC."** Always remember to sell too soon!"

(IMF, 10/12/97)

Sell recommendations from Wall Street gurus are scarce, for at least three reasons: a) **Self proclaimed geniuses hate to be proven wrong so they avoid telling their clients to give up on securities they've touted so strongly in the recent past.** b) On the other side of the scales, they are afraid to recommend taking profits (until after their in-house Mutual Fund managers do) for fear that the stock will continue to go up! Do they know human nature or what? Someone in the media could point out that they sold too soon and their reputation as a guru could suffer. c) Major firms can't say "sell" or "take profits" because of the investment banking relationship they have with the company in question!

(I just discussed this behavior with one of my "coverage" callers an hour ago! It was readily admitted

with no excuses offered. He just considered this to be business as usual; everybody does it! Unbelievable!)

Wasn't it a Vanderbilt who said that the secret of his great wealth was "selling too soon"!

I remember a situation a few years ago when a hotel chain I owned stock in for a number of my clients was the target of an unfriendly takeover. Well the stock price shot up and I instantly made the calls to sell all of the stock and to reel-in the 45% "instant winner" profit! A few days later, I got a call from a client who was extremely upset that I didn't wait around for the offer to be sweetened! Believe me, had I waited (which I absolutely would never recommend under any circumstances) and the deal fell through, I would have received a call from the very same person. **There is no room for hindsight in any management situation, and there is no such thing as a bad profit!**

Frequent selling is also frowned upon by Wall Street regulators and (more importantly) looked upon by client Attorneys as evidence of "churning". Aren't lawyers wonderful? An investor calls the shots in his portfolio based on advice he can either accept or reject, he gets caught with his speculative pants down and goes crying to some Attorney. It reminds me of some of the kids I went to grade school with! Its even more amazing how Attorneys are willing to sue for absolutely anything! Here's a "real lifer":

A South Jersey doctor hires me to manage one of his portfolios. I instantly had the broker stop reinvesting income in a bond fund (which had been described, in error, to the doctor as: "similar to a Money Market Fund"!) The broker convinces the doctor to purchase a large amount of the same fund in another of his accounts (an unmanaged account). Interest rates rise, the market value of the fund goes down, and the doctor finds an Attorney willing to sue the brokerage firm on the grounds that they took advantage of a poor unsuspecting, and inexperienced investor!

The doctor explained to me that I would be his "key" witness. I was supposed to corroborate that a broker who should have known better, had sold him this "bad investment" under false pretenses. After all, it must have been a bad fund because I had stopped him from buying it elsewhere. Quite a stretch, huh? But it wasn't a bad fund at all; it was just a bond fund that had reacted exactly as it should have in the face of higher interest rates. He was a very sophisticated investor indeed, and he knew as well as the broker did that I would not invest in it. The only thing the broker had done wrong was to say that the fund "acted like a higher yielding Money Market Fund", and the doctor was extremely well versed in both bonds and Money Market Funds.

The doctor was also very well experienced at throwing his weight around with threats and promises to get his way with big companies where he was a big client. His lawyer was willing to play the game and he (the doctor) expected me to fall in line as well, or else he said, "he would be very disappointed". I understood what he meant. If only more lawyers would just say "NO". Lawyers who get paid "win or lose" need to be punished for bringing frivolous lawsuits like this one would have been, if the doctor could have found a willing "witness" (or accomplice?).

Unfortunately, Attorneys are supervised by (you guessed it), other Attorneys.

In constructing your portfolio, 15% or so should be the high end for representation in any one industry. Not as much for fear of total loss, but for a lessening of your ability to take advantage of opportunities elsewhere. One really never knows which groups will move in which direction, or when such movements will occur.

Diversification Level Four: By Country

Overseas investing demands a level of knowledge that is beyond most individual investors. Investment textbooks single out this type of investing as particularly speculative. Someone should produce a documentary on the story of the development of foreign country mutual funds! Packaged products from a thousand different vendors appeared almost overnight, just so you could feel like you've done your duty and properly covered this slice of your "Financial Advisors" multi-colored pie-chart diversification plan.

Here are a few clues: an asset allocation formula needs only two numbers (fixed income % and equity %). An asset allocation formula that includes a target % for "cash" is the confused product of someone who thinks he can predict the future OR who is waiting for his boss to tell him what to think. An asset allocation formula with multiple "cap" classifications, precious metals, or decimal point percentage breakdowns is the work of a sick mind.

There is an easier and more fruitful way to invest in the global economy with considerably less risk. The vast majority of investment grade companies are international players with proven track records of success in foreign markets. Additionally, the very best foreign companies trade their ADRs (American Depository Receipts) on our own hometown stock exchanges. Don't make this more difficult then it needs to be. **Boutique funds for foreign investing won't find a home in most sophisticated portfolios.** Have you seen the TV commercial where the Mutual Fund "big shot" is poking around the streets of Hong Kong or Manila? "This proves, Mr. Investor, that we 'know' how to find the very best overseas investment opportunities!" Now there's one to test your GQ (Gullibility Quotient).

Here's a "True" or "False" Wall Street Quiz: the following Mutual Funds could be sold to the public, legally, and successfully as worthy foreign investments.

1. The South American Political Stability Fund.
2. The Arctic Refrigeration Industrial Reclamation Fund.
3. The Middle East Peace and Security Fund.
4. The Tiger Woods Absolutely Anything Anywhere Fund

If you must invest in foreign companies, apply the same "quality tests" as you would with domestic companies. Stick with the best and you'll rarely lose money. Try Phillips, Dupont, Royal Dutch, Sony, Unilever, etc.

The Case for Income

Maybe it's the tax code or perhaps it's just a misconception people have about investing, but I've always gotten a chuckle out of seriously well employed people who (pompously) say: "just invest for growth, I don't need any more income!" Can't you just hear the tone of their voice? **Income is good. It pays the bills, particularly at retirement time. Never discount the importance of cash flow, especially if you can arrange for the bulk of it to be tax-free! What's better, tax-free or tax-deferred? BOTH!**

Pretend that you are a corporate hot shot, making and spending a huge salary while you accumulate all of those prestigious, over-priced status symbols that the newly rich love so well. You have millions of dollars in company stock that you refuse to sell, and much more in stock options that you won't exercise until the company "splits" a few more times. BANG! Suddenly, your company's buggy whip is replaced with the new and improved "Pentium Twelve" buggy whip perfected by your competition! Surprise! Now how does the million in municipals you shunned last month sound? That $60,000 in tax-free income

51

would certainly pay a few bills while you find a new employer. **Quality, Diversification, and Income strike again!**

My father was big into Real Estate. He didn't trust the Stock Market, and hated the thought of anyone else earning a commission from him! He said that he had no use for things that fluctuated wildly in market value. Actually, he was more of a "trader" than he would ever admit to anyone. It was not uncommon for him to sell a house or a property before he even owned it, and cry about the taxes all the way to his Accountant's office.

You can behave similarly in the stock market with a transaction called a "short sale". You are guessing that the price of a stock will fall so you effectively borrow the shares from the brokerage firm as they sell it from their inventory. You cannot collect interest on the proceeds of the sale, so the cash sits idle in your account, and any dividends that are declared by the company belong to the brokerage firm. You then "buy the stock back" after the price falls (covering your short position). **This is an extremely speculative and dangerous strategy that must be avoided, no matter what you think you "know".** It could be where the expression "lose your shorts" comes from, or is that your shirt?

Many rallies are temporarily magnified (toward their end?) as speculators "rush in to cover their short positions" and to cut their losses. **I don't think I've every heard any one report that a rally has been started as a result of (profitable) short covering!**

So in bad real estate markets, brought about by recession, high interest rates, whatever, DAD WOULD FEEL "BROKE". I never cared for developing real estate. There are just too many rules and regulations, an illiquid market, having to deal with the petty dictators who live on local planning boards, etc. Still, over the years, I have grown to appreciate the usefulness and profitability of well-positioned real estate, as a portion of a person's fixed income investment portfolio. (Here's another area where a seasoned Professional is worth ever dollar you pay him in fee or commission. Find someone you can trust, check the references, and apply the same rules as you now do in your equity selections.)

Once our family was out for a fancy dinner, and Dad thought that we should all pass up those wonderful lobster and crabmeat cocktails because they were so expensive. Real estate wasn't selling, and cash flow wasn't nearly at normal levels. Corporations, on the other hand, weren't stopping, or even cutting, their quarterly dividend payments. Municipalities didn't default on their bond interest payments, and there were still trading opportunities in the equity markets. I was happy to pay for the fancy appetizers.

The lesson is simple. I can buy a lot more meals with my Municipal Bond Interest and trading profits than I can with a vacant rental property, or with a thousand acres of raw land. I can pay for more vacations with interest, dividends, and capital gains than I can with a portfolio full of securities that don't produce income or that are subject to a "buy and hold" mentality. I also can't buy more "growth" stocks without cash flow from somewhere. Just what is a "growth" stock anyway? It must be one of those stocks that only go up in price, because its numbers go up every quarter and will forever!

Liquidity. Note that the "liquidity" of an investment is a factor in determining its inherent "Quality". A portfolio comprised solely of even the highest quality real estate is as poorly diversified as the junk bond portfolio mentioned earlier. Liquidity is definitely a factor that must be considered when developing the fixed income side of the portfolio. Don't load up on securities with a "thin" (non-liquid) market. But, at the same time, you should be purchasing fixed income securities with an "I may never be selling this investment" mindset.

Income Must Increase Annually. Not only must a portfolio generate income, it is important that a conscious effort be made to actually increase the "base" income level each year. **"Base Income" is the sum of dividends and interest only.** The reason for the exclusion of "capital gain" income is that you cannot actually plan on any particular level. This is certainly a conservative way of planning your cash flow, but it seriously reduces your risk level in a very important area.

The easy way to increase annual income is through an asset allocation formula that has a fixed income element of at least 30% and which is seriously applied in investment decision making. The formula itself need never be changed and the base income will still increase, absolutely.

Make sure you understand the math! Here goes. A $100,000 portfolio produces $7,000 in base income in 1997. None of the income is spent and it is all reinvested in fixed income securities at a 6% rate of interest. Our base income would increase to approximately $7,420. Right? ($100,000 x .07) + ($7,000 x .06) = $7,000 + $420.

The classical portfolio objective is to have enough base income at retirement to preclude the need to invade principal. You just can't do it with a Microsoft home run and nothing else, and you don't want to wait too long to get started!

Risk Management

An awful lot of wisdom has been packed into the education phase of this book! Your appreciation of how Wall Street functions; your understanding of how easily the media is manipulated to suit the long-range plans and objectives of the Institutions, and some familiarity with what makes a "Commissioned Financial Advisor" tick are all elements of Risk Management. An insistence on **Quality**, strict adherence to the fundamental Rules of **Diversification**, and a constant pursuit of increased annual **Income** are the fundamental tools you should use to protect yourself, not only from the bad guys, but also from yourself. **Must humans are very much alike; they can resist anything except temptation. Wall Street owns about the sweetest** smelling candy store on the planet; temptation is the corner stone of their business plan!

It's important to understand that investing is in no way an intellectual pursuit in which "research", "information" and "business degrees" are more important than common sense, greed control, discipline, and experience. Every investment involves some element of risk, and you would be well advised to stay far away from any person or institution that even suggests to you that they have solved that problem. **You just can't eliminate risk. FORGET ABOUT IT! But you absolutely must manage it!**

This section has provided much of the investment insight that an up and coming millionaire needs to preserve the wealth he or she accumulates. You would do well to review the preceding sections periodically as a wake up call for your portfolio. Here are the key words and concepts: Trading, Fixed and Variable Costs, Quality, Diversification, Income, and Liquidity. If you're confused, do not pass Go. Read it again. Look at your portfolio structure frequently to make sure it is positioned in accordance with "The Plan."

Break Time: Financial Professionals and You

It's nearly as important to distinguish between Financial Services professionals, as it is to understand the motivations lurking beneath the recommendations they make and/or the advice that they give. 99.9% of you will need the assistance of some form of Financial Pro at some time in your investment life. We'll look at a few of these very superficially, just so you will know to whom I am referring throughout the remainder of the book. You'll find that several categories of professionals are missing: Accountants, Doctors, Attorneys, Bankers, and Media Commentators among them. They are professionals who are certainly worthy of your respect for their professional opinions, but the vast majority of them are absolutely not qualified as financial professionals no matter how wealthy or influential they happen to be. Even a license to sell securities is not qualification, in and of itself.

I have a great deal of respect for the honest financial professionals I have been fortunate enough to work with over the years but, unhappily, I have found that most (in order to feed their families) are less than interested in what is best for you. It's easy to test your professional with money. Tell your Life Insurance agent that you want a $1,000,000 policy and see if he tries to talk you out of it. Tell your stockbroker to sell all your municipal bonds and buy a Foreign Aggressive Growth Fund. I'm sure you get the picture; what was that "oldest profession" again?

Stock Brokers, Financial Advisors, and Investment Brokers: Every brokerage firm has some euphemistic title that they use to describe their retail stockbrokers. Most stockbrokers are also given the title: "Vice President of Something" to further impress you and to gain your trust. When I use these terms, I am referring to the person you speak with when you are placing orders to buy or to sell securities. If you are not speaking to someone, you emphasis is on the wrong syl-la-ble.

These are also the people who "cold call" you at dinnertime to sell specific stocks, funds or other investment products. Some of these people can, and often do, fall into other categories since they are encouraged to learn as much as possible. Learning is geared toward passing specific tests that (you guessed it) qualify them to sell additional products.

Financial Planners, and CFPs, Investment Advisors and RIAs: Stockbroker types often try to achieve additional status by becoming either a "Chartered" or a "Certified" Financial Planner; most are required to become RIAs. Anyone, even a plumber (and some plumbers probably know more about investing than some Financial Planners), can call himself or herself a Financial Planner or an Investment Advisor. "Qualified" Financial Planners and "Registered" Investment Advisors will have a designation such as CFP and RIA after their name that sets them apart from the unqualified variety. They have education.

Most Financial Planners are also Registered Investment Advisors, which merely means that they have passed some securities examinations, and that they have registered with the Securities and Exchange Commission. If they haven't gone to the trouble to obtain the education, I would question their ability to fully understand their own experience, since that has to be their primary claim to fame! Your first search should be for the Financial/Investment, Planners/Advisors with the designations.

That group can then be divided into three sub groups. First there are those that just plan and advise, and for a fee only. They make generic recommendations that you can implement on your own with whomever you like. If you ask them to point you to a salesperson, and they do, remind them that they are legally bound to disclose any financial arrangement (soft or hard dollar) that they have with that person. ***(It would be unethical, and illegal in some circumstances, for any of these professionals, NOT TO DISCLOSE such a financial arrangement.)*** It's best if you don't ask for names.

One of my clients introduced me to her Accountant, at his request. He had been impressed with my handling of her accounts, and wanted to recommend me to some of his other clients. "How much of my fee would I be able to share with him as a referral fee", he asked? "Investment Management fees are much smaller than Mutual Fund commissions," I explained, "and, I could legally make such an arrangement ONLY if I disclosed it to the SEC and if he disclosed it to the client." This was fine until I told him that I had to have a disclosure document signed by his client in my files and that my client files were subject to SEC audit. The arrangement never happened, and the client was eventually moved into "load" mutual funds! This guy was recently elected to a local government position. Go figure!

Other Financial Planner/Investment Advisor types primarily will be product salespersons. They want to sell you whatever benefits them the most from among the many products they have in their bag that will absolutely satisfy your goals. They will always have a product that perfectly suits your needs, whatever those needs happen to be. What a coincidence! Unlike the Stockbroker group, these people always sell Life Insurance and Annuities. In fact, **no self respecting Life Insurance Salesman would ever refer to his profession as anything but "Financial Planning"!** It has a very respectful and confidence-building ring to it, doesn't it? Once or twice in my career, I've met product selling Financial Planners/Investment Advisors that I thought I could work with and trust. I was wrong.

Finally, there are Planners/Advisors who are fee based if you want them to be, or commission only if that's what you would prefer. These guys and gals want it both ways, and should be avoided at all costs. There is no need for you to deal with a person who is having such an identity crisis.

Note that all of the professionals listed above (Stockbrokers and Financial Planners) think of themselves as Investment Managers and will try to convince you that they are literally managing large sums of money for their clients. For the most part, they are really just kidding themselves! They sell Investment Management services that are provided by others, and for a hefty commission.

Investment Managers, Money Managers, Asset Managers, and Fund Managers: One word separates these professionals from all of the others. "Manage!" **They run the investment program** in a manner that they hope will achieve certain identifiable objectives and goals. (Even a Mutual Fund prospectus "talks the talk" as though a certain directional strategy will be adhered to.) Managers make all of the decisions with regard to securities selection, buying and selling, and so on. They may or may not be involved in "planning" the program itself with the client, but they absolutely run it! For some reason that is unintelligible to me, "packaged" (Mutual Fund) money management is much more popular with investors than individualized management. Somehow people think it's safer to trust people they never meet than to meet with people to determine if they should trust them!

Personal Investment Management is facilitated by a legal document called a "Limited Power of Attorney", which permits the brokerage firm to take the Manager's directions with regard to a specific investment portfolio. It is very specific and very protective of the owner of the securities. A Mutual Fund manager is tacitly given exactly the same powers, but without the same protective covenants.

Mutual Fund Managers have one other serious, and often fatal, problem: when the going gets tough, they get fired! That's right ladies and gentlemen, and it's the Mutual Fund shareholders that do the firing! "Deep Pockets" will tell you all about it!

"Being in the right place at the right time often provides some of life's greatest opportunities. Agree? We all know stories where someone got the "BUY OF A LIFETIME" on a boat, plane, house, or whatever. Sometimes, just by chance, life gives us a shot at making the really big deal at a "CHEAP" price. We often pass these opportunities up because of ignorance, fear, or lack of money."

"The most frustrating reason to forego GREAT opportunity is the lack of money! In the case of ignorance you don't feel bad because you have no idea that you are missing out on anything. Fear makes one more comfortable to pass the BIG DEAL up. Lack of money haunts you for a lifetime as the ONLY IF scenario plays over and over again in your head."

"Peter Lynch (manager of the famous Magellan Fund) expressed that frustration after the "CRASH" of October 1987. On one of those "RESEARCH" trips we spoke about earlier, on the other side of the Atlantic, he got the news on the faltering markets. Oh yes, it was the end of the world back then also. Life as we knew it at the time was over and we were on our way to economic disaster with no way out. The lemmings were very busy selling all of their stocks (at any price) running as fast as they could from the monster (CAPITALISM). It was the biggest one day drop in terms of points and I believe also in percentage. The party was over as the selling pressure was so great that even the "Specialists" on the New York Stock Exchange panicked. We were close to a 'MELT DOWN'."

"Old Peter wasn't fooled. He was a seasoned professional who saw the glass as half full (soon to be refilled). What did he see in all of the chaos? OPPORTUNITY! What did he do? Buy up all the bargains? WRONG! Knowing that the stocks of the greatest companies, in the greatest economy the world had ever seen, were at "fire sale" prices, what did he do? SELL! SELL! SELL! BUT WHY?"

"Because the lemmings (investors) were giving orders to exit the market (fear). As redemptions come in, even the brightest fund managers are FORCED to sell stock. But what about buying all that CHEAP stock at once in a life time prices? Managers have to wait for the lemmings to reverse course and buy when the prices are high. Why? Because that's what the lemmings "think" is best (ignorance)."

"The fund managers can't buy low (lack of money). I read somewhere that Mr. Lynch said it was one of the most frustrating times of his life. Not the crash, but the inability to take advantage of the OPPORTUNITY!"

*   *   *   *   *

All of these professionals are required to pass securities tests similar to those required of the other Financial Professionals. But, those who are running their own Investment Management

Businesses must achieve a higher grade to become a Registered Principal. What don't any of them do? ***They Don't Sell Products, or anything else,*** other than their own skills and experience. How are they compensated? They get a fee based on the market value of the assets they manage. Obviously, their incentive is to make the value increase.

Any commissions or similar compensation they receive for directing investments to particular places or products would be considered an illegal conflict of interest! Also, there are specific rules that prohibit any performance or profit based incentives for smaller investment clients.

Most professional Money Managers are employed by the major Wall Street Institutions because you just have to "have money" to survive the early years of building this type of business from scratch, without commissions! A million dollars "under management" generates less than $10,000 in gross annual income for the manager. Selling a million dollars worth of annuities and Mutual Funds would produce between $40,000 and $60,000 in commissions! (Does that help explain why your Accountant obtained a securities license?)

Additionally, major firms will pay big salary bucks to recruit fund managers (experienced or not) while the "Independent Manager" route will take years to develop a meaningful cash flow. They also pay big advertising bucks to promote the management business, making for a competitive environment that most independents can't survive.

Another reason why many investors choose "in house" or "Wrap Account" managers ***is just because they are affiliated with Institutional Entities.*** **These investors want to have someone with serious money to sue if something goes wrong!** It's a sad statement, but a true one...

Very few people can afford to become Independent Managers and even fewer are able to survive. Those that do survive, sacrifice more and more of their independence as they grow, and most do want to grow as much as possible. Competition in this field has become so fierce that most managers have had to become "fund managers". Many allow themselves to be used as WRAP Account Managers; most eventually become pawns or employees of the Institutions! Pity.

The bigger and more important they get, the less accessible they become. If you can't meet with the person who is managing your portfolio, or at least get references from other clients for whom he manages similar accounts, you should be looking elsewhere! Learn how to be "under-whelmed" by the hype of Institutional advertising. Commercial minutes at last year's (not so) Super Bowl cost millions, and many of those minutes were purchased by Financial Institutions solely to tell you about their wonderful "just an annual fee", no commissions, personal Money Management services.

Would you spend billions promoting a service that you expect to lose money on? I don't think so! **Find yourself a Totally Independent Investment Manager, with no affiliations with or dependencies on any other entity or professional! Talk to the real live person who will be making the decisions in your account, look her in the eye, and shake her hand. Get references and check them out. Formulate a plan and monitor the transactions. There are only two "don'ts". Don't be impatient and don't compare your performance with indices and averages that have absolutely no correlation with the structure of your portfolio.**

Just Testing!

Mutual funds have minimal requirements for starting an account, and that's perfectly fine because every Unit or Share that is purchased (you can't actually get the stock certificates and you don't actually own a piece of any individual companies) theoretically represents a fraction of the fund's assets. Thus, you will experience the same "performance" with a $2,000 "test" investment, as you will with a $2,000,000 commitment.

But, you can't do that with a real personalized portfolio Investment Manager because of the rules we've already discussed. You have to give the Manager enough of a commitment so that he or she can put your program into operation effectively. A Mutual Fund manager really doesn't care. They have no idea what your "plan" is, and they do only one thing that is supposed to satisfy a million "owners".

A personal manager though, has to set up a portfolio with a definite asset allocation and make appropriate selections of companies that you will actually own. You will see what he is doing immediately, (Every trade generates a confirmation notice.) and you should be able to tell if what you see is what you expected. **With a Mutual Fund, what you don't see is what you get! There is absolutely no way you can determine what you own at any point in time!** If something is done that is improper for whatever reason, or not in line with what you would expect, you'll just never know!

With a personal manager, the more of your program you allow him to control and to supervise, the better job he will be able to do to meet your goals and expectations! And, of course, you'll be able to talk to him about what he's doing for you, if you happen to have a question.

CHAPTER TWO: WALTZING AROUND WALL STREET

If you accept the premise that the Wall Street Institutions we tolerate combine to form a Financial Super Power that can take over our investment lives, and manipulate us invisibly and effortlessly, read on and learn how to harness that incredible power and use it to your own advantage for a change! Yes, you can get wealthy and/or remain wealthy investing on Wall Street, BUT only if you control the process, using the institutions and the media as your own private investment "counter-resource". We've begun your "know thy enemy" training; the process continues below.

If you disagree totally, turn off the TV (or your computer monitor) **STOP KIDDING YOURSELF** and re-read the introductory portion of the book!

We've talked about the development of a financial plan as a basic first step in the process of developing a successful investment strategy. **Management of anything involves identifying the goals and objectives of the enterprise and then planning, organizing, controlling, and directing the implementation of the plan.** Just in the off chance that you don't have an investment plan (an integral part of a "Financial Plan" and the part we are concerned with here) of your own, we'll use the one that I've been using to run money with for three decades. It was just outlined for you under the topics of Quality, Diversification, and Income.

You should be thinking that there really is a fourth basic principle of investing, just from the emphasis it has been given above. You're absolutely correct! I do consider PROFIT TAKING an integral part of the investment process, but it is an "operational" principal as opposed to a design principle. Sure it's as important as "The Big Three", but you're not going to have much use for it if you don't fully implement the others!

If someone were to approach you with an offer to give you twice the value of your "Benz" or three times what you paid recently for your Compact Disk collection, what would you do? Hold out for more or take the money and run? Only in the securities markets do most people take the wrong course of action most of the time! Conversely, what if you could buy that Mercedes at half price? Now there's a "no-brainer". Right? So why does the whole mind-set change when we talk in terms of Daimler Chrysler common stock?

Developing A Selection Universe

"Universe" is about as big a word as we really ever need to deal with isn't it? Its use here, in a (counter "Wall Street" culture) training guide about the process of investing, is interesting because the infinite size, scope and mystery of the universe is not unlike the infinite potential, confusion, and mystery of investing. Perhaps the most important bit of learning the investor can acquire is an appreciation of just how vast the possibilities are! And, the investment universe is growing every day.

What to do first, or most of, is one consideration. How to go about gathering an understanding of the variables that affect each of the different types of securities, commodities, options, indices, funds, new issues, and other investment products is another. Is it even possible to understand all this stuff? The secret to becoming unconfused is to operate only within defined limits. For example, if you are looking for investment grade stocks that pay a dividend of any size for your "Equity" side, and "tax-free bonds" (municipals) for your "Fixed Income" side, you can eliminate a whole lot of "product" type stuff that just doesn't fit. The less you intend to speculate the less confusion there will be in your investment future. My experience has been that no speculation at all is necessary for success out there.

And then there's the problem of who to listen to. There are bulls, bears, stock brokers, financial planners, discount brokers, radio and TV personalities, miscellaneous celebrities, co-workers, government officials, shoe shine boys, cousins, on-line brokers, sports personalities, Bloomberg, CNBC, Accountants, Attorneys, and of course, spouses. No two of these bastions of learning and expertise will agree regularly on any particular subject and most have an agenda that does not include you anyway! They all have one or three things in common: selling products, analyzing the past, or predicting the future. **The products will change periodically, the analysis and predictions daily.** Independent investment professionals are few in number, **particularly if you emphasize the INDEPENDENT! They recognize that investing is a long-term process, and they don't make their living predicting!**

There's another problem with the information and/or advice that you receive from the usual sources, and that is its inconsistency. The same people will advise one thing today and then a totally different approach will be recommended next week. Before you begin to act on something spread through the normal "Wall Street" media channels, find a spokesperson that seems to be heading in the same direction consistently.

This sounds like a logical approach, I know, but you're not going to be able to do it! Consistency doesn't promote transactions, and "the Street's" objective is to keep that money moving! You'll have to keep your filters active and only take actions that are in line with your stated objectives. Good luck!

Finally! What do we really have to read! The list of research and news services is endless. There are nearly as many self-proclaimed (or Media followed) experts as there are Mutual Funds. Incidentally, have you ever noticed that every Mutual Fund is the best performer in its class, whatever that means? If not, they just make up a new class!

Most Investment Managers, either independently or through their Mutual Fund companies submit "performance statistics" to rating services. A standard form is completed where you (the manager) indicate the types of products you are reporting on (the assumption being that everyone is selling packaged products), your performance figures for various quarterly and annual periods (it doesn't matter if it's all your accounts, your ten biggest, seven best, whatever), and other general questions that give a picture of your management style. All of the above are submitted in standard Mutual Fund jargon.

Early in my career, I submitted data to one of the major reporting entities for all of my clients, on a "Working Capital", annual figures only, basis. The portfolio asset allocation at the time was 65% Equity and 35% Fixed Income. Wow, was I impressed with myself when I learned I was 3rd in the country in "my class": diversified managers with ten years or more of statistics, and a "proven" track record! (One of the things I didn't realize at the time was how few managers there actually were with ten years of experience!) I immediately ran out and purchased several thousand dollars worth of "glossies" to distribute at seminars and trade shows, and to send to every lead, relative, and financial professional I could think of.

The following year was weak in the "quality" sector of the market and trading wasn't as productive as usual. "Working Capital" growth fell to about 12% and my rating moved down. It was then that I noticed that one firm's results were based on the "top 5 portfolios", and another's on portfolios over $1,000,000, etc. But, there was another surprise. I was # 2 in foreign equity investing!!!

Time Out! I trade a few ADRs, but that's hardly foreign investing. Picture a light bulb clicking on. These guys are selling printing services! No matter who you are, what you do, or how you do it, you are going to be good at something! They make sure of it; it pays the bills for an otherwise "free" service. I don't submit data to these services any longer, but Wall Street firms love them to death.

My college Statistics professor said it best: "there are liars, there are damn liars, and there are statisticians! Yes. You can add politicians (and Wall Street research analysts), but you get the point. ***Talk to the clients. Get live references. You would for a baby sitter. This particular "baby" is YOUR MONEY!***

What we really need is a manuscript written by a millionaire who has made the millions investing (not selling, predicting, writing, reporting, representing, or calculating). Just doing it. Every day. Up markets, down markets. Rallies, corrections. All those truly unfathomable, unpredictable things that comprise the enterprise we refer to so nonchalantly as investing.

How many Wall Street experts, fund managers, brokers, and the like have been into investing for more than ten years? What does it tell you when you realize that there are literally more mutual funds out there than there are stocks listed on the New York Stock Exchange? There are also more Mutual Funds than there are Money Managers with five years of investment management experience. Interesting…

Applying the "KISS" Principle

A basic principal of investing, and of life, is that the future is totally and completely unknown and unpredictable. I've always gotten a kick out of the incredible amount of useless information that is circulated. Why should I care that certain months are historically good or bad in the Market? Just today some technician was reported to say that a "rally" would begin early in 2002, because rallies often start a year after the Fed start's to cut interest rates! Now if you could tell me with absolute certainty what's going to happen tomorrow or even next week (and to which particular stocks) I'd be interested.

Once you separate yourself from this preoccupation with predicting; once you start to appreciate that the information you really want (but can't get) would only get you thrown in jail anyway; once you appreciate the absolute fact that YOU CAN MAKE MONEY and PRESERVE YOUR WEALTH in the market; then and only then will you be able to adopt this millionaire's proven method of investing in the stock market. We use the KISS (Keep It Simple, Stupid) Principle to avoid most of the investment land mines that have been buried in our brains by our friendly institutional "street"-walkers.

It's important to note that the stock market is the world's largest known breeding ground for hindsight, even larger than sports desks around the country! This is an indisputable fact of some significance. But of more importance by far is the fact that it (hindsight) is useless and counterproductive. Most users of hindsight would protest if you told them that they are addicted! It is a product once again of this human need for certainty that has been cultivated by Wall Street so unmercifully. Shoulda', woulda', and coulda' must be stricken from your investment vocabulary! Any manager of anything real will tell you that decision-making is always done under conditions of total and complete uncertainty; no matter how good you believe your information is. It's similar to risk. It's out there. Get used to it. More importantly, learn to manage it!

Developing A Stock Worksheet

The first step in organizing your attack on Wall Street is the development of a worksheet that really works! Get some good software, a relatively fast computer, and set up a spreadsheet that will help you implement the Investment Principles that you are going to use as your decision-making model! **Review <u>Table One</u>, at the end of this Section.**

<u>Column 1 of the spreadsheet</u> should contain the S & P rating of the stocks contained in the "Selection Universe". **Quality is the most important of the investment principles,** and this placement assures that it will always be the first thing considered. This should also be a reminder to you to obtain the current month's Stock Guide. Ratings change in both directions and you need to know about the direction of these changes. Some stocks will need to be removed (but not instantaneously) from the selection universe and others may occasionally beg to be added.

As a trader, you will become a bigger than usual brokerage client. Your broker will be happy to give you the latest copy of the guide. I've been told that you may not be able to obtain it from certain "on-line brokers". You get what you pay for sometimes.

Column 2 should allow space to record the number of shares owned of each stock currently in the portfolio. Those that are owned must be looked at every day to see if they've attained either their target "sell" price or their "buy more" price. **Notice that there is no place for a "stop loss" price. Similarly, there is no need to make any "purchase lot" or ownership distinctions on this worksheet.** Those stocks that are being watched closely each day, but are not yet owned, may also be listed. But in honor of The KISS Principle, limit the number of stocks on the list. (My list for nearly two hundred portfolios rarely exceeds 110 issues. I can usually go though it and make all buy and sell decision plans in about two hours.)

Let's observe a moment of silence for the "Stop Loss Order", an artificial tool developed by Wall Street brokerage firms to increase trading activity. There is no need for this device in a portfolio of high quality securities. We know that the prices of the stocks we are buying may go down since we are buying them when they are low, and we do not pretend that we know where or when the downtrend will end. Wall Street technicians will try to dazzle you with talk of support levels and so forth. This simply defines a price point where more shares would be sold at a loss than at a profit. Since professionals are in this for the profits, the likelihood of continued weakness is said to diminish. New "support levels" are forming all the time! Understand? You can confidently buy more (average down) of a stock that has fallen in price if you haven't "maxed-out" your allocation percentage too quickly, and if your confidence in the fundamentals of the company remains intact. (Has the S & P rating changed? Has the dividend been cut? Is the company making money?) All of this important information is at your fingertips, or in your broker's database.

Column 3 contains an alphabetical listing of the stocks that you have chosen to include in your selection universe. This is where the fun begins because now you actually have to identify companies that fit those very exacting selection criteria you established! It's really much easier than you think. **Table Two** lists the symbols of 105 companies that met my criteria back in 1999. Again, it's imperative that you follow the rating changes that are included in the S & P Guide each month! Note that many of the listed companies from 1999 are no longer listed in my universe for many different reasons. Many that are listed today will be gone next month, so you would be foolish to skip this important, educational, and creative step by just copying the list of symbols in **Table Two**.

No, this listing doesn't include every stock that fits the criteria because it would require much too much time to review every possible issue every day. And yes, it includes only New York Stock Exchange companies (one of my personal rules is NYSE only, it need not be one of yours). The list includes many companies that have been excellent trading vehicles in recent years, and a few excellent companies that haven't been "tradable" at all recently!

YOU SHOULD NOT LIST EVERY POSSIBLE CANDIDATE ON YOUR WORKSHEET! Only those that you own, and those that are getting close to your initial "buy" target, need to be listed. Periodically, you should scan a newspaper with a complete stock listing to search for new "buy" prospects. There is really no reason to exclude good quality companies that are traded on other exchanges, so long as you are able to keep things simple and manageable. But they must meet all of your selection criteria. **"Liking a stock" just because it hits you as a good idea or because the "story" in "Heard on the Street" is fascinating (AND adding it to your selection universe for that reason alone) will bring your investment program to DEFCOM I. It's called discipline; without it there is no program.**

By the time we reach the third fairway, any person who knows what my profession is will invariably ask me a stock market question. The brainwashing is a virus. It's everywhere! This was today's installment (July 28,2001):

"Hey Steve, Do you 'like' Intel here? Do you think we're at the bottom of this downturn?"

"Are you buying or selling Intel, John? You're retired aren't you? Should you own it at all? Why do you think there has been a downturn? Did you know that advancing issues have exceeded decliners over the past eighteen months, and that new twelve-month highs have exceeded new twelve month lows by a huge margin for more than a year? Haven't your fixed income securities risen in market value?"

"But they say it's been a terrible year... Don't you listen to CNBC? Just yesterday they were predicting..."

"I watch the tape on CNBC occasionally, John. But I avoid listening to the commentary like I try to avoid the flu...I'll send you a copy of my new book!"

Columns 4 through 7 will contain Month end closing prices, starting with the last December 31st closing price. I use this figure as a point of reference, for informational purposes, nothing else. The next three show closing prices for the three most recent months (i.e., May through July 2001 in **Table Two**).

If it is impossible to get your hands on a newspaper, use the Internet, the next issue of the S & P Guide, or some other reliable source. **Don't discount the importance of accuracy in this data. It's the "stuff" that decisions are made from, but not for the reasons you might think!**

This is a test of your "brainwashed level"! Do you think that these 3 months of price data are used either for trend analysis or to trigger some kind of "buy" signal? **Be honest, this is like golf. Recording a better score than you really achieved is only kidding yourself and will eventually cost you money!** Neither answer is correct, but the data is used in the decision making process, covered later.

Column 8 is the "Current Month" column and it will be used to show this month's price in "+ or −" terms. This column gets updated every day and is probably the most important decision making column on the spreadsheet. As you update this column each morning from your favorite newspaper, you will create your "Buy List" for the day AND determine which of your current holdings, if any, are in profit taking range. **Regularly updating this column will also help you appreciate your sixth grade math teacher. Finally, a chance to work with decimals!**

Column 9 is used to reflect the relationship between today's stock price and the 12-month high of each of the stocks you are watching. Any stock that is 20% or more below its 12 month high, for example, is considered a candidate for new buying, but there are other criteria to be considered, such as diversification.

Any stock that is _down 30% from your original cost basis_ is considered a candidate for additional buying, or averaging down. This process of reducing the average cost of your holdings allows you to "escape" from a holding far sooner than would be the case if you just held on and waited. For example, if my original purchase of General Electric was at $47 per share (down 22% from its 12 month high of $60.50), I would consider buying more GE at below $33. If I succeed, I can then sell the entire position for a 10% profit at around $45 as opposed to $52.

The final column of the spreadsheet is for the **Dividend Yield** of any stock that is being considered for purchase. The importance of the dividend information is absolutely not the dividend yield in and of itself. Rather, it is the fact that the company pays a dividend that we want to be sure of as yet another symbol of the fundamental strength of the company.

When interest rates rise (or are expected to rise), Utility Stocks become great trading vehicles, although the time between "buy" and "sell" will certainly be longer than normal. **Don't hesitate to add these boring stocks to your portfolio. They pay great income while you wait for interest rates to move back down.**

You may even want to consider categorizing them as "fixed income" securities rather than as equities. It is unlikely that you will be able to achieve your normal trading objectives with these stocks, and you don't want to skew your trading statistics unreasonably. Quality and Diversification rules absolutely apply!

Time Management

You should organize your morning routine so that ALL of your daily investment decisions are made and ready for implementation BEFORE THE STOCK MARKET OPENS at 9:30 AM, EST. This allows for the calm and quiet that most people find better for decision-making. If you're only looking at a few portfolios (Personal, Pension, IRAs, and your Mom's), only an hour or two is needed. You will find that "sell" and "buy more" decisions are more time consuming than "buy" decisions. Lately, I've found that I save a lot of precious morning time if I deal with those two decision types in the evening, after the market closes at 4:00 PM, EST. There are several places on the Internet where accurate closing price information can be found. I use AOL and Bloomberg regularly for this.

Record your planned decisions separately for each portfolio on a daily order log that separates buys from sells, indicates approximately how much cash is available in each portfolio, AND distinguishes between that cash which is allocated to stocks and that which will be invested solely for income.

The order log worksheet should be completed in pencil, because it will be changed to reflect the actual prices of orders submitted, etc. You should plan on "checking in" with your market contact from two to four times a day to see if any of your planned decisions will be changed into actual orders, and to determine if any of your actual orders have been executed. **You must be committed to spend the time necessary to do this properly.** Opportunities will be missed. This is inevitable. But the number missed is reduced in direct proportion to the attention you bring to the exercise!

One of the standard "Buzz Words" used by Wall Street firms that are trying to steal your business from some other firm is the promise of "good" or "better" executions". Just what kind of silliness is this? Don't believe any of it. **You are the master of your own "executions" simply with the way you place your orders.**

The order log can easily be used to control for the receipt of brokerage house confirmation notices, which should be checked for accuracy. It would be super helpful to you at tax form preparation time if you have recorded all of your transactions in a computer program designed to deal with securities transactions. The program I use provides a "Schedule D" that can be used directly in a tax return.

Heed the voice of experience! If you have the proper software and complete it properly, all the necessary tax information will be there. If your (hourly paid) Accountant asks to see the confirmation notices "to check them out" or for more detail than that which is provided on the brokerage firm year end summary report, he or she is: (a) padding your bill unnecessarily, or (b) trying to find a way to suggest that something else would be a better investment.

If your discount or on-line broker doesn't give you this information for free, you're kind of stuck. In life, what you get for "cheap" is usually worth it.

Stability vs. Volatility

The brilliance of "trading" is the use of market volatility to your personal advantage. You are looking for those stocks that are constantly making fairly significant gyrations so that we can "BUY" them "LOW" and "SELL" them "HIGH"(er). Trading is the process of implementing this most trite of all investment sayings. The more often we can do this, the more money we make!

Volatility has become more a function of what is reported by the media (and the particular spin it is given) than it is a function of the fundamentals of companies and economics! This is precisely what creates the opportunity for profit! **So long as big Wall Street Companies and the Media continue to pay too many people too much money to pretend that they "know" the impact of hundreds of different variables on one simple weighted average of 30 companies, these truths will exist.** Appreciating this, and avoiding the temptation to take any action based on Wall Street's self-serving interpretation of events, can help you become a successful investor. For example:

> **Most forms of market analysis and reporting are two to three steps ahead of themselves!** The predicted end result depends upon a chain of uncertain events. Caveats are always expressed in an "ignore me" manner, or not expressed at all. This is Standard Operating Procedure. The same analyst will often express a totally different opinion within days of his original statement.

> **The "Market" always over-reacts to news, good or bad, global or individual. Always. This is one thing you actually can rely upon with some degree of certainty.**

Defining Low and High

We have to define "low" and "high"(er) so that we can establish our trading rules. We also have to come up with some standard of measuring volatility. We can do all of this rather simply, and you should be starting to realize now that you don't need to be a rocket scientist to make money trading stocks. You also do not need any fancy or expensive computer programs, schools, trading floor simulators, newsletters, momentum analyzers, or witchdoctors! **Managerial skills are much more important than finance degrees, technical data, and research reports!**

"LOW" is a price that is at least 20% below the high point achieved by an issue during the past 12 months. "HIGH"(er) is a selling price at which we will realize at least a 10% net/net profit (net/net means "after all expenses"). Remember that, as traders, we hope to realize such 10% gains several times per year on many different stocks! At times when the vast majority of stocks are 20% or more below their 12 month highs, a higher number than 20% may be appropriate. But **absolutely never accept a price that is less than 20% below the benchmark figure!**

I know this sounds a bit boring and out of line with the type of gains that some individual issues will certainly make if held for longer periods. But if you apply these decision parameters to nearly every Equity Success Story of the past, you will find that more money would have been made trading the issue than just holding it! (Go ahead, review some charts.) Another issue is involved here. That of hindsight, the great Wall Street greed and guilt producer! Don't use it or allow it to influence your decision making process in any way. **Second guessing your disciplined trading decision model will bring your program to DEFCOM II.**

Identify if you can ten stocks, traded anywhere, that will increase 100% in the next 2 years, with absolute certainty. You can't, of course. On the other hand, it's pretty easy to come up with a list of 50 or 60 stocks that you can trade over and over again (for reasonable gains) during the same time frame! **(Revisit**

77

Table Two.) Trading is not a one-decision enterprise. It is a process of finding a potential short-term gain opportunity, capitalizing on it, and then finding another and doing it all over again.

I don't recommend the "hindsightful" type of analysis that "money trails" report upon, but such an illustration is useful to exhibit the raw power of a fresh concept. It would be foolish and pointless to try to do this type of analysis in the course of managing a portfolio. **Table Three** shows the actual trading activity in a "real life" managed portfolio during most of 1999. Follow the theoretical "money trails" and the power of this strategy becomes abundantly clear! Five separate trails from January through September included 30 profitable trades, or an inventory turnover rate of 600%!

Stability Is Not Welcome Here!

We are looking for volatility, which is casually defined as frequent (2 or more times per year) movement within our "buy" and "sell" parameters. Stability is identified by a portfolio management technique called "aging". Since our objective is to trade frequently, a security that refuses to cooperate by going up 10% or more in a reasonable amount of time must be considered for sale, even at a below average profit! What is a "reasonable" amount of time? If you can't sell a stock within twelve months, it really shouldn't be in your Selection Universe, and steps need to be taken to replace it with a more cooperative issue.

A trader's portfolio is different in appearance from a "Buy and Hold" portfolio in a number of ways. But the most important difference is the average age of the positions held. The objective is to move the stuff off the shelves and out of the warehouse as quickly as possible. If it isn't selling at the original "markup" it goes on sale at any profit. Finally, and on rare occasions, a loss may have to be taken.

Shopping at "The Gap"

Traders crave volatility, and they learn to love major movements, particularly to the downside. The worst environment for a trader is one where prices move broadly lower, and very slowly. Although we want to get invested "too soon", it's better for quicker trading when the market moves in big "gaps". Always buy into panic selling, and use your limit "day", "limit" orders wisely. (See Chapter Three)

Let's say you are driving down the highway when the radio program you are listening to is interrupted by an announcement of a 500-point decline in the DJIA. What do you do about it? Don't waste time going to "Bloomberg", or searching the airwaves for analysis or explanation. All you need to know is how much money you have available and where it is. Call your broker and determine the price of your "favorite" trading stocks. If they are in range (down 20% from their one year high), throw in a "day limit" order below the bid and see what happens!

Of Performance, Tools, and Rules

The "performance" of a trader's portfolio (actually, any portfolio) must be appraised in a different manner as well. And this will be the subject of Chapter 4. Think about it. There could be forty or more different investment entities in operation at the same time. **Table Three** identifies twenty-three distinct start-up points for new investment entities to be purchased. Very few of these would have the same starting point and, most importantly, the ending point is totally "uncertain"!

Wall Street uses models to measure "market performance". Their favorite models are the Dow Jones Industrial and the S & P 500 averages. Both of these "models" are really just computer games based on a "buy and hold" discipline. Such analytical comparisons are totally misleading in evaluating the performance of portfolios, especially those where trading is relatively frequent; it just has to be!

79

The content of the averages and indices that are being used as "benchmarks" may not change at all from one year to the next, while the funds that are being "rated" or "analyzed" are changing constantly.

A trading portfolio rarely compares favorably to a market index when the index is on the rise. And nearly always "performs" better than such an average when the index tanks. This is an observation that really has little or no relevance, but it may "learn you" what your expectations should be. Trading portfolios need to be analyzed differently, and you have to be able to explain this to your investment buddies, or they may succeed in undermining your resolve, believe me! Remember that if you are trading, you've already proven that you are operationally smarter than they are!

In fact, any planned investment portfolio with its goals, objectives, rules, constraints, and individual personality is just not measurable by normal Wall Street standards and procedures, whether or not it's traded frequently! Blasphemy, you shout! Absolutely. By what stretch of the imagination is your portfolio anything like any average or index created by Wall Street to make you transact? Investing is an objective directed exercise and the only valid performance analysis is one that compares results with your own personally stated objectives!

I hope you've seen now that with some readily available and not so complex tools (a newspaper, an S & P Guide, a spreadsheet, and a daily order log) we can gather and synthesize all of the data we need to create a selection universe. With an equally simple and precise set of rules, we can manage an investment portfolio quite productively and in an unusually low risk environment. There are three distinct types of decisions to make about every holding, every day: BUY, SELL, and HOLD. The HOLD or "do nothing" decision is actually the most common of all, and even though we go through the daily ritual of preparing a "buy list" and identifying stocks that are to be sold, nothing is forcing us to actually do something every day. Sometimes, even with fifty or more potential trades on my worksheets, no orders are actually submitted! In Chapter Three, you will learn how to develop a buy list and to prepare to do some trading! But first:

More "Inside" Information from "Deep Pockets" (My Questions, His Answers)

*   *   *   *   *   *   *

What are the basics of the stock recommendation process at most major retail firms? "At the start of the month every broker's paycheck is zero. Each day he comes in and looks at the "money run" (un-invested cash or money market). The next stop is the firm's hot list (the research department's list of stocks that shine above all of their other buy recommendations). Surely everyone with cash needs one of these stocks. The call is made to the client explaining just how powerful the story is and how perfectly the stock compliments their portfolio. Keep in mind that every other broker at the firm has been chasing the stock over the past few weeks. No regard is given to the recent price movement and the lucky client buys it somewhere near the high for the year."

"When the client has no cash available for the purchase, with just a little imagination, the broker can come up with a dozen reasons why one of the current holdings should be sold and a beautiful thing happens for the broker (double commissions). This is not to say that all brokers are bad or that all recommendations are based on the broker's greed (just most of them). Most firms would disagree with this scenario, but that raises some interesting questions: Why is it that 60% of most firm's revenue occurs during the last week of the commission month, and the largest day is invariably the last day of the month?"

Were the "good ole days" really all so good? Is tomorrow quite as bad as it seems? "During the good old days of '98 and '99, the growth rates suggested for earnings and revenue were outrageous.

The price targets for stocks were laughable. Everyone wanted in on the party. Some professionals resisted the temptation to join in the festivities and were punished by greedy clients who now knew everything about investing (from financial television and chat rooms). They left to go it alone. Over the last fifty years the return on common stock has averaged eleven per cent. **Get used to it; the get rich quick days are over!"**

"The bottom line is that none of the party crowd was smart enough to go home and the fortunes made on paper turned into financial disasters. **From April 2000 through June 2001, Five Trillion Dollars was lost in the stock market.** People who bought Juniper at $120 now hold it at $8. Priceline.com went from$100 to $1, and the beat goes on! What were people thinking? Oh, it's happened before. The 1920's and the late 1960s lost fortunes for the masses."

How about all of those "safe" Mutual Funds? "The gurus who run the trillions in Mutual Funds did no better. They were busy pumping up their funds with all the latest growth names; drunk with power, they tried to lead the pack in performance. Complete disregard for the safety of client capital was the order of the day as they tried to squeeze the returns to higher and higher levels. When the scam unraveled, growth funds dropped in value by half; technology funds by three quarters. Many of the new "Wall Street' darlings just disappeared (bankruptcy). Once again a new generation of investors had been duped. Quite frankly, greed is greed and those who ran with the fast crowd got just what they deserved!"

How can "The Street" bounce back from this embarrassment? "If your broker makes recommendations for selfish reasons and the Mutual Fund thrill rides don't seem appropriate, what should one do? Hire someone to do it all for you, an Investment Manager. It's logical! With the vast amount of information that flows through the system and all of the conflicting views, why not hire someone to filter through it all and make informed decisions? Take the emotion out of what should be a business process. You're in luck! Wall Street's new scam: MANAGED MONEY!"

There isn't a firm on The Street not trying to garner a share of this action. Charge a flat fee and do it all: asset allocation, security selection and management with no transaction costs. Put yourself and the brokerage firm on the same side of the table. Perfect! **WRONG!** Obviously, the lion's share of Registered Representatives (brokers), out there have NO SKILLS relating to Money Management. Then who's going to manage it? Of course, an elite group of hand-chosen investment professionals will do it. The firms charge up to 3% of the value of the client's account and basically do nothing! Let's look at this one."

"Just as trying to walk in someone else's shoes that are four sizes too big or small would prove to be difficult, one size fits all portfolio management doesn't work either. Once again "Wall Street" has taken a legitimate process and turned it into a scam. What is represented to be individualized portfolio management is nothing more than a Mutual Fund. In most cases, the performance has been even worse."

How do they disguise this so that it's "sellable"? "Clients are invited to complete applications to be accepted into Managed Money Programs. The questions are probing, giving the impression that this is truly a personalized program. Goals and objectives are established along with risk tolerance guidelines. An asset allocation is established and finally an investment management search picks just the right manager for you. Sounds individualized so far right? **WRONG AGAIN!** The information is fed into a computer program at the broker's desk and all of that personal probing information spits out a "Boiler Plate" (standard form) proposal that in most cases invests along only one investment style (growth, value, mid-cap, small-cap, large-cap, international, fixed income, etc.). The minimum account is $100,000 with any one manager. A typical investor "tries it out" with $100,000 because of the minimum requirements. The entire amount is invested in one style."

Doesn't that negate all the Asset Allocation work that was just done? "Let's follow the process for a typical investor, Mrs. Jones. Mrs. Jones filled out the long questionnaire and received a beautiful proposal that showed an optimal asset allocation personalized to her needs and risk tolerance. The allocation suggested 50% fixed income and 50% equities, with the equity portion balanced between large-cap value and large-cap growth. Mrs. Jones has $150,000 available for investment. Her only $150,000! Remember that each manager only manages one style with a minimum size of $100,000. By the book, this account is not suitable for a "Wrap" account."

"The broker reviews the situation and gives careful consideration to the client's needs and the suggested asset allocation that he has prepared for the client, and comes to the following conclusions: 'I need the commissions and the manager is putting pressure on me to market our "Wrap" programs. By dangling the impressive returns of "last year's hot growth manager, he convinces Mrs. Jones to "bet" the entire $150,000 with one growth manager. Keep in mind that the computer generated "plan" suggested that only a 25% "growth" weighting was appropriate."

"The forms are completed and signed by both Mrs. Jones and the broker. Her only hope is that the Office Manager will realize that this "aggressive" investment style is inappropriate and that it completely ignores the firm's own suggested allocation. **WRONG A THIRD TIME!** When the broker presents the new account form to the manager, he is praised for "going with the flow" and marketing the "Wrap Program". The manager is particularly happy because his salary is increased for each dollar of Wrap Program business produced by his office. He doesn't even look at the new account form or the allocation model. The broker is patted on the head and the manager signs off to open the account. From here the scam becomes even larger!"

*　　*　　*　　*　　*　　*

TABLE ONE: A SPECIMEN STOCK WORKSHEET

S & P Rating	Shares Held	Ticker Symbol	Dec 2000	May 2001	June 2001	July 2001	Current + Or -	Down %	Current Yield
A +	700	AFL	36.09	32.43	31.49	29.58	-.49	22%	0.7%
A +	2700	ADP	33.61	53.74	49.70	50.95	-4.01	33%	0.9%
A +	2300	AVY	54.88	58.48	51.05	51.26	-.18		
A	1600	BK	55.18	54.61	48.00	44.86	.27	24%	1.6%
A	600	BSC	50.68	54.35	58.97	58.15	2.45		
A -	3100	BLS	40.94	41.23	40.27	40.70	-.08	20%	1.9%
A	2200	BMY	73.93	54.24	52.30	59.14	-1.34	23%	1.9%
A +	2000	CSL	42.93	39.30	34.87	36.14	.09	22%	2.3%
A	1900	CLX	35.51	34.64	33.85	37.68	-1.28	23%	2.3%
B +	3400	CA	19.51	28.36	36.00	34.48	1.51		
B +	3000	DIS	28.94	31.62	28.89	26.35	.25	40%	0.8%
A +	900	HD	45.69	49.29	47.24	50.37	-1.25		
A -	1300	ICN	30.69	30.23	31.72	30.75	2.72	20%	0.9%
A -	2300	KMB	70.69	60.45	55.90	60.81	.29		
A -	1100	MEL	49.18	45.82	44.81	38.02	1.28	24%	2.4%
A +	2700	PFE	46.00	42.89	40.05	41.22	-.48		

TABLE TWO: HIGH QUALITY STOCKS

1999	2001	1999	2001	1999	2001	1999	2001	1999	2001
AFL	AFL	T	T	ABT		APD		ABS	ABS
ALD		ALL	ALL	AHP		ADM	ADM	ADP	ADP
AVY	AVY	AVT	AVT	AVP		ONE		BCR	
BSC	BSC	BLS	BLS	BMY	BMY	CWP	CWP	CPB	CPB
CCL	CCL	CBC		CTL	CTL	CB		C	
CC	CC	CLE	CLE	CLX	CLX	KO	KO	CL	
CAG	CAG	CA	CA	CDD		DH		DIS	DIS
DG		DLJ		DOV	DOV	DJ		DD	DD
EMR		EFX		BEN		FTU	FTU	GPU	GPU
GCI		GPS	GPS	GE	GE	G	G	GSK	GSK
GWW		HDI		HRS		HNZ	HNZ	HSY	
HRZ		HWP	HWP	HB		HOE		HD	HD
ITW		IFF		JNJ		JCI		K	K
KEY	KEY	KMB	KMB	KRI		LEH		LNR	

LTD	LTD	LOW		LU	LU	KRB		MRD	MRD
MCD	MCD	MDT	MDT	MRK	MRK	MOT	MOT	MYL	
NSC		NUE		PWJ		PEP		PFE	PFE
PNU		MO		ROK	ROK	ROH	ROH	RD	
SLE	SLE	SGP	SGP	SLB		SCH	SCH	VO	
SHW	SHW	SBH		LUV	LUV	TNB	TNB	TR	TR
UST		UL		VFC		WMT	WMT	WLA	

Note that the Selection Universe has changed nearly 50% since August 1999 for various reasons including: profit taking, mergers and acquisitions, downgrading by S & P, etc. Of the fifty-one stocks that are no longer listed, twenty-five are still looked at regularly for new buying (Bull Pen Residents) and thirteen were "taken over" by other companies. **Fifty "Replacement Parts" are listed below:**

AXP	ASO	BUD	BDG	BK	CTS	CAJ	CSL	DCX	DCN
DDS	DNY	EK	AGE	AJG	GT	HLT	ICN	IPG	JPM
LM	LZ	MAY	MCK	MEL	MER	NWS	NOK	NT	PHG
P	PBI	PCP	STR	RJF	RTN	REY	ROP	RCL	SBC
SFA	SNA	SON	SNE	TIF	USB	VOD	WAG	WCS	WFC

Take a minute to look at **Table Three** and to make a list of the symbols of the stocks traded during 1999. You will notice that there are about twenty-five stocks which aren't listed anywhere in **Table Two.** Thirteen of those that were sold profitably have returned. When you're trading, inventory can change rapidly, almost like produce in a farmers market. So it should be!

TABLE THREE: AN EXAMPLE OF TRADING

Bought	Sold	#	Symbol	Cost	Received	Short Term	Long Term	Money Stream	# Of Trades
12/21/98	01/04/99	100	BDX	3,863	4,338	475		1	
10/28/97	01/05/99	100	MOT	5,864	6,119		255	2	
12/14/98	01/11/99	100	C	4,850	5,800	950		3	
10/28/97	01/11/99	100	MOT	5,864	6,725		861	4	
08/26/98	01/15/99	100	DIS	3,256	3,731	475		5	
01/12/99	01/27/99	100	EFX	3,348	3,881	443		2	2

Bought	Sold	#	Symbol	Cost	Received	Short Term	Long Term	Money Stream	# Of Trades
05/21/98	02/02/99	100	HWP	6,612	7,225	613		6	
05/27/98	02/06/99	200	UPC?	9,425	10,338	913		7	
06/24/98	02/09/99	100	ROK	4,319	4,575	256		8	
01/04/99	02/11/99	200	BFI	5,675	6,225	550		1	2
12/23/98	02/19/99	100	CDD	3,550	3,875	325		9	
01/31/99	02/22/99	100	UHC?	4,150	4,700	550		2	3
03/01/99	03/10/99	200	BBC	5,012	5,713	701		2	4
12/07/98	03/17/99	100	RD	4,519	5,018	499		10	
03/11/99	03/19/99	100	JEF	3,712	4,756	1,044		2	5
08/06/98	03/19/99	100	PNC	5,262	5,906	644		11	
08/07/98	03/22/99	100	[GWW]	4,325	4,625	300		12	
03/25/99	04/09/99	100	LEH	5,775	6,350	575		2	6
04/07/99	04/13/99	100	EMR	5,200	5,725	525		5	2
02/09/99	04/19/99	100	BWA	4,575	5,100	525		3	2
07/08/98	04/19/99	100	NUE	4,594	5,568	974		13	
11/27/98	04/20/99	100	DCN	4,113	4,663	550		14	
03/13/98	04/20/99	100	DS	4,000	4,538		538	15	
03/24/99	04/20/99	100	PPG	5,075	5,850	775		4	2
12/01/98	04/22/99	200	AME	4,100	4,563	463		16	
02/16/99	04/22/99	200	BEN	6,550	7,550	1,000		1	3
06/16/98	04/22/99	100	HAL	4,231	4,488	257		17	
10/16/97	04/26/99	300	SHI	5,148	5,175		27	18	
10/28/97	04/30/99	300	TUP	6,736	6,993		257	19	
02/25/99	05/07/99	200	[RAL]	5,575	6,118	613			
05/18/98	05/11/99	300	ELY	5,181	4,519	-662		20	
01/22/99	05/12/99	100	CB	5,994	6,962	968			
03/26/99	05/17/99	100	HNZ	4,819	5,362	543			
05/14/99	05/28/99	200	PEP	6,875	7,675	800		1	4
04/01/99	05/28/99	200	TRW	9,050	9,962	912			
02/22/99	05/28/99	200	UST	5,538	6,113	575			
01/22/99	06/01/99	100	KO	6,325	6,887	562			
04/02/98	06/01/99	200	SNT	7,075	7,100		25	21	
05/19/99	06/07/99	300	PLL	5,250	6,038	788		2	7
05/24/99	06/08/99	100	GLW	5,369	5,500	131		3	3
05/17/99	06/11/99	200	[LBY]	6,025	6,575	550		4	3
05/18/99	06/15/99	100	GPS	6,106	6,538	432		5	3
06/11/99	06/25/99	200	[RAL]	5,350	5,863	513		2	8
06/07/99	07/08/99	100	BSC	4,056	4,756	700		1	5
05/21/99	07/08/99	100	SGP	4,656	5,344	688			
05/27/99	07/12/99	100	CAH	6,250	6,944	694			
06/29/99	07/23/00	300	FSS	6,037	6,693	656		2	9
06/25/99	07/23/99	100	G	4,188	4,706	518		3	4

Bought	Sold	#	Symbol	Cost	Received	Short Term	Long Term	Money Stream	# Of Trades
06/30/99	07/29/99	200	[LBY]	5,700	6,350	650		4	4
07/13/99	07/30/99	300	SUT	7,500	8,850	1,350		1	6
01/14/99	08/02/99	100	DF	4,044	4,313	269			
08/12/99	08/30/99	100	CA	4,500	5,275	775		1	7
07/23/99	09/02/99	200	PFE	7,150	7,825	675		2	10
06/26/98	09/13/99	100	TNB	4,888	5,100		212	22	
08/16/99	09/20/99	100	[GWW]	4,500	4,900	400		3	5
09/10/99	09/27/99	200	CC	7,400	8,275	875		1	8

TOTAL (NET/NET) REALIZED GAINS = $31,532

AVERAGE GAIN PER TRADE = 10.53%

AVERAGE HOLDING PERIOD = 3.76 MONTHS

STOCKS HELD LESS THAN SIX MONTHS = 78%

TOTAL INVESTED IN ACCOUNT = $170,000

NET GAINS AS A RETURN ON INVESTMENT = 18.5%; ANNUALIZED = 24.9%

[BRACKETED STOCKS WERE TRADED TWICE]

CHAPTER THREE: "BUY LOW"

The decision to become your own Investment Manager is a major big deal. It should not be done because you think you know something that others don't, because you've either done or intend to do "your own research", or because you've purchased some fancy software that gives you special trading signals. You should not be attempting to "beat the market" or to minimize your variable investment costs. The reasons for managing your own assets should be more personal than that! You're doing this to achieve the financial objectives that you have identified, prioritized, and organized within your investment plan.

You are taking on the same responsibilities (albeit in miniature) that the Mutual Fund descriptive documents profess are being dealt with personally by that "bepedestaled" superstar Investment Manager, earning millions per year to make you money. Actually you should be a lot better and much faster than he or she is! You don't have to answer to an Investment Committee, or buy and sell under the pressure of what one of the company's analysts has to say. You are not competing with any other managers either in-house or out-house (your supposed to smile at that one) or with the market averages. You aren't being "told what to do" by the emotional decisions of unit or shareholders. Hold these truths to be self-evident; YOU ARE FREE! If you aim at your own targets you just might hit them; if you follow your rules religiously you will succeed. **The only individual authorized (if not qualified) to second-guess you is your spouse!**

Developing a "Buy List"

On the weekend before you implement this new approach to running your investment portfolio, go out and buy yourself a reliable alarm clock. There's a lot of wisdom in that "early bird gets the worm" idea, particularly when planning what you would like to do during the trading day! Getting an early start will allow you to find the nearest Deli with good coffee and a wide selection of newspapers.

Contrary to popular belief, daily investment decisions can be made from a well constructed Selection Universe without 47 pages of listings, statistics, and drum beating. Pick one that you know you can get your hands on early in the day. Barron's, The Wall Street Journal, and Investors Business Daily are excellent publications, but you just don't need that level of detail on a day-to-day basis. And why spend a buck per day when you can get the job done for 35 cents? Sure they are impressive, and I'm confident that every subscriber to "Investor's Business Daily"(IBD) is now a mega-millionaire. In reality, you don't need the majority of the stuff they publish at all! If you pay too much attention to the stories, you will develop "investment decision impotence"! Sorry guys.

Have you heard the rumor about the real cause of that recent brokerage firm failure? It seems that every employee was required to "keep current" by reading "The Journal", "Barron's", and "IBD". Nothing ever got done!

I have seen too many people develop that dreaded investment disease "analysis paralysis" from spending the bulk of their time trying to interpret, categorize, and synthesize all the investment related materials they can get their hot little calculators and computers on! They don't wind up prepared, they become confused, mesmerized!

Excessive analysis is extremely dangerous. It results in chronic indecisiveness, a curable condition that limits a person's ability to identify present investment opportunities. At its' worst, it can cause irrational, knee-jerk like loss taking behavior accompanied by many of the standard symptoms of panic!

The cure is a simple one, but the withdrawal period is susceptible both to self-doubt, and to occasional bouts of "speculative relapsia". Phase One: limit the daily intake of business news and information to thirty minutes. Phase Two:

cancel all business newsletter and research subscriptions. Phase Three: establish reasonable, personalized goals and objectives... You know the rest.

This point does bear repeating. **The purpose of most analysis is to explain the past somewhat intelligently, a worthy endeavor. The purpose of "Wall Street" flavored analysis is to create an image of a wisdom so profound that it can predict the future, and help you pick the "right time" either to invest, or to liquidate, or to just wait and see**.

What you must learn to accept is that investing is not an "either", "or" proposition. Buying, selling, and holding are all going on everyday and they get along really well together, operating, as they do, in the land of ignorance. **Investing is not something that one should do at a certain time; it's something that just has to be done ALL OF THE TIME!**

Barron's, by the way, is totally overkill. It lives by snob appeal like Jaguar Motor Cars. Did you know that if you don't pronounce Jaguar or Porsche properly, the snooty salesman (How can he look you in the eye with his nose so far up in the air?) wouldn't even let you own one at all! All you really need is a newspaper that lists ALL of the stocks that were traded yesterday in a convenient manner of presentation. Otherwise, you'll have to get "on line" periodically to obtain closing prices, either for the stocks you own, or for others that you've become interested in. Incomplete listings are inconvenient at best, and you just have to question their reliability. Obviously, a news resource that doesn't provide all of the decision-making data you need is undesirable. I tried to make this point with the Business Editor of one of New Jersey's top papers on several occasions, but he didn't seem interested in publishing a really useful investment tool!

By the same token, I could never understand why the New York Times has never included symbols in its quotations. On Saturdays, the Times or an equivalent local paper will just have to do. **The Wall Street Journal is a bit pricey, but without a doubt the easiest tool** to work with, particularly at month end. Just don't try to read it all!

To be at all useful, a newspaper listing must include all of this information for every named security:

- The 52-week "high" and "low".
- The Amount of Dividend paid.
- The Daily Sales Volume.
- The Daily "high", "low", and "last" prices.
- The amount of daily change.

Other useful information includes: dividend yield and P/E ratio.

A Daily Ritual

Trading in the stock market is a unique enterprise because it actually is different every day! And every day we have to sit down with our paper and coffee to study yesterday's "action" in order to **develop an "action plan" for today.** There are two key thoughts here: This is *a required daily exercise* that should be completed before the market opens (this relieves the pressure that comes from "knowing" what type of day it is in the market.) Secondly, *it is just a plan* based on the last day's results in the marketplace. This means that we are merely creating a list of stocks that we will consider buying should the market price cooperate.

This does not mean that you have to re-invent the wheel every day! Most often, the same selection decisions will be appropriate for the portfolio in question, with a slight change in target price.

Let's assume that we have money to invest in Equities right now and that our portfolios are all properly diversified so that we don't have to make a conscious effort to avoid a certain industry or issue. We will also assume that our Selection Universe contains about 100 names. Our goal is to come up with a list of between 10

92

and 15 buying opportunities. We select opportunities from the Universe by applying a very strict set of rules. Never force the issue. There is no guarantee that as many as 10 opportunities will exist, and there is also no requirement that we buy something every day. The larger the portfolio, the more likely it is that something will be going on all of the time, but there is no pressure to transact.

Buy Low

The Stock Market is the only place in the world where the standard sales pitch is something like this: "We like this stock a lot! It has been attaining new "highs" nearly every day, and we expect that trend to continue!" My interpretation is: "If you buy this stock right now Mr. Investor, you will pay more per share than anyone in the entire world has ever paid!" Additionally, you will be encouraged to buy the issue immediately before it goes any higher. (Note that your "Financial Advisor" will buy you as much of it as you want without question.)

I wonder if this approach would interest someone investing in a business, a piece of real estate, or a normal automobile (not really an investment, sorry Porsche)? Ever hear this one at the mall: "Attention shoppers! Prices for our most popular fashions have just been raised to their highest levels of the year, literally twice what you paid for them last season! Hurry to the Ladies' Department now!" Now I recognize that there are people who feel good about themselves when they pay too much for something, but try to stay "real" when you're considering an investment strategy!

You should only be looking for *stocks that are down in price by at least 20% from their highest level over the past 12 months.* All this requires is a simple comparison of the "Last" price column with the price that appears in the "52-Week High" column. Depending on an enormous number of factors, this alone may not be enough to identify the absolute "best" opportunities. Frankly, there is no "best" way to do that, because the word "best" connotes a level of knowledge that we humans (and our electromechanical creations) are incapable of achieving. **Selecting the stocks we feel have the "best" short term gain potential involves a study of the month-to-month data on your "worksheet", your personal experience, and good judgment.**

Even if you do not listen regularly to the popular business radio stations, you have undoubtedly heard advertisements for software, or systems, or training guides that will let you "trade like the pros"; with faster, smoother, cleaner, "executions". (Whatever an execution is!) The latest and greatest information, facts, and opinions culled from all over the "virtual" universe so that you can trade better! WOW! Don't get caught up in this. Information of any kind is out-of-date the moment you receive it anyway. Stick with the fundamental trading rules described here and you'll make fewer mistakes. **Didn't some human just like you and me program that computer? If you are serious about investing, you are not in the market for what they are selling.**

I have a friend who has purchased every conceivable gimmick possible in an effort to improve his golf game (training tapes, fancy new clubs, swing trainers, special golf balls, hypnosis, you name it). If they all worked, he'd be a PGA touring professional. They haven't, and neither will the myriad of "investment tools" you can buy to improve your investment performance! Stick to the fundamentals for the best possible results.

Good Judgment, that quality our teachers and parents knew we would never have any of, now has to be exercised! How do we determine which of these good opportunities are actually the ones we should be looking at today?

I once worked as a manager in a large New York City based Life Insurance Company. My boss was the same one that most of you have worked for in your past experiences as someone's employee. This guy would constantly give me assignments and

94

projects that were "to be considered high priority"! So I went into his office one day (after dutifully trying to organize my time) with my list of projects and assignments, asking for guidance. "Which item on this list should I attack first since each will take several days and each has to be done ASAP?"

He just didn't get it, or take it well when I pointed out to him that I really had no high priority projects at all! Poor Judgment strikes again! The point is this: if all or most of the stocks in the Universe are down 20% or more, we need a way to distinguish the better opportunities from the other opportunities. This will happen quite often, and it's not a bad thing either!

Good "Buys" vs. "Best Buys"

I have used two different methods to make this important distinction. As the number of stocks meeting the basic "buy" parameter rises above 15% of the Selection Universe, "ratchet" the parameter up 1% at a time until the list of opportunities falls back within the acceptable range. During the "Market Melt Down"/computer loop of October, 1987 for example, I was buying only those stocks that had fallen 40% or more from their highs! If you're basically a technician (an engineer type) this approach should satisfy your need for structure, BUT I really think that it is too limiting, and that another, less structured, approach will produce superior results.

For the past several years, I've been exercising that "Good Judgment" thing by matching my success experience against the raw list of stocks down 20% or more. I select the opportunities that my past experience tells me offer the fastest turn around times. For example, from the partial list included in the **Table One** Spreadsheet, I would buy AFLAC (-22%) before Disney (-40%) or Bank of New York (-24%) before Automatic Data Processing at (-31%). This approach worked particularly well in the 1999 to 2000 crash in high quality securities that was engineered so beautifully by those brilliant Wall Street Institutions.

There are no guarantees that either approach will work. But applied consistently, they have both worked very well.

Of "Bulls" and "Bears"

You're right! That is too easy. There are two types of investment animals out there and I don't mean Bulls and Bears. I'm referring to the "Buy and Holders" and us, the "Traders".

Actually there are several other animals that you should learn to identify, particularly if they are you! "Pigs" and "Sheep" come to mind instantly and there will always be schools of "Sharks" (not Attorneys) out there ready to swallow anything you have in your wallet. "Pigs" are investors who refuse to take profits as a result of their greed. It can take a while, but they always wind up slaughtered. "Sheep" are investors who buy whatever becomes popular on "The Street". They just have to have those "Zero Coupon" Venezuela Hyper Inflation notes or Hong Kong 500 stock index fund futures. If any of their buddies own it, they have to have it too! Shish Ka Bob anyone?

Now who are the "Sharks"? They are the ones who fuel the avarice of the Pigs and the vanity of the Sheep. You know who they are!

We are walking our way through a "managed trading strategy" so temper your "Good Judgment" with your knowledge of what the average trader is likely to do. He or she is going to take profits. When adopting a trading strategy, you accept all the responsibilities of membership. One of these is to **become one of those fearsome Wall Street "villains", the PROFIT-TAKERS!** I know that the media has taught you to hate these people; "those dirty rat" rally killers. But hate them for the right reason. They will always make money while you lament in your beer (or single malt whatever) about what coulda' or shoulda' been. This is a success club that anyone can join, even if you drive an old Rambler.

These guys, the professional big dollar traders, are probably going to set their profit goals quite a bit lower than the 10% that I recommend and their "turn-around time" is likely to be a bit quicker than the average of below six months that I like to talk about. They are trading hundreds of thousand of shares, in their own commission free trading accounts. A one-dollar move can mean a serious profit!

So look at your spreadsheet carefully and eliminate from the "Buy List" any stock that:

a. Went up a point or more yesterday.

b. Is up a point or more from last month's closing price (column 7).

c. Is up two or more points from the previous month's close (column 6).

d. Is up three or more points from the price appearing in (column 5).

The approach to selection and trading I'm describing here is somewhat unique, but the idea of trading large quantities for small per share gains is not. These simple rules will keep you from paying too much more often than they will cause you to miss a "best buy" opportunity, and there absolutely will always be another buying opportunity. Have I mentioned that successful Investment Management requires patience?

You should be developing a list of important words (not "Streetese buzz words") but human emotion control words

97

like discipline and patience, and management words like objectives, strategy, and planning.

Hot Tips From the Investment Management Forum (03/12/01)

"The "Market" always overreacts! Direction really doesn't matter. This is not a "Bear Market" and it certainly is not being reported in the media as a "Bull Market". It is nothing more than it always is, a Market of Sheep and Pigs! The "rally" in Quality Issues produced an abundance of "Smart Cash" just waiting around for new opportunities."

"Well, the opportunities are arriving right on schedule! The buy list is growing and, for the first time in nearly a year, I have only one stock ripe for profit taking. What do investors do when prices go down? They BUY! It's the Sheep that sell. What did the investors do as prices went up? They SOLD! What do you think the Pigs did? Here's a clue for you that, in an admittedly oversimplified way, contains all you need to know to be a successful investor: Wall Street (and the Media that pretends to know about Wall Street) is not about Bulls and Bears. It's about playing with the emotions of Pigs and Sheep!"

What's In A List?

Smile if you were just about to kick back, print the "Buy List", log on to some discount broker, and submit a bunch of market orders. First of all, **no self-respecting trader or millionaire will ever submit a Market Order** so erase those words from your investment vocabulary forever. Secondly, the "Buy List" is not a "damn the torpedoes", full speed ahead, action plan. It is a selection of possible actions that we may or may not choose to implement during the trading day.

Most of **you are going to have a little trouble with this, depending on your "BQ" or "Brainwashing Quotient"**. The idea that there is a rush to buy or to sell is part of the hysteria Wall Street has programmed within you. This devil must be exorcised for success to be possible. You are the decision maker. You have set the rules and you will implement the strategy. Contrary to what the Street (and your Accountant) wants you to believe, your investment life doesn't run from January 1st to December 31st. If you choose not to pull the trigger today, there's always tomorrow.

From the "Buy List" you will select no more than three stocks to purchase in any one of your portfolios. The guideline is one potential selection for every 10% or more of your portfolio that is not invested (i.e., in cash or money market). But never more than three! You have to put the brakes on your enthusiasm. There are no good reasons to fill up your portfolio quickly, (particularly since you know now that you do not "know" just how low the prices of your selections will go). Additionally, the less available cash you have, the more selective you have to become. **Beginning to see why cash flow is so important?**

One test that you should eventually apply to see how well you are doing is a cash availability test. **You should want to run out of available cash while there are still a large number of stocks on your buy list!** Why? Because it proves that you are not caught up in any type of "Market Timing" fantasy. Market timers are plentiful, but I dare you to find a satisfied client who would refer you to one. **Not even Wall Street (who really does sell anything and everything it can conceive of) tries to sell the Market Timing story! I'm not even sure if a "market timing" fund exists, but I know that it would sell (and that it would fail)!**

It's OK To Be Arbitrary

Why is "three" the magic selection number? This is absolutely arbitrary, but it is based on a principle that has been flowing between the lines all along. This is the "Principle of Ignorance" that I will address in more depth in Chapter Six. In a nutshell, **we don't ever want to make a decision that even appears to be made under conditions of knowledge or certainty** about the future, either of the stock market, or of the individual stocks we are thinking of buying. Such knowledge does not exist, period! It may well be a great time to buy the listed stocks, but we really cannot know this. **It is extremely unlikely that we will ever buy a stock at its low and we have no intention of even trying to sell them at a new high.** Therefore, we will control our enthusiasm by establishing constraints (rules).

Here are some more arbitrary but time tested buying guidelines. On an order sheet or "log" of some kind, make a notation of the stock or stocks to be selected for each portfolio today. (Yes, in pencil.) Since we are interested in buying stocks as they move "down", **the price we are willing to pay today must be below yesterday's closing price by:**

a. **$.35 or more if the stock is trading below $20 per share.**

b. **$.50 or more for stocks ranging between $20 per share and $49 per share.**

c. **$.75 or more for stocks ranging from $50 through $70.**

d. **$1.00 or more for stocks above $70 per share.** (How big a portfolio is needed to support the purchase of a $70 stock: $70,000; $140,000; or $235,000?)

e. **Don't even think about buying a stock selling for $90 a share or more.** It just has to be overpriced.

Question. How big must a portfolio be to support a purchase of 100 shares of a stock selling for $100 per share? The answer is not $200,000.

The Daily Routine

About two to three times per day, check in with your broker to see if any of the planned decisions is ready for implementation. This

100

involves an examination of the three prices that make up **"the trading range"** of the stock for the day. Isn't new information fun? Most of you are used to this: "Hi George, I want to buy 100 shares of Pfizer. (If your broker doesn't know the symbol for a stock like Pfizer, he's either a Mutual Fund salesman or a speculator, find another guy.)" "Sure, Steve, just hold on a minute and I'll be able to confirm that purchase at the market." (This sounds like great service, doesn't it?) That bell you hear is **Portfolio "DEFCOM THREE"; it sounds on market orders!**)

A "market order" is what Wall Street wants you to use to buy or to sell securities. It simply means that you are willing to pay whatever price the owner of the stock is willing to sell it for. Consequently, you always get what you want, but at a price that you have no control over. The same is true with a "sell" order at the market; you get what ever the next buyer is willing to pay.

Do I hear the whirr of those gears? Of course you wouldn't transact business in this manner anywhere else. "Hey George, I want to buy a hot new yellow Corvette." "Sure, Steve, just hold on a minute and I'll be able to confirm that purchase." "OK, Steve, we got the "vette" you wanted for $180,000. It was the only one for sale today" "Great George, that was sure a great execution".

Here's the new way you interrelate with your broker:

"Hi George, give me a quote on Pfizer, please."

"Sure Steve, just a second. Pfizer is at $37.50, last trade, that's down $.88 for the day. The "bid" is $37.10 and the "asked" is $37.75."

"Great, get me 100 shares at $37.40, "day". Thanks".

This is a "day", "limit" order. It precisely specifies the maximum you are willing to pay, and for how long your offer is valid. Thus you will try (and succeed most of the time) to buy the Pfizer for less than you would have paid otherwise, with one of those "other" orders.

Your broker absolutely has all of this "complete stock quote" information at his fingertips. Most often, market orders will "go off" at the "asked price", but they can "execute" at higher or lower prices, and often will. Most often, a higher price will be paid because the security is being aggressively marketed by Wall Street and even more furiously reported upon by the media. This creates a demand far in excess of supply and results in an upward price spiral. This is why people often get "killed" when attempting to buy a new issue.

Heed the voice of experience: Any time the market seems to be in a state of "free fall" for whatever reason, throw in some limit orders well below the "bid" price and see what happens. (Only for stocks on today's "Buy List", of course.) I've used this tactic on several occasions in the past to pick up some real bargains! You'll know when to do it; the media will report that the sky is falling!

The "bid' price is what buyers such as yourself are offering to pay for the stock. The "asked" price is what sellers want you to pay for their stock. Somewhere at or between these two numbers there will be a "last trade" figure and this is the number we are most likely to use in our buy order.

Yes, Virginia, there is a "seller" for every "buyer". Believe it or not, there are people out there who think you can just sell something to "The Market". Not so. Wall Street "specialists" in a particular security match the buy and sell orders (electronically, of course) to create the "auction market" that we all misunderstand so well, at very specific prices and with very detailed rules of behavior that I will not go into. This is one of the reasons that you should stay away from securities that have a limited "float" (number of shares outstanding) and are therefore not very actively traded (local bank shares, for example).

On stocks that trade enormous volume, we can often go in below the bid and succeed. Most stocks in our Quality range are in this category. A "day", "limit" order such as this can execute below the limit ($37.40), but never above. On the sell side, the order can execute above the limit, but never below. If you place such an order and it is either placed or executed improperly, you have a right to have it "busted" at the broker's expense, not at yours!

As you might have guessed, brokers are trained to have you place market orders. Many "sales assistants" that I've dealt with in the past have entered market orders on my trades because they had never placed a limit order! I understand that at some brokerages, limit orders and day orders are more expensive than market orders. Make sure your broker understands that every order you submit is a "day, limit" order EVEN IF YOU FORGET TO SAY SO. Send him a certified letter if you have to.

Only "day", "limit", orders are placed, ever! The price of the order must be at or below the price we planned to pay before the market opened. There is never a reason to pay more, ever! Day orders expire at the end of the trading day if they are not "filled". Limit orders may only be "filled"("executed") at the price indicated on the order "ticket" OR a better price (for you, not the brokerage firm).

Wall Street discourages this type of order because it requires more effort to control and because it is not an automatic commission. **Do not let this concern you.** If you cannot simply and quickly obtain all this information AND submit your order(s) within a matter of seconds, find a different service or a new broker. If the broker (or the on-line prompt) says "market", it is not a day-limit order, ever!

One other type of order exists, and it too should be avoided. An "open order" never expires. It just hangs out in the computer until executed. "Stop loss" orders are open orders. Open orders do have another interesting (insidious may be a better word) wrinkle. When the price on the order is reached, it miraculously becomes a "market" order.

"I Have A Client"

I have a client who insists on using a certain well-known discount broker because of the lower commissions. The process is very complicated, cumbersome, and time consuming, even before I reach a person (which itself is not guaranteed). And all of this (the recorded message parrots endlessly) is for my protection!

Believe me, it's for their protection, not yours. By the time they get done checking passwords and names, reading back numbers, and realizing that you want a complete quotation, the price on the order may no longer be realistic! When they end their spiel with "Is this correct sir?" and I respond: "Well I really don't know. Have those prices we spoke about earlier changed in the last few minutes?" They just don't get it!

Service, I've heard, can often be a more important consideration than price, especially since this particular price (the commission) is a variable cost of the merchandise you eventually will be selling! If you value your time more than they do, either arrange for a direct inside line (I've been able to make such an arrangement if the relationship is big enough.) or move your account to a firm that's a bit more considerate. On general principles, you should never be forced to do business with a telephone menu monster. Enough said?

Sometime before the end of the trading day, the brokerage firm should let you know whether or not your order was executed. You can then update your cash position and prepare for tomorrow. If your broker (or on line service) doesn't provide a "verbal" confirmation service, find one that does. **YOU NEED THIS INFORMATION before you attempt to make the following day's decisions!** Service strikes again!

Stock prices change quickly, particularly in the "best" trading vehicles. **Don't ever let the commission "tail" wag the portfolio "dog".** It is significantly more important to get the order in at the right price than it is to shave a few pennies off of the c(rate! Try to think about it this way: If you buy 100 shares of a stock at $40 per share "at the market" and pay a $35 commission, your cost basis is $4035 ($40.35 per share). If you buy the same 100 shares at $39.50 per share "at your limit" and pay a $75 commission, your cost is actually less, $4025 even though you paid the larger commission.

Yes, you can use limit orders at some discount brokers with no extra charge for that specific service. (Most? I just don't know.) Make sure that the overall service is adequate.

Never Violate the Rules

In the Investment World, there are deadly emotions that we have to recognize and protect ourselves against. Fear is one. Greed is another. Pride (are you familiar with the term "hubris") can also be financially fatal. Emotions have about as much use in an investment strategy as multiple swing thoughts have in a tee shot. Investment decisions have to be made objectively, so make sure that your judgment is not being influenced by outside forces! If you find yourself thinking something like this: "issue breadth has been negative for three months, maybe I'll just hang loose for a while and see what happens", STOP! Do the opposite! This is a day-to-day exercise; don't allow your emotions to complicate things!

A new "Buy List" must be developed every day, using all of the rules we've discussed, religiously, without exception. The "down 20% from the 52 week high" rule itself is inviolate. 19.875% is just not acceptable! Of equal importance are the rules about big daily movements and month-to-month changes in price. Otherwise, some of the major players will be selling to shift positions before you are in a position to sell!

Out of town; overslept; tied up in meetings? If you haven't been able to do the work, either don't do anything at all, or look at the same securities you planned to look at the day before. But base your decisions on the previous day's closing price, not yesterday's. You'll wind up paying less than you originally intended if you do actually place an order.

Issues you may be ready to sell? Remember those college "crib sheets"? Write down the pertinent information, and call in between flights, nines, meetings, etc.

What about vacations? Your money works every day; your equity portfolio is "in business" five days per week. Even though we human beings do require some R & R, the equity side of an investment portfolio can be managed easily from anywhere in the world. (You could do this even before the Internet made it super easy!) I've traded from Athens, London, Rome, Hong Kong, and other neat places without missing a beat.

This is your money remember, and your responsibility. None of your traveling companions (whoever they may be) will begrudge you the few minutes a day you spend taking care of business. Actually, they'll be impressed!

All you need to do is have an inventory of what you own, a relatively current newspaper (or Internet access) for current quotations, and a telephone. You should be able to get an international 800 number from your broker or insist that he take your collect calls. With the Internet, just use e-mail. (Again, you may not be fortunate enough to have either of these luxuries with some discount brokers. NO EXCUSES! You absolutely need to be able to trade from anywhere you happen to be!) Selling (profit taking) opportunities just can't be allowed to slip away, even if you have. **Your performance will absolutely suffer if you fail to** take care of business when you're away from home! It's all part of **YOUR RESPONSIBILITY!**

There is one other thing, particularly for you Mutual Fund and Wrap Account fund owners to understand. None of these investment managers or your Accountant, Financial Planner, Investment Executive, or "employee" Investment Manager would even consider doing this while they are on vacation! You can bet on it.

Don't be in too much of a hurry to fill up your portfolio. There will always be new opportunities. Think about it. If there are no new opportunities, your account should be full of profit taking cash ("smart cash")! If it's not, you are not following your rules. I have never experienced a time when there were both no buying, and no selling opportunities in the stock market. (The smaller the portfolio though, the more likely it is that this could occur.) Don't press yourself to find new opportunities just because you feel that you have too much cash in your portfolio. You'll wind up adding marginal issues to your "Selection Universe" for the wrong reasons. There is no harm at all in holding this **"smart cash"**. The more of it you accumulate, the more likely it is that some serious institutional profit taking will happen, giving you plenty of new investment opportunities. Think of it as a form of "compounding": You've already made 10% on this money, and now it will compound at Money Market rates until you find a new home for it.

The Selection Universe is hallowed ground and it will prove to be counterproductive if you become less "selective" for any reason. Be patient, your investment life is a long one. The shorter your buy list becomes, the more likely it is that your type of securities are becoming overpriced. In August of 1987, for example, a month or so before what proved to be the best buying opportunity in the history of the financial markets, my buy list contained only two stocks. My inventory of stocks owned amounted to only forty or so, with 50% of those being utility stocks, because interest rates were very high at the time. Continue to take your profits (See Chapter Four) and smile, new opportunities will be along soon enough.

Just what is "smart cash"? The oracle of Wall Street always recommends that a portion of your investment portfolio remain in cash. Banks will advertise their "CD" (Certificates of Deposit) and "Money Market" interest rates, and suggest that you "invest" in these high yield vehicles! Other financial types will tell you to move into cash quickly because this or that is about to happen, and you should wait and see what is going on before you make any further commitments.

None of that cash is "smart cash" for two basic, and I mean extremely basic, reasons. This direct from the "oracle of reality" so make sure you thoroughly understand it: a) by definition, cash is never an investment! It is a temporary holding area for dollars that are destined for placement in either the equity or fixed income portion of the investment portfolio. And b) the future is an unknown.

Even those superstar Harvard or Wharton MBAs, with their million dollar salaries, have no more of a clue about tomorrow's stock market than you or I. **A recommendation WITHOUT "CASH" would be an admission of this ignorance, and they can't afford to admit to that.** Actually, their fixed vs. equity numbers have nothing to do with asset allocation either! It is just guesswork about what these two classes of investments are going to do in the short-run.

They advise you to hold cash until they tell you that the time is right to do something with it. **Don't take the bait, put your right hand over your heart and recite the Investor's Creed! (See below.)** There is another, more subtle, motivation for Wall Street firms to recommend a change in the "cash" portion of the portfolio. This just has to generate some transactions! Right? Right! Something either has to be sold to raise cash, or purchased (their latest "hot" stock, no doubt) to alter the amount of cash in the portfolio.

Smart cash is simply that which results from the taking of profits. The only reason it is in cash is because we haven't gotten around to doing anything with it yet. We don't rush around doing things that are outside the plan, just because the pinstriped piper of Wall Street is playing a different song. This is the overall concept at work, and it is the answer you should learn to use when asked about the amount of cash in your portfolio. I call it:

The Investor's Creed!

"My intention is to be fully invested in accordance with my planned equity/fixed income asset allocation. On the other hand, every security I own is for sale, and every security I own generates some form of cash flow that cannot be reinvested immediately. I am happy when my cash position is nearly 0% because all of my money is then working as hard as it possibly can to meet my objectives. But, I am ecstatic when my cash position approaches 100% because that means I've sold everything at a profit, and that I am in a position to take advantage of any new investment opportunities (that fit my guidelines) as soon as I become aware of them."

How Much to Buy

We've talked quite a bit about diversification already. (**What are the three basic principles of investing?**) If you don't spit out this answer instantaneously, return to Chapter One, do not pass "GO", do not place any orders!

It goes without saying that "The Big Three" are inviolate! But in smaller portfolios, keeping positions below 5% can become difficult since purchases should be limited to "round lots" (i.e., 100 share increments). Remember that the 5% rule is a total investment "program" consideration, which means that three separate $70,000 portfolios are one $210,000 program! 10% might just have to be acceptable in extremely small portfolios, but you can always raise your "Quality" parameter to A- or better to offset some of the increased risk in the "Diversification" element. Portfolios of less than $20,000 should be started in Closed End Equity Mutual Funds. Check the back of your S & P Guide, and look closely at GAB, BLU, PEO, and others.

This type of security (the closed end fund) is much less complicated than the "open end" variety, generally produces a nice dividend, and trades like a stock. You should be aware of the fact that the bulk of the dividend will come after January 1st. As soon as the "cost basis" (working capital) of the portfolio exceeds $20,000 dollars, ***commence the move*** into individual stocks. Even though the fund itself is a diversified entity, be careful not to establish any one position that represents as much as 20% of the portfolio.

A move from one type of security within a class (closed end equity fund to individual equities), or from one class to another (fixed income to equity) is orchestrated over time and in accordance with our basic trading standards. Take profits or accumulate income in one area and then reinvest in the other.

Since we are buying stocks that have moved down 20% or more from their 12-month highs, it is likely that they will continue to move down after we have purchased them. This is a fact of life that is dealt with through a strategy called "Averaging Down", which was illustrated earlier and simply refers to the purchase of additional shares of a stock you already own, but at a lower price. **Please don't confuse this strategy with the popular "Dollar Cost Averaging" concept or even with "DRIPS" (Dividend Re-Investment Plans). Their popularity should be your first clue that they are bad for your financial health!** Think about it!

Dollar Cost Averaging is a mechanical process where a fixed sum of money is invested in the same security or fund at a regular time interval (monthly, for example) either through direct deduction from a bank account, payroll, or by regular cash payments. I can't think of a single reason why this type of investing makes any sense at all. It certainly doesn't fit into a program that involves any kind of personal decision-making! Obviously, it doesn't fit into a program that is based on quality and diversification, nor does it allow for a selection process based on price. **Finally, there's no provision to sell!**

This is probably an idea that developed through the Life Insurance industry, where systematic insurance premium payment made life easier for the sales person, by decreasing the amount of time spent trying to "conserve" lapsed policies.

Dividend Re-Investment Plans are much more popular, and those who use this "forced-feeding" approach are cult-like in their support and enthusiasm for it. People somehow seem to feel less manipulated and abused with this approach (since it is controlled by the companies themselves and not the brokerage firms) but they are really just kidding themselves. The popularity of DRIPs, believe it or not, is occasioned by a nominal reduction in the price per share and the absence of a commission on the purchase. Added to the issues that make this form of Dollar Cost Averaging so unproductive are these: participants are saddled with a horrendous record-keeping job! Cost basis determination is nearly impossible (as it is with automatic reinvestment in all Mutual Funds). Additionally, participants are buying the shares under demand conditions that are being artificially increased.

The individual decision-making approach is completely different than these "programmed buying" methods of becoming disproportionately invested in (and falling in love with) a particular security. **Consequently, when we make our initial purchase of any stock, we must allow "room" to add to our position by buying more of the stock at a lower price, at least once!** So in response to a question raised earlier concerning the amount of an initial purchase

111

in a $200,000 program, the answer would not be $10,000. Right? In practice, initial purchases should be controlled at about 3% or even lower.

Accountants love to create work for themselves because they bill by the hour and, thus, they have no reason to recommend things that would cut their billing totals. Tax payers have the option of determining the "cost basis" of their securities in either of two methods: by individual "lots" or by average pricing. You have to be consistent in the use of one or the other. **If you intend to "average down", as you must to be successful; you must also use the average pricing method!** You'll save yourself a lot of record-keeping time, and keep your Accountant's bills in line!

When to Buy More

When to buy more of a stock (and just how much more) becomes the key question. Most of you have probably been told, at some time in your investment life to "sell your losers and let your profits run". That type of thinking will eventually sink your portfolio, particularly at a time when issue breadth runs negative for an extended period, or if you don't have some pretty good "when to sell" rules to apply! It is a basic principle of speculating, not investing, just another transaction generating tactic developed to enhance commission levels. It also just has to make you broke!

Nowhere does it say "stop buying! So you dutifully take a loss in ABC, and buy DEF. When DEF drops, you sell it and are moved into GHI, which then starts to fall. Wait a minute, the XYZ stopped going up so now we have to sell it. Sorry, but this process just has to end at zero eventually. *Never Forget*: **no matter how sugar coated or rational the advice sounds, it is motivated by a powerful lust to separate you from some of your dollars! If it were legal for these guys to just take your money all at once, they would!**

The "buy more" decision is certainly one of the most difficult to learn to implement confidently. It takes some successful experience and a lot of courage. Take some time to review the historical charts of some of the companies that have been used in the Chapter Two Tables, particularly **Table Three,** which is a "study" in the profitability of buying those "losers" and turning them around profitably!

Since we are dealing only with "Investment Grade" securities, it is far more reasonable to say, for example, that Merck is a better buy at X-25% than it was at X. Particularly if we've planned ahead and allowed room to buy more within our diversification limits! Well, you might observe, if the market price continues to fall, more and more can be purchased without exceeding the diversification limits. We could wind up investing too much in a company that really is in trouble!

HAVE NO FEAR! All such problems are avoided through the use of "The Working Capital Model", an approach to portfolio design and management that I developed in response to observations such as this. Simply, "Market Value" is just not an acceptable measure to use for questions of diversification. The important number is the amount actually invested in the security or securities under review. The Working Capital Model is covered in complete detail in Chapter Five. All portfolio design considerations should be based on "cost basis" not on market value. Thus, we avoid putting too much money either in a faltering company, an unpopular sector, or a weakening asset classification.

How Many Stocks

A properly diversified equity portfolio would have at least 20 stocks in it. One with more than 50 stocks would be a bit unwieldy, but it certainly is "doable". In my management business, I have several $1,000,000+ portfolios that typically contain between 35 and 45 issues. This millionaire's program had 43 at the time these words were written. Similarly, the fixed income portion of the portfolio need not contain a huge number of issues. Most Mutual Funds contain much larger numbers of securities than this, making one wonder if the underlying strategy is merely to "mirror the market" rather than to follow a diversification model of some kind.

Now Warming Up In The "Bull Pen"

As you move down the columns of the newspaper each morning, you will notice companies that are moving into your buy range even though they are not currently in the Selection Universe. You'll notice that many of your very best trading experiences will fall into this category! Every Saturday morning I take the extra time needed to look for this kind of new/old opportunity. Today, Saturday July 28, 2001, I noticed Bank of New York, Colgate Palmolive, Emerson Electric, and Roper. It is now August 26th, and both the Roper and the Colgate are gone (i.e., sold for profits)! WOW!

Eventually, as you become more experienced, you'll take instant notice of a few stocks that you feel you really should buy ASAP! My personal favorites include Pfizer, PepsiCo, Schering-Plough, and a few others. When they move down to that 20% level, I make a mental note to check the price throughout the day for the opportunity to re-establish a position.

Remember to control your enthusiasm. The "Bull Pen" is just for your very best "traders", and one such item per day should be enough (I'm looking at four because I am managing more than 100 portfolios). **NOTE that no change in the normal purchase guidelines is warranted!** As important as buying is, experience will show you that it should not be done in a hurry. Fill up your portfolio slowly! Selling, on the other hand, needs to be done much more quickly. We'll look at that process in the next Chapter.

Two Important Numbers/Two Important Lists

Keeping "in touch" with what is going on in the investment world each day is important but it can be dealt with sanely. There is no need to be "at the tape", watching each trade as it goes by on the screen. You really don't need flashing numbers, bells, and whistles to get the job done! Wall Street wants you to believe that everything (buy, sell, panic) has to be done immediately. "This deal just won't be available tomorrow!" In this respect, securities salesmen sound an awful lot like automobile advertisements, don't they? Commission based sales people get paid based on sales made through a specific cut-off date each month, quarter, and year; usually the last Friday or Thursday of the reporting period. **So unless they know they can't "sell" you, you'll be hearing from them around that time. Still, as a trader, you are probably their best customer so don't feel at all uncomfortable leaning on them for all the information that you need.**

Wall Street does have great "real-time" information that you would be foolish not to use to your advantage. If you are looking to add a Preferred Stock, Treasury Securities, or a Corporate Bond Unit Trust to the Fixed Income side of your portfolio, your broker has all the information you need at his keyboard. Make sure he looks at "call price" and the first "call date", too. But it's still up to you to be knowledgeable and careful. **You absolutely do not want anything brand new or "just coming out" with no sales charge or commission! WHAT!**

There is no such thing as a "freebie" on Wall Street. There is no such thing as a "freebie" on Wall Street. There is no such thing as a "freebie" on Wall Street! There is no such thing as a "freebie" on Wall Street! You are paying the "underwriting mark-up" and the "Financial Advisor" is getting special points toward a bonus or campaign prize of some kind, you can count on it! *The next time he tells you he's going to a conference in Maui at the company's expense, ask him why they aren't sending the clients?* The old "Show me the customers' yachts" scenario…

Depending on the type of security you are after, and within a Quality Range that you specify, he or she should be able to get you a good sampling of the fixed income opportunities that are out there.

Just as an aside, **here's an interesting difference between the Financial Institutions in New York City and the Gaming Institutions of Atlantic City.** Wall Street is a bit subtler in its efforts to take your money. They don't do it quite as quickly, with the exception of a few products, and they certainly don't advertise themselves as gaming establishments. Still it doesn't keep them (the banking divisions of the Wall Street institutions) from putting ATMs every place you look, even in the casinos! Yet another Hydra head appears! Is there an "ethics" department?

The interesting difference is that the Casinos reward the losers and the winners impressively. Wall Street just takes the money! There is as much competition for "high rollers" in Las Vegas as there is for Wrap Account money in New York. I don't know about you, but I want in on that next trip to Vail!

Make sure you avoid paying a "premium" (more than the face value at maturity), check on the "call date"(keep this two or three years out), determine current yield (yield right now at the last trade price), yield to maturity (coupon or contract rate), yield to call (securities may be redeemed early), and so on... You should become familiar with these terms and your broker must be fluent in them! All textbooks on investing will have a section that explains all of the terms you need to understand when you invest in bonds. You best resource is an experienced broker you can trust, if you can find one! (The longer a broker has been around, the more "honest" he is likely to be, for fairly obvious reasons!)

Attention, discount broker fans and direct Internet traders! Most of these entities will have no inventory of fixed income securities for you to select from!

WARNING! WARNING! WARNING!

DON'T BE FOOLED INTO BUYING BONDS (OR PREFERRED STOCKS) WITH SHORT-TERM MATURITY DATES! One of the oldest "cons" out there is the one where the broker tries to sell you bonds that are maturing in a year or two, even though the yield can be a percent or more less than longer term bonds. He'll try to convince you that this makes your portfolio more "flexible" in response either to changes in interest rates or to other opportunities. What it actually does is: a) assure you of an unnecessarily lower yield on investment, b) guarantee the broker a constant 6% return on your money, and c) assures the broker of special bonuses and incentives for pushing the firm's new underwritings!

That's right, he gets up to a 3% mark up on each side of the trade! Flexible cash flow can be assured by using Corporate or Municipal Bond Unit Trusts. They pay out principal and interest on a monthly basis.

DON'T BE FOOLED INTO BUYING BONDS, PREFERRED STOCKS, OR ANYTHING ELSE THAT THE FIRM "IS JUST COMING OUT WITH"! It's really just common sense. If you have 100,000 brokers selling the same security, what do you think happens to the price? On the flip side, why are these 100,000 brokers focusing on this particular security? Just one more question; what will happen to the price of the security next month, when the 100,000 brokers stop pushing it? Note that the price of a Unit Trust is fixed by the institutional trustee, and not by an institutional marketing department. I'd like to believe that there is a slight difference there. This may be the reason why the Unit Trusts aren't pushed quite so hard.

*   *   *   *   *

Finally, make sure you have a feel for what current interest rates are and, equally as important, the recent trend in interest rates. Avoid any security that has a current yield significantly higher than normal (Compare with Utility Stock yields or some other benchmark.), there is a reason and its called higher than normal risk. This higher risk can be well hidden, but it's in there for sure. The recent trend in interest rates is usually very well publicized. If the trend is downward (prices of interest rate sensitive securities are moving higher), wait until a week or so after the Federal Reserve makes a move before you shop. (Don't buy on good news.) If the move in rates is a "disappointment" or part of an upward trend, buy just after the announcement. (Do buy on bad news.)

Now I know you are thinking: If rates are going down, why buy at all? If rates are going up, why not wait? Good questions! Interest rates generally move very slowly and in 25 or 50 "basis point" (A "basis point" is one 100th of a percent.) increments. **"Wait and see" is "market timing" jargon with interest rate sensitive securities just as it is with equities.** (All Fixed Income Securities are interest rate sensitive securities, as are equities that pay high dividend rates.) If interest rates are now 6%, money market rates are probably about half that. That's a lot of interest to give up on a directional guess.

Remember that if you buy properly, you will have room to buy more if rates increase significantly, thus increasing your average yield. If rates go down significantly, a selling opportunity will materialize!

One more point should be considered in selecting securities for your fixed income portfolio. If you are digesting all of this, you will realize the importance of establishing positions in fixed income securities that are readily added to such as "closed end" Municipal Bond funds and Preferred Stocks (so that you can "Average Down"). Unit Trusts and self-liquidating Government securities (Ginny Maes, Treasury Bills, etc.) are difficult to buy more of but they demand a place in the portfolio because they return principal on a regular basis. These cash flow machines give you monthly checks that can be used either for new position purchases or for adding to existing holdings. And, don't forget that a portion of this cash flow is destined for equity investments too; our asset allocation model applies to all of our income, regardless of its source.

Managing your portfolio in this new, low (er) risk, environment is different. Two or three times a day, when you check in with your broker for prices, ask for "issue breadth" statistics and "market stats". These should be at his fingertips, "real time". Yeah, service again!

Issue Breadth

Issue breadth is the single most accurate barometer of what is going on in the stock market on any given day, period! Issue breadth is the single most important number you need to know about to understand your portfolio's (equity) value performance in the real investment world. Issue breadth undermines the validity of the popular market averages and is, therefore, rarely reported loudly enough from Wall Street. *Issue breadth is a true indicator of what is going on today in the market place and an even better indicator of what has happened in the recent past!* Interestingly, this measurement tool was designed to be a "stock market" indicator; the DJIA (Dow Jones Industrial Average) was not.

Issue breadth compares the number of "advancing issues" with the number of "declining issues" on the New York Stock Exchange (also on the other exchanges). A rational person would expect rallies to be accompanied by positive breadth (more winners than losers) and corrections to be evidenced by the opposite. Wall Street just doesn't care!

In July 2001, Wall Street was still successfully selling its Market correction/bad economy scenario; it had been doing so for about 18 months. On the NYSE (New York Stock Exchange), where most true investors live, advancing issues had exceeded declining issues by more than 22,000. That works out to a positive monthly differential of about 1300 "ticks". ("Wall Streeteze" for a price change, either up or down, is an "up tick" or a "down tick", respectively.) The trading strategy presented here calls for buying only on "down ticks".

During the same time period, NYSE issues achieving new 12 month "highs" doubled the number achieving new "lows"! (See below.) Only twice during this fictional "correction" did monthly new lows exceed monthly new highs! It's kind of like that old nursery rhyme, "The Emperor's New Clothes"! I once had a boss who used to say "Don't confuse me with the facts, I've got to make a decision!" He could have made it big on Wall Street!

Numbers provide information that adds to our minimal understanding of what is going on "out there", in the stock market. No single number does it all and weighted averages are about the most confusing numbers ever developed. If IBM, for example, was up (or down) by 3 points, and the other 29 DJIA stocks were unchanged, what would the change in the average be? What should it be?

Similarly, 1998 was a year in which the rise in price of just 10 stocks accounted for 70% of the gain in the S & P 500 stock average! Of the other 490 stocks 60 % or so were DOWN, many significantly! **We either need a new collection of averages and indices, or seriously better reporting of their meaning in the Wall Street media!**

New Highs vs. New Lows

Another number you have to become fluent in is the differential between stocks achieving new 12-month highs and those falling to new 12-month lows. I know it sounds somewhat simplistic, but rallies should be accompanied by a greater number of stocks achieving new 12-month highs than new lows. Don't you think?

You would have to page back all the way to the '80s to find a time when there were days with no new 12-month lows! You'd have to reach back even further to find a time when such information was given any attention on The Street! **Table Four** (below) teaches a lesson that SEC Regulators need to know about. During the NASDAQ run up from 1998 through early 2000, new lows on the NYSE more than doubled new highs! Where did the "Gold Rush" money come from? **Who encouraged investors to switch from value investing to no-value speculating? ANSWER: Those Wall Street Institutions!**

"Market Statistics"

Market statistics will give you a current idea of what is happening with individual items. **The Most Active List and The Most Declining List** tell you about group activity, lead you to individual news stories, and provide potential additions to the "Bull Pen". The Most Advancing List gives similar group information and will also make you aware of new selling opportunities, the most important information of all, and the subject of Chapter Four. The following "Market Statistics" listings come from the August 4, 2001 issue of the New York Times. (The same information is available free on the internet.)

Most Active List   Most Advanced List   Most Declined List

Stock	Volume (100)	Last Price	Chg	Stock	Last Price	$ Chg	% Chg	Stock	Last Price	$ Chg	% Chg
Lucent	598,766	6.60	+0.29	Sensor	23.12	8.18	54.8	FstCwel	11.75	1.18	9.1
Sensor	343,035	23.12	+8.18	Oakley	13.18	2.15	19.5	SLI Inc	5.25	0.50	8.7
GlblCrs	234,357	5.97	+0.29	FostrWh	7.48	1.00	15.4	FibrMrk	9.95	0.87	8.0
Cabltrn	152,901	20.75	-0.05	Oakwood	8.50	0.90	11.8	ColeNatl	12.30	1.00	7.5
GenElec	152,538	42.75	+0.55	Cabltrn	14.25	1.50	11.8	AsiaGlbl	4.90	0.35	6.7
QwestCm	146,665	24.40	+1.30	ExideTec	7.27	0.68	10.3	MCS Sft	20.50	1.45	6.6

FamDlr	130,787	26.24	-0.79	ElderTrs	6.65	0.59	9.7	Gensco	27.48	1.87	6.4
EMC Cp	96,733	20.48	+0.02	TrinityIn	26.16	2.14	8.9	AdMkSv	15.69	1.06	6.3
Disney	94,249	26.60	+0.10	Guess	7.43	0.56	8.2	TycomLt	13.63	0.91	6.3
TycoIntl	90,344	53.29	+0.51	ScaniaB	17.00	1.25	7.9	Wipro	32.50	1.99	5.8
Exxon	88,348	41.26	-0.47	WHX	5.50	0.40	7.8	UtdMicro	8.35	0.51	5.8
Motorola	84,049	18.63	-0.77	Checkpnt	12.25	0.85	7.5	StdPac	22.64	1.31	5.5
MicronT	73,018	43.45	-1.45	ColeMyr	26.50	1.80	7.3	RyersTul	12.15	0.70	4.4
SprntPCS	72,711	25.43	-0.62	UCAR In	12.34	0.81	7.0	CornrRlt	10.78	0.62	5.4
Pfizer	71,292	40.74	Unc	Satyam	8.10	0.50	6.6	Encomps	6.15	0.35	5.4

As a trader once again, you will be a very good brokerage client! Over time, a "bright" Account Executive will learn your strategy, and let you know when something important occurs, particular when he knows you will be able to sell something profitably! He might also clue you in on a downward "gap" in a stock he knows you love to trade. And he will make it a point to have the statistics you want available at all times.

Be careful though, I have found that the majority of brokers do not have enough of a spine to support their inflated egos. If an "outside manager" is running your program, your (insecure) broker will make every attempt to undermine his judgment in either buys or sells. Whatever criticism you come up with, right or wrong, he will support, even magnify. Then he'll try to sell you his firm's WRAP account managers or Mutual funds.

I could never understand this (but I guess it boils down to the tremendous incentives brokers have to sell product). Here they are blessed with a lucrative relationship, and absolutely no accountability for the decisions that are being made. They can devote 100% of their time to soliciting new business, and still be assured of a steady cash flow. **It's a mystery why they are not standing in line to sign up their clients with independent managers. Can the commissions and benefits from their product sales be that huge! I guess so!**

The **Table Four** spreadsheet shows actual NYSE Issue Breadth numbers from May 1998 and High/Low numbers starting in April 1999. It will be an eye opener if you spend some time looking it over and comparing a few time periods with Wall Street analytical propaganda. I'm hopeful that after a few more chapters you'll be totally "deprogrammed" and ready to go forward in the investment world with some knowledge that really will help you to succeed. How're you doing so far?

Table Four: Statistics That Really Matter

Month	Up Ticks	Down Ticks	Net	Total	Up Days	Down Days	New Highs	New Lows
May '98	27,944	31,418	(3,474)		7	13		
June '98	32,394	33,870	(1,476)		10	12		
July '98	28,187	35,980	(7,793)		8	14		
August '98	24,829	39,978	(15,149)		5	18		
September '98	33,929	31,291	2,638		11	10		
October '98	35,830	32,682	3,148		13	9		
November '98	31,623	29,176	2,447		11	9		
December '98	33,486	33,687	(201)		11	11		
--------	------	-----	------		-----	---		
May thru Dec, '98	248,222	268,082	(19,860)		76	96		
--------	-------	------	------		-----	-----		
January '99	27,087	31,336	(4,249)		7	12		
February '99	25,786	31,947	(6,161)		4	15		
March '99	33,812	35,101	(1,289)		9	14		
April '99	31,251	26,396	4,855		15	5	1,546	1,099
May '99	29,282	30,561	(1,279)		11	9	1,227	739
June '99	32,172	34,041	(1,869)		12	10	1,439	1,777
July '99	29,377	34,343	(4,966)		7	14	1,783	1,365
August '99	30,165	36,455	(6,290)	(6,290)	6	16	1,046	3,247
September '99	28,070	35,699	(7,629)	(13,919)	8	13	892	3,820
October '99	29,578	33,696	(4,118)	(18,037)	8	13	835	5,176
November '99	30,022	34,235	(4,213)	(22,250)	9	12	1,476	3,316
December '99	32,592	35,695	(3,103)	(25,353)	9	13	1,882	7,098
--------	------	-----	------		-----	---		--------

Month	Up Ticks	Down Ticks	Net	Total	Up Days	Down Days	New Highs	New Lows
Jan thru Dec, 1999	359,194	399,505	(40,311)		105	146	12,126	27,637
January '00	28,912	32,956	(4,044)	(4,044)	8	12	1,388	2,224
February '00	27,611	32,952	(5,341)	(9,385)	7	13	1,298	3,821
March '00	35,558	35,758	(200)	(9,585)	11	12	1,847	2,667
April '00	28,225	29,782	(1,557)	(11,142)	10	9	750	1,120
May '00	28,494	33,258	(4,664)	(15,806)	10	12	1,157	1,497
June '00	36,154	29,746	6,408	(9,398)	11	11	1,521	1,185
July '00	29,357	27,996	1,361	(8,037)	12	8	1,478	824
August '00	34,738	29,820	4,918	(3,119)	15	8	2,268	818
September '00	27,682	28,739	(1,057)	(4,176)	8	12	2,356	1,489
October '00	29,698	33,872	(4,174)	(8,350)	8	14	1,172	2,543
November '00	27,239	33,744	(6,505)	(14,855)	8	12	1,510	1,611
December '00	32,716	25,937	6,779	(8,076)	12	8	3,956	1,840
Jan thru Dec, 2000	366,484	374,560	(8,076)		120	131	20,701	21,639
January '01	34,777	27,591	7,186	(890)	17	4	3,626	228
February '01	28,670	30,972	(1,402)	(2,292)	8	13	2,749	386
March '01	32,835	32,844	(9)	(2,301)	11	11	2,139	1,408
April '01	32,407	28,969	3,438	1,137	12	8	1,883	849
May '01	35,956	31,848	4,108	5,245	14	8	3,294	357
June '01	31,165	30,555	610	5,885	9	11	2,434	749
July '01	34,565	33,456	1,109	6,964	15	8	2,275	1,109
August '01	30,998	26,838	4,160	11,124	13	6	3,034	756
Jan thru Aug 2001	261,373	242,173	19,200		99	67	21,434	5,752
From May, 1998	1,235,273	1,284,320	(49,047)		400	440		
From August, 1999	778,284	792,513	(14,229)		259	265	48,266	50,048

Finding This Information On-Line

Your broker should not say "Huh!" when you ask him to recite the Most Declined List! Again, cheap trade executions will save you some pennies but lack of information could cost you thousands of dollars! If you have trouble getting what you need from your trading place, you can get this information on AOL for free, but with about a 20 minute time delay. By the way, you don't have to join AOL to get the information.

"The Emperor's New Clothes" (Appearing in The IMF, January 1999)

"'Cyclical Stocks had one of their worst years ever relative to the overall market as the Morgan Stanley cyclical index ended the year exactly where it began 1998'"

"'Through late December, about 86% of fund managers were trailing the S & P 500. That was only a little better than the performance in 1997, when fully 90% lagged the index.'"

"'Make no mistake, 1998 was a year that humbled the mightiest of managers.'"

"'...growth stocks in the S & P beat the index's value contingent...by an unprecedented 28 percentage points...'"

"'If your Mutual Fund wasn't invested in Internet stocks or the best handful of big stocks, you probable didn't do well in 1998.'"

"'Tech stocks increased their weighting in the S & P to a record 19%...'"

"These quotes are from the latest issue of "Barron's" and they support (the contention that) conservative investing in quality companies...and emphasis on Managed Asset Allocation couldn't compare with indices and averages that are 100% hype and 0% plan. **Like the Emperor's New Clothes, a child can tell you that: when losing issues outnumber advancers and hundreds of "Investment Grade" NYSE companies finish the year below where they started, "The Market" is really not as well dressed as you've been led to believe."**

Wall Street has no preference; it will mislead you in either direction! [Right now (August, 2001), for example, Wall Street still won't admit that there has been a "rally" going on for at least eighteen months!] Issue breadth (sometimes called the advance/decline line) at that time (January, 1999) had been clearly negative since early in 1998! It is also interesting to look inside the individual quotes from one of the most respected mouthpieces on Wall Street. If the columns were understood, goal orientated people would appreciate why their portfolio values were lower for the period. (Note that interest rates had been rising as well, producing a "double whammy" effect on the bottom line numbers that Wall Street wants you to focus on.) They would also understand that the change in emphasis on Wall Street would have no permanent damaging effect on the achievement of their investment goals. It's simple: only speculators could possibly "win" during this hysterical surge in the "no value" sector of the market!

Unfortunately, if the columns weren't understood, investors could be tempted to change strategies, and try to board a train that was speeding by at hundreds of miles per hour! Many did. The train crashed. There's a lot of sadness in the world!

Another observation that one should make about these seemingly harmless quotes is their typical Wall Street focus on performance "as compared with the S & P 500 average or some other index. What's in the average? One quote shows a weighting increase for "tech stocks" to nearly 20%. Another speaks of "cyclical stocks", and yet another the "growth component" as compared to the "value component". No one seems to care about how a portfolio (Mutual Fund or otherwise) fared when compared to its own stated objectives. Should a fund manager have changed the focus of his portfolio just because Wall Street Institutions decided to promote dot-coms? I don't think so. (Of course, many did.)

Trite? Yes. True? Absolutely!

Every business, institution, sport, or other popular activity has its trite little phrases that everyone has heard, but that few people really take the time to understand or to appreciate. Investing is certainly no exception. For Example:

Buy on Bad News

The Market always overreacts to bad news causing the prices of otherwise high quality securities to go down quickly (a "gap" opening), often after a lengthy trading halt in anticipation of the news. (And they say that there is no longer any Insider Trading going on!) In most instances, this will prove to be a good time either to establish a new position or to add to an older one. (But never violate the rules.) In addition to the other statistics we just looked at, every broker has instant access to the most recent news stories on any equity.

So after you find out that the "drugs" are weak (because six of the fifteen "Most Declined" and eight of the "Most Actives" are in that group) lean on your broker for the news, and get some current prices to see if any of your favorite traders are ready for action! Now this is research that makes sense at the "local level"!

Always Buy Too Soon

Market Timing is impossible in the aggregate, extremely unlikely with individual issues, and patently unnecessary to be concerned with at all. Yes, the price of the stock you are buying will probably move lower. That's perfectly OK when you are dealing with quality securities and when you have a game plan.

Buying too soon doesn't mean "hurry up"! It simply means to apply your rules to today's price movements without trying to guess what may or may not happen tomorrow.

Don't Be In A Hurry to Buy

Don't allow your self to get all caught up in the hype and fluff of "Wall Street" gurus and CNBC interviewees. If you don't get what you want (at the price you want) today, you can buy it or something else tomorrow. It is unlikely that there will ever be a day in which nothing meets your buying requirements, no matter how restrictive they are.

Never Buy a "Hot Tip"

Don't even think about it. **Every stock idea someone presents to you has its own special story. It has a new product or technology, a different niche for an old something or other, a new spin, a different twist, better management (We've just got to talk about that one!), etc. Don't you believe it!** First of all, why would anyone share this good poop with you (or with anyone else)? Secondly, do you think you are the first one to hear about this special opportunity? Check out your source. How much did he buy? Even if it's an impressive number, don't do it.

How do these geniuses determine what "better management" is? Is it the aggregate dollars paid by executives for their impressive post-graduate degrees? Or perhaps it's their aggregate salaries. Management involves four things: planning, organizing, controlling, and directing (or leading). That's all! Just ask Drucker. (If you don't know that name, just go to the library and look up books on management.) Sure we can look at the corporation's long and short-term planning methods, its organization structure, and control mechanisms. We can be appropriately impressed with the influential super stars that sit on their boards of directors.

But how can we predict what any of them will do under fire? Who is the ultimate decision maker?

Some "great managements" include an "Office of the President", or "Co-Chairmen of the Board". We have Chief Operating Officers, Chief Executive Officers, and Chief Financial Officers. If you can't identify "the boss", you don't have good management. Most organizations are run at the lower levels of management. Now that's a good thing!

I've seen hundreds of portfolios filled with worthless "story stocks". The following paragraphs will provide some insight about why.

Break Time Courtesy of Vanity Fair

One of my clients sent me an article, from the August 2001 issue of "Vanity Fair", in which **Nina Munk** has presented an exposé with regard to the analysts that make things happen on Wall Street. I don't know the writer personally, and have never read any of her other work, but she is "right on the money" here! I have excerpted a few pieces that are meaningful to me, and that support [naturally] the thrust of this book. You should make it a point to keep this article on your desk for the next time the "greed monster" starts blowing in your ear. And there will be a next time. You can count on it! **Please note that any commentary of my own will be [bracketed]:**

"Before the 1990s, research analysts were neither queens nor demigods, nor even stars. Instead of being featured in the media, they quietly advised clients on the long-term prospects of public companies. However, with the emergence of the bull market of the 1990s, and especially the mania for technology stocks, that all changed. As record numbers of Americans began investing in the market **[not the fist time this or the subsequent rout and withdrawal of the individual investor had occurred]**, what counted was not a company's balance sheet but the short-term performance of its stock. Who had time to be patient?"

"Financial-news outlets—particularly CNBC, the cable network watched obsessively by traders—needed provocative sound bites; analysts whose views could send a stock soaring quickly became media stars. [One analyst] was 32 years old, a history major from Yale who'd taught English for a year in Japan and worked as a proofreader at *Harper's* before landing on Wall Street in 1994. **[Now there are credentials for you!]** Quokka Sports, an on-line sports information network whose stock [he] once predicted would hit a split-adjusted $1,250 is in Chapter 11 bankruptcy."

"[Another analyst] has done just as badly. In March 1999, her employer underwrote the I.P.O. of Priceline.com... Despite the company's enormous losses, its I.P.O. was strongly promoted by [this analyst]. 'This is a time to be rationally reckless,' she explained to *The New Yorker*. Rational? Not exactly, but reckless she was **[not to mention the incredible conflict of interest! Caveat Emptor, indeed!]**"

"So what's the bottom line, as they say in the trade? Investors lost huge sums of money by following the advice of so-called celebrity analysts; the analysts, meanwhile, got famous and rich."

"...In Washington, Representative Richard Baker...has launched a congressional investigation of analysts; specifically, he wants to know if some manipulated the market for their own gain. **[Don't be naïve. Even if they didn't own shares in the companies they plugged, their employers made fortunes and they benefited through huge bonuses and sports superstar salaries!]** New York State's attorney general is studying conflicts of interest among analysts."

"...leads us to the heart of the matter: many of the picks and predictions of analysts weren't just dead wrong—they were compromised. As long as they made money, few **[greedy]** investors **[speculators]** bothered to consider that the [analysts] were no longer objective observers of the market: they were insiders with inherent conflicts of interest, making money for themselves and their firms by promoting their…clients, bringing in deals, pushing big I.P.O.s, and even owning shares in the companies they covered and recommended."

"As professionals on Wall Street know, analysts rarely issue "sell" recommendations. Why? Because the company concerned could get petulant [and] …cut off the analyst's access to information; …refuse to do its investment banking with the analyst's employer; …the analyst could get fired for undermining one of his firm's important clients." **[In other words, analyst recommendations are 99% financially and politically motivated, Jack, and it's not the prospective investors financials that are considered to be important!]**

[Please note that the bracketed portions above were mine.]

It goes without saying that the analyst/underwriting/media/investor relationship is one that can only inflict financial pain on the final consumer, and that a whole lot could be done to control and to regulate the way securities are analyzed and brought public. But none of this is new, it's business as usual discovered, uncovered, and (finally) reported. Will it lead to meaningful change? You can help. (See Chapter Seven.)

And, if you allow yourself to be manipulated like this over and over again; if you consistently let your own personal greed "Harpy" lure you onto the rocks; if you are that incapable of learning from your own mistakes and the wisdom of other, more experienced, people, who is really to blame? **It is (or was) your money! It still is your ultimate responsibility!**

Don't cry "foul" and go out and sue somebody. It's your own fault. **You don't blame the croupier for your losses when you throw "craps", and that's pretty much what you've been doing when you threw your money on those Dot-Com ponies.** Grow up, little leaguer, you lost the game and it wasn't the referee's fault. End of story, learn how to invest.

CHAPTER FOUR: "SELL HIGH (er)"

The market was just breezing along during that summer of 1987, enjoying one of the broadest rallies ever experienced on Wall Street. From the very start (twelve consecutive up days in the DJIA) equity prices just didn't seem capable of going down! The mystical "2000" barrier was shattered early in the year and upward the market soared! On through 2100 it rumbled, then 2200 and 2300. All aboard the street "engineers" shouted! It seemed like even the comic strip "dart board" approach would be successful, and many subscribed to it. The Institutional Hydra was still very young then, with too few heads to be scary and, with only the dark cloud of rapidly rising interest rates in an otherwise clear sky, the small individual investor was once again lured back into the market. (A decade earlier, a "bear" of some kind had attacked the portfolios of small investors and they had had little or no presence in The Market for years.) 2400 on the DJIA by July and on it went. No end in sight!

The Institutions introduced hundreds of new Mutual Funds; their CEOs could remember the Glory Days when the small investor (suckers) believed in the safety of the markets, the integrity of their Stock Brokers, and the sound investment advice emanating from the granite bastions looking out on the Hudson. The Institutions pumped up their marketing efforts and pushed the rally onward through August. 2500, 2600, 2700, just incredible! Get in their quick boys and girls, we're headed for the moon!!!

Nowhere did you hear even a whisper of the words "take profits", "sell", "lock in these super high interest rates". How stupid would that sound? How dumb would we look? No one even suggested what would happen in the two months that followed the Market's peak that August (Although many would claim later on that they had predicted a major "break in the market", no written documentation ever appeared, and no Wall Street firm ever uttered the "S" word.) The short term trading approach we are describing here (which was twelve operational years old at the time, and which had its practitioners sitting on mountains of that "smart cash" we described earlier) may have looked like "we" knew something was about to hit the fan. Not at all, I didn't have a clue, and truthfully, I didn't even care.

The weakness hit the NYSE around August 18th, immediately after the peak at 2722 the day before. **No one on Wall Street today would be able to tell you the date of the 1987 peak, and no one under the age of forty or so would be able to describe what I've just related to you.** (By the way, the average age of a Wall Street portfolio manager is well under thirty. Scary?) **But nearly everyone has heard of the climactic events of October 19th! Not a big deal really...** Hindsight? Nope! At the completion of this Chapter, you'll understand why it was just another day on Wall Street!

DIVE!   DIVE!   DIVE!

The market had been dropping steadily since mid-August as the Institutional Money Managers took profits for their own accounts while continuing to encourage participation in stocks that were still selling near their highest prices in history. The IPO market had enjoyed one of its greatest years. No one suggested to anyone that they sell anything, except those lousy bonds (which had gone down as they should have in the face of rising interest rates).

Here's a "pop quiz": If you had an active asset allocation plan at this time, what were you doing in the weeks leading up to the October 19th "crash"?

a) **Reinvesting in stocks that had fallen back into "buy" range.**

b) **Watching profits disappear as prices fell.**

c) **Taking advantage of historically high interest rates by adding to the fixed income side of my portfolio.**

d) **Smiling a lot to see a plan "come together" in what others perceived as a blood bath.**

e) **Waiting to see what would happen next.**

The "buy low" strategy described here kicked-in early in September as the list of opportunities began to grow from two to four and so on. As prices continued to weaken, analysts began to mumble. Most were too young to remember earlier downturns, and the economy certainly didn't "look" like a doom and gloom scenario was appropriate. Just those pesky rising interest rates. And then it happened! Technology bombed the market (Ironic isn't it that technology would have a "crash" of its own a "lucky thirteen" years later!) when those "programmed trading" sell signals ran fast and furious down the cables, resetting themselves lower, and lower, and lower.

Wall Street panicked (or pretended to for public consumption). Inflation fears, higher interest rates, tension in Europe, foreign oil, war in the middle east, and so on. All of the usual suspects were paraded in front of the media as the culprits that caused "The Crash Of '87". With all due respect for "The Street's" ability to analyze and predict (and there should be none!), a simple program "bug" got the whole thing going, and going, and going... It just doesn't take a whole lot of impetus for Speculative Greed to turn into Investment Fear! Wall Street had done it again. Those poor unsuspecting "individual investors" had just gotten pulled back in when the rug was swept out from under them!

Unlike the "real" economic crash of the '20s none of the Institutional "biggies" fell from their penthouses!

If your answer to the "Pop Quiz" included either b) or e), go back to Chapter One and PAY ATTENTION this time through!

RELAX, A Volatile Market Is Your Dearest Friend

Most people, including myself, never forget their first love; but I'll never forget my first trading profit either, sometime in 1970! Ah, I remember it well, Royal Dutch Petroleum. The $300 or $400 dollar profit I realized was not nearly as significant as the conceptual realization it signaled! I was amazed that someone out there would actually pay me more for my stock than the newspaper said it was worth just a few weeks ago! I couldn't think of anything that had changed that much. But it happened, and it began to happen often with nearly every well-known company I purchased.

I had taken over my own equity portfolio a few months earlier, and really had no idea what to do with it. I was fortunate to have a stockbroker at that time who "mothered me" through my investment adolescence. She didn't take advantage of my ignorance, and schooled me well! I had about a dozen stocks, all "Blue Chips" at the time, and I proceeded to chart their price movements. Up and Down, Up and Down, over and over again with what appeared to be an upward long-term bias.

What if I were to buy some IBM or International Harvester (both Investment grade at the time incidentally) at or near the "troughs" and then sell them at or near their "peaks"? *It sure seemed easy enough*, and after the successful "RD" experience, trading became the foundation for an investment strategy that has remained fundamentally unchanged for thirty years!

A volatile equity market creates opportunities with every gyration. As a trader, you will find that you do best (i.e., realize more profits) when there is what Wall Street would describe as either a "Mixed" or "Wait and See" market or one that is "directionless and full of uncertainty". **Uncertainty is the real "investment world" so you might just as well learn to work with it. Here's a "toast" to uncertainty that appeared in the IMF late in 1996.**

A TOAST TO UNCERTAINTY...REALITY! (IMF 12/07/96)

"When the Market stops going up in a straight line, it becomes a little more difficult to decide whether to buy, to sell, or to hold. Questions become more abundant than answers and "predictors" start to mumble about a future that was crystal clear to them a month earlier. (Ever notice that there is very little difference between the spellings of predictors and predators?) Is this a correction, or just a pause? What's going to happen next?"

"The problem with most investment strategies is that they rely on answers to questions like these! The problem being that these 'answers' exist only in 'Wall Street' promotional materials and investor fantasies. I propose a New Years' toast to uncertainty. The reality that separates investors from speculators!"

"Equity investing is soooo easy when the Market goes up for months at a time. Geniuses and experts are everywhere. Shoulda's and coulda's become performance analysis tools and greedy eyes see 15% gains as under-achievement! But what happens when the engine starts to sputter? Is "the grinch" going to steal the Christmas rally? **AHA, THE MOMENT OF TRUTH...**"

<u>"FORESIGHT HAS TO REPLACE HINDSIGHT!"</u>

"The scenario that began to unfold...is not a new one. Nor is it a scary one if you have a strategy. The distinction between a strategy (action plan) and a hunch, knee jerk or "they-say-ism" is one of the differences between investing and speculating. Investing requires understanding, valid expectations, patience, and a level of discipline that most individuals never acquire."

"...strategy is based upon a knowledge of the purpose and nature of the securities we own. We know why rate sensitive securities are lower in price than a year ago. We are pleased that the Market has provided...trading opportunities... If the Market plunges, we have (money) to recycle into new/old investments. If the rally continues, we will take more profits and find high quality situations that have fallen from grace with the 'experts'."

"...we accept reality and deal with it. This is not a time to worry; it's a time to act. This is not a time for concern; it's a time for understanding. This is not a time to 'wait and see' ...IT NEVER IS."

"My prediction for tomorrow? It will be Sunday."

The "Sell" decision is the most difficult for most investors to make. A number of emotions are involved, but the primary ones are:

Greed, Hatred (of both taxes and commissions), Pride, Fear, and, of course, Love. **You absolutely will recognize yourself in one or more of the five paragraphs that follow. By the end of this section, it should never happen again!**

Investors won't take their profits because they fall head over heals in love with a stock that has gone up in market value. They become complacent, thinking that they "know" the company and its management. The strongest love of all is reserved for a company that employed the person for a long time and/or where stock (purchase) options are involved. Shareholders will actually read the annual and quarterly reports (now there's a real waste of time) religiously, complete proxy forms (there's another) and honestly believe that the price will continue to rise forever. They add to their holdings in this "Mother Lode" by taking advantage of the Dividend Reinvestment Program. Surely they will be rich and famous, having solved the mystery of the stock market. Life is good! Love is blind!

Investors won't take their profits either because they hate to pay taxes or because some "Neanderthal" once told them that commissions would somehow make their profits disappear. Why pay now when we can wait until our earned income is lower (i.e., in retirement)? The fallacy becomes clear when these retirees try to construct an income production plan. How much "Base Income" (Interest and Dividends) is for sure going to be generated annually by $1,000,000 worth of the Magellan Fund? Hate is counterproductive. It clouds the rational mind. Not enough? What's it worth after taxes? Still not enough?

Investors won't take their profits because they love to have a winner that they can brag about to their buddies. They need to talk about the "home run' they just made on Conglomeration Suspender Co. They've done better, they think, than Cousin Bill who insists on clipping those boring Municipal Bond coupons. Who said: "death (financial) be not proud"? Perhaps they meant: pride can be dangerous to your financial health.

Investors won't take their profits because they have no clue as to what they will do for an encore and because they don't want to miss out on any additional paper profits. These "Buy and Holders" are smart enough to realize that they have just been lucky, but their limited experience keeps them from appreciating the fact that there are no guarantees "out there" in the real world. That stock price could tumble. It could tumble quickly and wipe out their retirement plans in one fell swoop (see below)! "But I don't know if I can do this again, or if I can trust anyone else to help me," they cry. Fear conquers all! Or was that love. No matter!

Investors won't take their profits because they are greedy so-and-sos. Enough said!

The "Take Your Profits" recommendation is not something that the average "Financial Advisor" is comfortable with. They too understand investor love, hate, greed, and fear and have learned how to deal with it. Suggesting a "profitable sale" is dangerous because of the hindsightful and litigious world we live in. What if the price of the sold stock continues to go up? Worse yet, what if the price of a new purchase goes down? Sounds like "churning" to a lot of Attorneys!

Brokers learn to take the easy road, the path of least resistance. It's much easier to convince a client to sell a "loser" than it is to get him to dispose of a "winner". Greed runs the "keep a winner" mindset; fear causes loss taking. Brokers learn early to "go with the flow".

Rags to Riches to Rags

I bumped into an old college friend while vacationing in New England in the early '80s. It seems that Bill had done extremely well with an up and coming software company, even before the technology blitz of the 90's. He had become a millionaire practically over night!

After learning that I had become an Investment Manager, he asked me to review his portfolio and give whatever advice I could.

Quality, Diversification, and Income

The company he worked for had been increasing its sales 30% or more per quarter for eleven consecutive quarters. **It paid no dividend whatsoever and was rated "B" by Standard & Poor's Corporation.** (Some would define this as a "growth" company under the premise that all operating profit is reinvested in the company itself to produce future growth. To a limited extent this could be true, but under closer examination, you are likely to find more growth in executive salaries than anywhere else.) **Bill's portfolio was invested 100% in the company's stock, with options for much more at about 25% of the current market value!** The "portfolio" was worth a little over one million dollars!

Quiz Time: What is wrong with this picture? How many of those bad emotions are involved here? What would you advise Bill to do? When?

STOP: Answer the questions yourself first, then proceed!

(Don't think for a minute that this is an uncommon scenario. I've encountered it quite frequently and it is nearly impossible to convince people that they are in serious danger. Did I just hit a chord with you? If so, pay attention and don't even think anything that begins with: "but my company...")

My advice to Bill was to sell 50% of the portfolio first thing in the morning (at 10:01 AM in those days) and then to unload at least another 40% of the shares after January 1st of the following year. He should have a "mental" stop loss order in mind at a price about 10% below current market, just in case the stock's price began to come under selling pressure sooner, rather than later! (A "mental "stop loss" order is the same as tying a string around your finger as a reminder do something.) Ten percent of the final portfolio would still be in his company's stock, and he could create a well-diversified and productive portfolio with the proceeds. At the time, his portfolio could have generated nearly $75,000 a year in tax-exempt income! He was young and so were his children. He could be set for life if he took the proper steps.

Greed, Fear, Pride, Love, and Hate

Bill was one of the company's most productive salesmen and he was "certain" that sales would continue to grow at a good clip (his personal production was up, for sure). He knew all the senior management and they were confident that the stock price was going to continue to rise. (Sounds like love to me.)

Bill was not happy with the suggestion that he should take his profits and secure his future income. He concluded that I was jealous, thinking that I had never had such a big winner. I pointed out that my (larger than his) portfolio had been produced safely, if not quickly, in the manner I described for him. "This was the company that would replace IBM as the industry leader and he would be very rich indeed!" Bill bragged. Watch out, Bill, your greed and (foolish) pride are showing.

Bill was finally convinced to sell some shares to put money away for his children's education, but he wasn't going to pay the taxes that would be incurred if he were to sell a large block of stock. A friend had convinced him to wait for a wonderful Oil & Gas Tax Shelter that he and his associates were putting together. Then he could sell the stock, buy the shelter, pay no taxes at all, and make even more money! And besides, he was genuinely afraid of investing. He didn't understand it, and he thought it was risky. Could I find him a Financial Planner that would review his situation and come up with alternatives? "And by the way Steve, I've got some Company Stock Options that I have to take advantage of right away…" (Hey, is ignorance an emotion? I guess not.)

No Happy Ending This Time Folks!

Five days later his company reported a "disappointing" 20% gain in Quarterly earnings and the stock's price fell more than 30%. It never recovered. Bill's employer was eventually taken over at a fraction of its former value. Then the new company was absorbed by Computer Associates, which (appropriately) has become one of my favorite trading stocks. Bill left the table with about 10% of his original wealth. The friend who took his money for the tax shelter did better! He left the country, never to be heard from again. The wells never even existed. There's more, but you get the point!

Here's that old "voice of experience" again. There's an important lesson within Bill's story that I know you noticed. Bill's company had reported a "20% gain in Quarterly earnings" and the stock price tanked! They were a profitable company before the announcement, and they remained profitable afterwards, but never again did the stock "perform". "Disappointments" like this one happen all the time, really, so don't be lured into the "growth of earnings/buy at any price" trap. In it's infinite marketing wisdom, Wall Street knows how to push those greed buttons. It will do the same thing with an earnings "surprise" to the upside. Take the profit you targeted and move on to the next opportunity.

Do the math using a 30% growth rate! How long is it before the numbers become unsustainable? Is there such a thing as an infinite market for a product or a service?

Establishing Reasonable Targets

If you intend to make money in the stock market you have to protect yourself from your emotions and those of your friends, family, and associates. Although Wall Street, and others in the financial products industry would like you to believe differently, one size does not fit all! You have to establish a selling discipline that works for you, based on your goals, asset allocation model etc. You should learn to "fear" the prospect of leaving any profits on the table. You must learn to sell out of "love", not "hate"! You can continue to "hate" to pay taxes, but not to the extent that you will consider losing money to reduce them. "Greed" cannot be allowed to overpower "good" judgment, and "pride" ...Well, you just have to grow up a bit if you want to be successful in the investment world!

Why 10% is a Reasonable Number?

On Wall Street, there are hundreds of thousands of MBAs being paid hundreds of millions of dollars to convince you that their employers and their wonderful analysts can predict the future! In the process, they assign target prices to securities that are most often significantly higher than the stock price has ever been. These assumptions are often "good news" for the stock's price but they do little to dampen the speculative tone of equity investing. In many instances, the target prices set by Wall Street analysts have nothing to do with a company's profit potential, just with the price of its common stock! This is a very real distinction that you need to be aware of. We've addressed a few of the reasons why Wall Street firms rarely go public with "Sell" recommendations. Can you imagine what it would be like out there if speculators reacted as negatively to "sells" as they react positively to "buys"? (Actually, they do. An "earnings surprise" to the downside, is every bit as potent a sell signal on Wall Street as a "sell recommendation" would be, but it's "politically correct"!

If you still salivate when you listen to Wall Street propaganda; if you still start to sweat before each Federal Reserve meeting; if you still twitch when you hear that the DJIA is falling; if you still believe your twenty-three year old "Financial Advisor" as he confidently tells you what "we think"; then you still need to be seriously desensitized!

Targets must be both reasonable and quickly attainable for a stock to be a good trading vehicle. The 10% "Sell" target is reasonable in three ways: (a) it is a price that has been achieved within the past 12 months (Understand?); (b) if we can do this twice in 12 months our annualized rate of return will be excellent; (c) it is not uncommon for 10% moves to occur very quickly. **(Have another look at <u>Table Three.</u>)**

(a) Since you bought the stock at least 20% below its high of the past twelve months, it can obviously increase by 10% above your cost basis without breaking through into any new price territory.

(b) If you can accomplish this twice in a twelve month period (with the same or different stocks, by reinvesting the total sale proceeds), your gain for the period will be 21% without including dividends received. You should be able to live with that.

(c) If you are fortunate enough to get an "instant winner" you can experience even better yields on a given "money-line". I really don't recommend that you spend your time with this type of research or analysis, but you will see the results after just a few trades. **If you insist, take a colored magic marker and create your own "money lines" in <u>Table Three.</u>**

<u>Managing Targets</u>

A "target' is a goal. It is an objective that may be totally or partially achieved, even exceeded with some regularity. But it is by no means a number chiseled in stone, and it is never something that should be translated into a "Stop Loss" Order!

Profit targets are managed as part of the daily worksheet routine. You will see a stock price approaching its target, and you simply check up on it periodically. When the goal is achieved a notation is made that we plan to "Sell" if the "bid" price falls by ¼ point from yesterday's close. If the price refuses to go down today for whatever presumed reason, we "ratchet" our goal up to ¼ point below the new closing price. This process (hopefully) can be continued, but not indefinitely! If the gain approaches 20% or if a gap increase of several points occurs, sell the stock and don't look back!

Also, if buying opportunities are abundant, "fire when you see the whites of their eyes"! [Take the profits immediately because: (a) you have a wide selection of good investments to choose from; (b) a growing "buy list" is evidence of weakness in the type of stocks you invest in, so it is likely that profits could evaporate; (c) if assumption (b) proves wrong, you will probably be able to take profits in the new purchases relatively quickly anyway.

Looking back is something you have to wean yourself from, especially if you intend to be a successful trader. The principle should be relatively easy to follow. Simply, what difference is there between a $10,000 profit made from one 60% gain and the same $10,000 made from several trades averaging around 10%?

None is the correct answer (and yes, I am always talking about profits after those "variable cost" commissions). But which of the two would be easier to attain?

Wall Street has labeled the years 2000 and 2001 as just plain "lousy". Not too many stocks sitting in portfolios with 60% profits. The 10% target approach, however, has enabled profit taking on over 100 different stocks in both years, and that was before the end of July 2001!

There are two very common situations (Takeovers and Stock Splits.) that will cause the price of a stock to rise rapidly, most of the time. I have seen many investors have great difficulty dealing with their good fortune! **It doesn't matter in the least what the perceived or actual reason for a price run up happens to be! Fast or gradually, based on rumor or fact, SELL ON THE "GOOD NEWS". No exceptions, no "buts", no "what ifs". SELL! SELL! Be Happy, and Move On!**

Just because a takeover is announced, there is no assurance that it will actually happen. Many companies have been the subjects of takeover rumors periodically for years. The price runs up. (SELL IT!) Nothing actually happens. The price goes down. (BUY IT AGAIN!) One client didn't want to sell so that he wouldn't have to pay a commission and reduce his profit on this sure thing, which was to settle in six or seven months, if the Government approved the merger. Let's just let this $25,000 sit around doing nothing for up to a year to save $100! What was he thinking!

Another client was outraged that I had sold a stock just a day or two after a split had been announced. The profit was about 17%! "Didn't you know about the two-for-one split?" he whined. "What difference does it make if I sell 100 shares at $50 per share or 200 shares at $25 each? We'll probably be able to buy the stock back again some time in the future anyway, below $25.00 per share." I explained. "Why will the stock price go to $25? How could that happen so quickly?" were the real live questions!

Profit taking on the "good news" is smart investing. Actually, it's the primary purpose of investing! You are not an "arbitrageur! Look it up if you need to, but please don't try to do it. They're the ones who helped push the price up for you. Say "thank you" and move along.

To Sell Quickly or Slowly, That is the Question

What dictates how quickly or how slowly you will sell? You have a managed trading program that is logical and based on sound principles. It is a methodology that has produced millionaires and, more importantly, maintained them at that level. It is an autonomous system. Run with it! In other words, you must absolutely stick with the rules when the profit level is at or above your target. "Above your target" should only happen when there is nearly nothing to buy, and/or you don't need to add to the fixed income portion of the portfolio. **Accepting less than a ten percent profit makes entirely good sense in situations where the buy list has grown**, and where there are a lot of stocks on it that you would really like to get back into. The profit potential of some of these issues may make them a better idea than waiting for an older position to "mature". **But see the second highlighted paragraph below!** Remember that faster turnover of the hamburgers and French fries accelerates aggregate profits.

For example, if I make two 10% trades in a twelve-month period, my total gain is 21%. If I make four trades averaging 5% or 6%, I can generate a little more total profit and find room in the portfolio for some new "best buys".

$$1,000 \times 1.10 \times 1.10 = \$1,210 \text{ or } 21\%$$
$$1,000 \times 1.05 \times 1.06 \times 1.05 \times 1.07 = \$1,250 \text{ or } 25\%$$

Absolutely never borrow on margin to buy securities no matter how many there are that have piqued your interest! Absolutely never take a loss on a perfectly acceptable holding to switch to another holding! In other words:

DO NOT TAKE UNNESCESSARY LOSSES! AND DO NOT BORROW!

You Have All the Ammunition You Need!

As you go through the daily routine, you will become totally aware of what has been happening in "your territory". Today's plan is ready for implementation. You can't wait for the opening bell! Where are "they"? What do "they" recommend? What do "they" see happening? How do "they" explain what has been happening? Just who are "they" anyway?

You don't need them anymore. You have become a "they"! No one else's opinion is relevant, knowing what you know now about what they really don't know at all! Upon completion of your daily "buy" list, you are aware of the opportunities that are "out there" today. The more "buys" there are, the more quickly you will want to take profits. How else will you be able to take advantage of these new opportunities? **If there are more "Best Buys" than your cash position would allow you to purchase, a profitable sale below target is totally acceptable, especially if it is fast!**

Pull the Trigger (Click Your Mouse!)

This is it, profit-taking time! The time to pull the trigger and take a profit!

At first you're going to want a second opinion. You may have heard a good report or seen a favorable write up. Merrill Lynch says it's a $60 stock! **Don't be confused by Wall Street Greed Food!** There are no facts, remember, only speculation and opinion. The only thing you really "know" is that if someone buys your shares of XYZ Widget International at this price, you will have made money! It is also very likely that you will be able to reinvest the sale proceeds for additional future profits in some other widget manufacturer.

Pull the trigger and move on to the next opportunity!

Your Accountant Will Not Be Happy

First of all, if your accountant has obtained his license to sell securities, fire him! You are no longer a client. You are just a commission! You would be foolish indeed, if you thought for one minute that the "license to steal" he has obtained has anything to do with what is best for his clients. Did I say "steal"? Sorry.

This is something you are going to have to deal with. As I'm sure you are aware, Accountants (and Attorneys) "know" all there is to know about all subjects, including investing. Keep in mind

148

that it is our expectations (of them) that have turned them into what they are. Unfortunately, most Accountants are so caught up in the "tail" (lowering the tax paid number) that they allow it to wag the "dog" (making as much money as possible). Another problem is that the very nature of accountancy is "hindsightful". The focus is on the financial transactions of the past and observations (especially of stock trades) are totally hindsight. And hindsight, as you know, has no place in investing! At you next meeting with your Accountant, count the times he says coulda', woulda' or shoulda'.

Keep in mind that it is the Accountant's job to make you happy and not vice versa. It is his job to find a better way to classify or protect your earnings, not to reduce or to delay them. **Would he be as quick to tell you to cut your salary, as he is to suggest that you not take short-term profits?** Would you be as willing to consider it? Will he guarantee the long-term profits he says you should be waiting for? Would he let you become a "bad debt" write off instead of a paid account?

Never sell a stock at a loss just to offset profits, never. I have 100 different clients with as many different accountants. **None recommend indiscriminate loss taking just to reduce taxes.** (Maybe they know by now that I wouldn't consider it!) If the Accountant insists, try this out. Tell him that you will accept his advice if he will! Offer to help him reduce has taxes by not paying his fee.

Finally, as a last resort, if you can't get over your hatred of taxes, just send me a check for the amount of your gains and I'll pay the dreaded taxes for you! I'll even pay at the "ordinary income" rate!

What To Do About the Real Losers?

There are going to be some losers, but because of the nature of the trading strategy, it is vitally important to define what we mean by a loser. We are buying stocks during a downtrend in their market price in anticipation of an eventual turnaround. We even buy more of them from time to time, to reduce our average cost so that we can exit profitably sooner. A "loser" is a stock that no longer fits within our basic, qualitative, fundamental, selection criteria. (Which are?) A "loser" is also a fundamentally sound stock that we have been unable to trade within a reasonable amount of time. We're built to trade, not to hold.

A Matter of Quality

A reduction in the S & P Quality Rating or a cut in the dividend is a clear indication of problems ahead. **(This is why you want to focus on such things in the selection process. Un-rated securities don't become "un-rated minus" and non-existent dividends can't be cut. You must depend on fresh information from a company spokesperson, from a report in the media, or from your "Financial Advisor"; I'm sure that they all have your pager number with them at all times!)**

When fundamentals deteriorate, any profit becomes acceptable and small losses become tolerable. We do not want to hold on to companies once their quality becomes suspect. Still, it may not be necessary to take a huge loss immediately. Judgment again! A small loss under these circumstances is acceptable, but there is no need to rush into a major loss. Be patient.

A case in point is Seagram. The September ('99) S & P Guide reported a reduction in rating from B+ to B. At the time, I had several clients with positions in the stock. Some were at minor gains, which were taken immediately. A few positions were sold with minor losses. The others were watched closely for sale as soon as possible. IBM went from A+ to B several years ago and the price went from one hundred something to forty dollars per share. Panic selling just never seemed necessary. **Avoid "averaging down" (see Chapter Three) on a stock once the Quality rating has fallen below investment grade.**

A Matter of Time

We are looking to trade stocks frequently. Therefore, a stock that we have been unable to sell profitably after a reasonable period of time is one that we should be looking to sell, even if we do so at a minor loss. Twelve months is about the limit. Ironic isn't it? The time period that most people want to wait before they'll consider taking a profit is the trader's bail out point! Similarly, by some convoluted kind of logic, a short-term loss is more attractive. The tax code, which changes periodically, should not be a factor in investment decision-making!

You've probably noticed that I say "twelve-month period" more often than I say "one year". I'm not trying to add to the number of pages, believe me. **The distinction between the two is a very real and important one.** The Institutional Hydra's hypnotic stare has created a "calendar year" worship that is totally out of control. As a trader, an investor who thrives on and prays for volatility and movement, the last thing you want to compare yourself with is some easily manipulated index of what happened between January 1st and December 31st! It is entirely possible that the entire equity portion of your portfolio was just purchased in November! (Remember the November Syndrome?) I refuse to do calendar year analysis either for my clients or for any of the "analytical tools" (I meant it that way.) that feed performance fodder of this kind to the data mills.

Again, given sound fundamentals, there is no rush to take a major loss. But any profit or a small loss should be taken without a second thought. And of course, the "poip" (how's your Brooklynese?) should be removed from the Selection Universe with a disdainful click! Individual stocks have a "volatility index" all there own. (Actually I don't think they do, but I'm surprised that no one has thought to come up with one similar to the "beta" index that is so ridiculously used in some kinds of portfolio volatility analysis.)

This new index (the one I just made up two sentences ago), and which will be very real in your mind after trading for a while, will change periodically. Take General Electric for example. Over the past several months I've been able to trade GE successfully, and quickly. It has to be six or seven years since the last time that was possible! Personalities change, group and individual popularity changes, and you have to be able to change as well. That may mean getting back into a stock that you tossed out of the Selection Universe in the past!

The "ATH" (All Time High) Profit Level Decision

Traders look at trading statistics to determine "how they're doing" just as "buy and holder's" watch their market value so closely that most have chronic migraines. From time to time, however, a trading portfolio will sport "All Time High" (ATH) market value numbers. An ATH in market value alone can simply be the result of new cash being added to the portfolio; an All Time High Profit Level is different. A portfolio is at an **"All Time High" Profit Level** when the difference between the market value and the amount invested (i.e., the total lifetime profit) is at a new "high water mark".

Generally, an all time high profit level will happen in a market environment where rising stocks outnumber falling stocks and where more are achieving new 12 month highs than lows. Sounds like a better definition of "rally" than some percentage rise in a weighted average, doesn't it?

I've actually experienced situations where the market value of all the individual securities in the portfolio were below their purchase cost but the overall portfolio value was still at an All Time High Profit Level. Ah, trading!

Here's a great analogy to use on your friends at "the club" when they are skeptical about your new investment strategy, particularly in such "a volatile market". The "waves" of the stock market are similar to those at sea. The ocean can go from a dead calm to roller coaster ride in a matter of minutes. The trading strategy you are learning smoothes the waves and allows you to surf the crests like a Hobie-Cat buzzing by a Day-Sailer. Trading gets you to your objective more quickly and with less risk (financial, not nautical).

Any time a portfolio achieves a new ATH (profit level); the worst "performing" stock (or security) in the portfolio should be looked at for elimination! You will be able to tell when this (an ATH) occurs without putting your hands on a monthly statement. Your equity buy list will be shriveling up. You will be taking profits on more things than you are buying, maybe even on a Preferred Stock or two or a closed end municipal bond fund. This is hard evidence. It's rally time, a time for "Buy and Holders" to expand their hat size, and time for you to expand your working capital.

Selling a "loser" at a time of strength is good for the portfolio in the long run but it is a strategy that must not be applied blindly every month that your account statement goes up! Look at everything carefully; you'll know which positions you want to unload! If there aren't any, that's a good thing.

Major Losses

Major losses absolutely will happen too, no matter what strategy you employ, but it happens very infrequently when you manage the amount of risk you take during the security selection process described in earlier chapters. **(You can actually expect to be successful nearly 95% of the time if you follow the rules that we have talked about religiously, or if your own set of rules is as conservative as those I've described here.)** It is generally safe to use the "buy more" strategy until a stock falls below $10 a share, assuming that the quality remains intact and that diversification rules are not seriously violated. (Strange, isn't it, that a stock rated "Investment Grade" can be reduced to a single digit price while others rated far below that level can be at lofty valuations. That's the Stock Market!) At that point, you have to be prepared to cut your potential loss by selling before it becomes $4, $3, or less. I "cut bait" from $7 to $4. Below that, I pray a lot.

I hate taking losses (and you should too) even more than most people hate taxes and commissions but I recognize their inevitability, cry a lot and move on. **Somehow it's easier for me to rationalize a loss at a time when everything else seems to be moving forward according to "the plan".**

Two Important Lists

Market Statistics should be looked at periodically during the day, not only to see if it is time to implement your planned "Sell" decisions, but also to identify new selling opportunities. *Unlike buying opportunities (which are abundant more often than not) profit-taking opportunities are precious and must not be squandered. It is critical that you don't miss your profit-taking opportunities!*

The Most Active List and The Most Advanced List will help you identify important intra-day movements. If your broker can't provide this information real-time, switch. You can get it on-line yourself and free, but with at least a 20-minute delay in the numbers. With the advent of the Internet, you are now in a position to get relatively current quotes from practically anywhere. When you hear that there is a big move to the upside, login or call up your broker to check all of your positions. You may discover a profit taking opportunity that could disappear if those institutional profit takers get there before you do!

A typical newspaper presentation of "Market Statistics" appeared in the previous Chapter.

Trite But True

Sure you've heard all of these little witticisms before, but now you should be well beyond familiarity. You should be leaving appreciation and heading toward understanding.

There's No Such Thing as a "Bad" Profit

You will be using two types of computers to manage your investment portfolio. The one that requires a keyboard is used to provide information to be analyzed by the one that resides between your ears. You will be making your decisions in the world of uncertainty (the only one available to mortals), so try to avoid looking over your shoulder or second-guessing yourself when something you've sold continues to rise in price. (Remember all those times in your past when you "forgot to sell", and watched your profits vanish into thin air!) Hindsight is a sure killer of an otherwise productive investment strategy.

There are people out there (mostly Accountants and Financial Planners) who will review the past year's transactions and point out how you could have done better here or there if you had waited or, better still, if you had purchased one of their products. First of all you should complement them for their excellent hindsight. Then ask them why they didn't call you before you did whatever it was they criticized, to advise you about their idea. Naturally they were willing to guarantee the results in advance! Sure.

The only decisions that should be subject even to discussion are those that blatantly disregarded or circumvented the rules you established for yourself. Go to the "chalk board" and write 100 times: "I will not disobey the rules!"

One Doesn't Become Poor Taking Profits *And/Or* One Should Always Sell Too Soon

I'm not at all certain who is responsible for these succinct bits of wisdom, but someone, when asked how he had managed to accumulate such tremendous wealth responded simply: "I was always fortunate enough to sell too soon." So much wisdom in so few words! "Profit Taking is good for your financial health" is an accurate translation of the first remark.

Never Count Your Winnings While Your Sitting At The Table

Not only is it rude (in poker), it's pointless (in investing). Even the IRS knows that a profit doesn't "count" until it is realized. They are not your winnings (profits, values) until you take the action necessary to remove them from the threat of loss (i.e. the table). You will always have many positions out there at some acceptable level of risk (measured by S & P quality ratings). It takes disciplined decision making to move them from the table to the pocketbook!

I like to think of the fixed income portion of my portfolio as "the bank" (not that I would ever buy CDs or have a Savings Account in a bank). But, the idea that is comforting to me is that I've taken a portion of my newly created capital (profits) and placed it in a safer place for compounding.

Have you ever "experienced" the "Weakest Link" Television Game Show? Its one redeeming feature is the need for the contestants to "bank" their winnings if they want them to "go forward to the next round"! Not a bad way to look at the profits you should be taking on your equities!

Sell on the (Good) News

The market always overreacts to news, good or bad. In the previous chapter, we talked about buying on bad news for that very reason. Take advantage of an upward spike in a stock's price when it provides a quick profit on a new purchase, a small profit on an old holding, or a significant reduction in loss on a position that was targeted for an eventual ATH sale. **If you find it necessary to determine what the "Street" thinks it knows, get the current news from your broker and take your profits anyway! Don't ever look back!**

Sell Out of Love, Not Hate

Here's a classic story about how a combination of ignorance and brilliance can lead an otherwise sophisticated investor to panic (not in the face of the countless unknowns that existed after the computer loop/market melt down discussed earlier) but in response to what he perceived to be happening in the political and social environment at the time. In a sense, he was "blinded by the light" of his own background, intellect, and experience.

He had made a "killing" in the first eight months of 1987, and at the market peak was about 75% in cash ready to pounce on the many excellent opportunities that appeared daily from mid-September on. On the fatal October 19th, his portfolio was invested in twenty-five of the very best companies in the world, by nearly any measure. His "Working Capital" was ahead by nearly 20% for the year, but current market value had suffered under the weight of the correction. He was perfectly positioned for another round of impressive gains as the market rebounded (the "quality" market has always rebounded from corrections of all shapes, causes and sizes).

He appreciated all of the facts; he understood that this would normally be the correct scenario; he "knew" though that this time it was different. The government was in a shambles, crooks and thieves ran the country, hyperinflation was just over the horizon, staggering unemployment was imminent, and political/ economic chaos were just around the bend. The sky really was falling, this time. He was absolutely "certain" that this would play out from conversations he had had with well-placed, knowledgeable people around the country.

Every thing in the portfolio was liquidated and the rest is history. He had been "selling out of love" willingly and fruitfully for years. But an overdose of "know" and "certain" created a hate for "the system" that could not be dealt with rationally.

There has never been a correction that has not succumbed to the next rally!

You Can't Make Too Much Money

This is what you want to be complaining about every year of your life! The next gripe is that you're getting too thin or too healthy. **Never lose sight of the fact that the very object of the investment exercise is to make as much money as you possibly can in a manner that emphasizes the minimization of the inherent risks involved in the process.**

Break Time, Part I: Investment Perspective (IMF, 04/08/93)

"Few novels contain the drama, suspense, and excitement that the 'Shock Market' plays out routinely every day. There is violence, intrigue, and greed, for sure, but hope, trust, love, and passion as well. Yesterdays' heroes become today's villains, and scenarios developed by expert "critics" often explode in unsuspecting investor faces!"

"This is a story without an ending; where no human being can predict events occurring on the next page, much less in the final chapter. The point is that you must understand the medium in which you invest your dollars. You must have realistic expectations, and an Investment Perspective that creates more opportunities for success than it does for failure (i.e., one based on Quality, Diversification, and Income)."

"For example, can you appreciate the concept that there is absolutely no difference between a Merck, Kellogg, and U S Surgical today, and the Citicorp, Chase, and Chevron of a few years ago? The former group will be on a future…list of stocks sold for profit. Will the later group be in yours?"

"Every downturn in the market, or in an industry, presents an opportunity for future profit. Think about how you hated…bank stocks in 1990 (and don't forget to sell them now). There is a huge difference between the erosion of the market value of your securities and the erosion of their quality. Their ability to generate future profits is just not a function of current market price!"

"[This] trading approach to equity investing, using the unique "Working Capital Model", moves [investors] into out-of-favor positions while the experts foolishly pick their "bottoms". [You] are making investment decisions (and taking profits) while the others are trying to predict the future!"

"Some things just never change."

Break Time, Part II: WHEN TO WORRY (and WHAT TO WORRY ABOUT) (IMF 11/03/94)

"Investors are the strangest breed of animal on the Planet. Nervous and Jerky, they lose sight of the 'purpose' and 'nature' of their investments as soon as 'market value' numbers stop going north, for whatever reason. **Impatience, even with securities that are doing exactly what they're supposed to do, causes unfounded anxiety attacks and often results in irrational decision-making.** The investment community encourages this behavior because it generates transactions…"

"Part of (your) responsibility is to protect (yourself) from the tendency to behave emotionally and irrationally. …Emphasize the development of valid expectations, and performance evaluation that is in touch with the realities of the market place. For example:"

"**REALITY ONE:** Business is good, corporate earnings are up, inflation is low, unemployment is down, etc. Expectations are that this good news will produce higher interest rates and higher inflation. This is not a 'new' economic scenario."

"**REALITY TWO:** The Purpose of fixed income securities...is the generation of income. Growth in the market value of these securities is "bad news" for the income investor and it cannot happen in a rising rate environment. Under no circumstances should you sell high quality, interest rate sensitive securities to realize losses or to find 'better performing' ones..."

"**REALITY THREE:** The Nature of the stock market is price fluctuation. The engines that move stock prices are many, and include news, political events, expectations about hundreds of economic things, 'guru' statements, etc. These movements are totally and completely unpredictable. Not one of the experts has even the slightest clue as to what will happen, or when. But their opinions do move the market!"

"This has been a difficult year for equity mutual funds (both open and closed end) because they require broad market movements to produce "growth". With all the market indices around even, or negative, you should not expect your stock portfolio to be ahead! Under no circumstances should you sell high quality equities or equity mutual funds to realize losses or to find better "performing" ones. Sound familiar?"

"**REALITY: There is no appreciable difference between today's market and those of the past. Investment opportunities exist in both fixed income and equity markets. Deal with it.**"

*   *   *   *   *   *

<u>MID-TERM EXAMINATION TIME</u>

Management involves about the same number of principles as investing, and we've dealt with each of them to a certain extent. You should know by now that the trading approach described here is a synthesis of the basic investment principles with management's Planning, Organizing, Controlling, and Directing (Decision-Making). Before you move on to the final Chapters, make sure that you have the answers to these important questions highlighted somewhere:

- What are the three basic principles of Investing?
- How many "classes" of Investment Securities are there?
- Of what investment significance is the calendar year?
- What is more important, current income or current market value?
- What is "analysis paralysis"?
- What is an Investment Product?
- What differentiates an Investment Manager from other Financial Professionals?
- There is no such thing as a bad [   ]!
- Why aren't CDs or Money Market Funds Investments?
- Wall Street is [   ] driven?
- What "tails" often wag the investment "dog'?
- What is a WRAP Account?
- Consumers buy products, investors buy [   ]?
- Name three levels of diversification?
- Who should be broken up: The Yankees? Wall Street? In Sync?
- What is the "purpose" of a fixed income security?
- Why are dividends important?
- What is Issue Breadth?
- What human emotions have to be controlled most rigorously?
- What is a "day", "limit" order?
- What is the gist of "The Investor's Creed"?
- What's a DRIP?
- Of what importance are "Market Stats"?
- Why does "Wall Street" hate volatility? Do you?

161

- Why are investors reluctant to take profits?

CHAPTER FIVE: PERFORMANCE EVALUATION

Dangerous Fixations: Fatal Attractions (IMF, November 1999)

"I just spoke with a client who is unhappy with the 'performance' of his portfolio over the past year or so. How could the value be 'treading water' when 'The Market' has gone up so much? Reasonable question? Only if you know the portfolio asset allocation percentages and the type of equity securities allowed in the portfolio. Staying even in a Growth Mutual Fund would be terrible. Staying even in a 75% municipal bond portfolio would be wonderful!"

"A fatal mistake made by many investors is a fixation on the bottom line number, regardless of the makeup of the portfolio itself. Dangerous errors in judgment are made when an investor improperly evaluates performance because his expectations are inappropriate for the securities he owns and/or for the investment strategy he uses."

"Few investors are willing to admit that they don't understand fixed income investing. Even fewer know how to evaluate the performance of an equity trading strategy! And no one seems to have the courage to look at performance in a non-calendar year context!"

"When your focus is on high quality/low risk securities in a balanced portfolio which seeks annual increases in 'realized' income, most of which is generated by short-term equity trading, a simplistic look at the change in 'Market Value' from point 'A' to point 'B' makes no sense at all!"

"There are really four separate numbers to look at:

- **Trading Results:** For stocks sold, what was the average yield on investment and the average holding period? Was the annual yield acceptable for the level of risk in the portfolio?
- **Income:** How much realized ('spendable') income was produced? Is this acceptable for the asset allocation? And (as a

163

percentage of invested capital) is it significantly more than the one year CD rate at the beginning of the analysis period?

- **Working Capital:** The amount invested in the portfolio's assets must increase from year to year at a 'beat-the-bank' rate. No exceptions are acceptable! Do you understand why?
- **Market Value:** This figure should beat comparable (apples to apples) market figures over significant measurement periods, not months, quarters, or a year. Try 'peak to peak' or 'trough to trough', etc. Note that in balanced portfolios, there are no comparable figures!"

*   *   *   *   *

The purpose of this chapter is to make you re-think the way you look at the performance of your portfolio. You will be replacing the transaction generating "Wall Street" method with one that is about 1,000% more personalized.

This "piece" appeared in the Investment Management Forum nearly eight years ago! It's still "current", and it should start you thinking in the right direction. Although older, it reinforces the "newer" release used in the Chapter introduction.

"At the end of every calendar year, investors and investment professionals alike, rush around to determine how they "performed". Bottom line growth is expected to be better than the gain in the Dow Jones Industrial Average, no matter what, end of discussion. Every mutual fund marketer, brokerage firm, and major investment management firm will find a way to be best in 1993, again!"

"Try to avoid all the "hype" and concentrate on the more important things that keep lofty paper values from disappearing as new heroes come forward during the next calendar year's campaign. First, ...recognize the importance of income, particularly that which is generated by profits. Secondly, ...have realistic expectations for each individual security owned. Income investments are asked only to produce cash flow, not growth in market value. For growth, ...buy under-valued stocks and wait patiently for profits to happen!"

"TO MAKE MONEY IN EQUITIES, YOU HAVE TO DO THREE THINGS:"

"Think of your equity holdings as 'work in process'. Evaluate their Quality, Diversification, and ability to generate Income (in the form of profits). That's all!"

"Take reasonable profits as often as you can. Find another high quality stock that 'fits' in the portfolio."

"Measure performance in terms of the trades you've completed, not in terms of market value at the end of some meaningless time interval... It takes a 'buy' and a 'sell' to complete an equity transaction. In a trading environment, only completed transactions can be compared with the averages."

"[This strategy] operates much differently than the typical equity mutual fund... Sell 'winners' and buy companies and groups that have become unpopular for various reasons... Avoid the high-risk elements (IPOs, small-cap, foreign, OTC unknowns, etc.) that propel most funds to high levels, one fad at a time.

(IMF, 12/31/93)

A Working Definition of Performance

By definition, performance ["functional effectiveness producing a desired effect"] is a measure of how well one did in accomplishing his or her objectives ["something aimed at"] and goals [an end that one strives to attain]. Wall Street strikes again! You have been taught that Investing is a race against an index or an average. You have been schooled that investing is a competitive event. You have been force-fed the idea that the calendar year is both an appropriate venue for analysis of the "event" results, and a meaningful stop watch for beginning and ending the competition! All of the above is untrue, totally. The un-learning process starts here.

Most investors think that the benchmark for performance evaluation is: **how their change in market value for the calendar year compared with the change in the Dow Jones Industrial Average, the S &P 500, or the NASDAQ Composite!** For an "index" mutual fund this may be acceptable, but not for real life portfolios, like those that I have been encouraging the readers of this book to construct. Even index mutual funds cannot keep up with the averages that they "mirror". Why? The invisible costs to run the thing. Ask this question of your Financial Advisor: "If the S & P 500 Average remains unchanged for a year, will the value of my index fund remain unchanged as well?

Here's Deep Pockets' "Words of Wisdom" on Index Funds:

"Index Funds, the "NO-LOAD" answer to everything? Enough about no-load! What is an index anyway? Simply a list of stocks that someone feels is representative of the market as a whole."

"The "S & P 500" is perhaps the most widely recognized average. An index fund marketer put together a portfolio that represents the weighting of that list. In theory, if the index goes up or down a dollar, the fund will respond exactly in kind. WRONG! The funds have serious internal expenses that have to be covered. Thus the performance of the index, less fund expenses, equals return to investors."

"THEREFORE, the index funds must under-perform the underlying average. Let's talk about the S & P 500 for a moment. Remember that this is a list compiled by Standard and Poor's that "THEY" feel represents the overall market. The key is the word "represents". The list is not Standard and Poor's buy list! How does their own research department feel about the companies included in the S & P 500 average anyway? Lets look to the "STARS" for the answer!"

"S & P research uses a rating system that uses 'STARS' (one to five) to rate stocks. 'Buy' rated stocks get five stars; 'Accumulate' rated stocks get four stars; 'Holds' get three; 'Avoid', two; and 'Sell' rated stocks get only one star."

"Only 10% of the stocks represented in the S & P 500 are five star rated, or 'buys'. Many of the stocks in the average are rated 'sell'! This is an 'average' of stocks, not a buy list! Spent much time lately telling your children that average is good enough in life? Should you decide to invest based on a 'list' of S & P stocks, at least buy the good ones (buy/five stars)."

*   *   *   *   *   *   *

I have been unable to find any one average, index, or model that even comes close to reflecting what is or should be going on within a diversified portfolio built on the conservative principles discussed here. Actually, you shouldn't be able to use such things for analysis at all, ever, if your portfolio is as distinctly your personal creation as it should be!

But, the transaction driven Wall Street "power brokers" pretend that the "popular averages" are so sophisticated that they can be used for performance evaluation by anyone at all. No matter where you go or to whom you speak, the questions "How are you doing in the market?" or simply "How are you doing?" really mean: **"How does the January 1st to date rate of change in your Market Value compare with that of the S & P 500 average, or the DJIA, or the NASDAQ Composite?"** Why should I even care would be the proper answer. Are you there yet?

And of course you should be insulted by the question itself! Hydra Head # 37 just told you how important diversification is and # 22 suggested that a retirement annuity (more on Annuities in Chapter Seven) would help satisfy your retirement income needs. Now, some other division of "the beast" is telling you that your performance is lousy because you didn't keep up with either the DJIA or the S & P 500!

Even Institutional Insiders should be offended by the rash assumption that Hydra Head # 64 is making with regard to the nature of all the other firms' public consumption and "proprietary" products! [A "proprietary" product is a Mutual Fund owned and managed by a brokerage firm for its clients alone. Although this sounds like a special service, it is really just a ploy to keep the money in the firm. Such securities are generally not transferable to other firms custodianship and can only be liquidated with severe penalties.] But, think about what this type of performance appraisal connotes!

There are at least one hundred Mutual Fund houses selling ten thousand Mutual Funds. Simple math says that there should be at least one hundred unique fund types, either by general direction, focus, geography, asset allocation, managerial style, income level, degree of aggressiveness, etc. Why else would so many even exist? **It stands to reason that there are significant, and distinct differences between funds or our "trusted" Financial Advisors would have counseled us to invest in only one of them!**

There are two questions just begging to be answered: **a) How can all of these "different" entities be compared to the same sets of arbitrary,** transaction insensitive, **index numbers and averages?** (They are "transaction insensitive" since it is assumed that their content remains the same from the beginning to the end of the period.) **And b) how could they all possibly "perform" so consistently with one another, and with the indices themselves, unless they all really** (on an operational level if not on a prospectus level) **own the same groups of securities?** A brief look at a few of the more popular NASDAQ Mutual Fund names in the monthly **S & P Stock Guide reveals some pretty scary numbers under the column headed "Shares Held by Institutional Investors". They really do all own the same**

stocks, and you get the speculative ones in your "value fund" whether you like it or not!

There is also one important observation that needs to be made. The average individual investor/speculator buys into this total misrepresentation without even the slightest doubt as to: a) the absolute reliability of the indices and averages, and b) both the calculation accuracy and the presentation honesty of the mutual fund performance numbers. **Then, with this handful of contrived statistical and verbal debris, he gleefully makes investment decisions and purchases products. I'm also convinced that many of the salespeople who perpetuate the Mutual Fund performance myth, actually believe the glossy sales hype that the Mutual Fund vendors provide! WHY? Only "The Shadow" knows!**

Here's another incongruity that you put up with and ignore. Any performance number you ever see coming from Wall Street, or anywhere else for that matter, must and will include language to the effect that **"past performance figures are not, nor are they intended to be, representations, guarantees, or predictions of future performance"**. Still every brokerage firm, every media (side) show, every Financial Advisor, and every Financial Planner sells these products strictly on the basis of how the fund performed last year! No "buts", no caveats, included.

At the end of each calendar year, thoughts of Program Objectives, analysis of Asset Allocation formulas, and consideration of Investment Strategy tune-ups are all tossed out the window while intense scrutiny is given to some irrelevant index that has absolutely nothing in common with the portfolio itself! Additionally, this "performance" comparison is done for a time period that has no relevance in the investment world. Throughout the year, analysts and other assorted experts talk about business, interest rate, and economic cycles. Then, all of a sudden, performance becomes a function of the calendar, and a popular index whose composition is totally irrelevant!

Financial Planners will talk of the long-range plan. Investment Advisors will counsel you to think of performance over the long run. Mutual Fund salespeople will emphasize the three, five, and ten-year performance numbers of their best Investment Managers. **Unless, of course, some one else constructed the plan!** (Note that they rarely have any 10-year statistics to brag about.) Long range is fine for them to talk about when they are selling or conserving business, but not when they are engineering a switch!

All of this contradictory behavior is designed to generate action, and it works remarkably well. It's your responsibility to back away and handle the performance evaluation sanely, systematically, and by yourself. **How do these people manage to talk out of both sides of their mouths at the same time anyway?**

The whole standard and expected year-end performance evaluation scenario makes no sense at all! Could Wall Street be doing this to manipulate unwary investors? To make them unhappy where they are so that they will switch into something else? (Switching produces transactions, and every firm gets its share of the other firms' turncoats.)

Market indices have become less and less "tuned in" to what is really going on among the equities that are traded out there anyway! In 1998, for example, about 70% of the entire gain in the S& P 500 was the result of the rise in price of just 10 stocks! That's just 2% of the stocks! In 1999, The Dow Jones Industrial Average grew at a pace 5 times that of the New York Stock Exchange Index. In 2000 and 2001, all of the indices and averages have tanked, but conservative, quality portfolios are up nearly 30% and both (NYSE) breadth and New High vs. New Low numbers are overwhelmingly positive!

While the indices were reaching new highs during the previous 20 months or so (January '98 through August '99) "down ticks" exceeded "up ticks" on the NYSE by tens of thousands, and stocks falling to new one year lows outnumbered those achieving new highs by a wide margin. **If you are comparing your portfolio's performance to the movement of the popular averages, you will eventually become confused, disillusioned, and unhappy; but only if you actually take the time to back away and think about it. And you really owe it to yourself (and your family) to do so.**

There really is a better way to examine performance!

The Objective Function

The objectives of the portfolio are the key to determining just what measurement tools need to be used. No legitimate Financial Plan or Investment Plan will have "beat the DJIA" or "beat the S & P 500" as an objective, nor will any legitimate investment professional suggest that doing so is necessary. Typical objectives would be: "to prepare an education fund for my children", "to have an investment portfolio that generates $60,000 per year in disposable income by the time I retire", "to take diction lessons and make enough money to afford a Jaguar", or perhaps, "to preserve the capital I have accumulated so far, and make it grow at approximately 12% per year". A 12% annual growth, incidentally, would "beat" the DJIA over the past few decades! Every portfolio will (and should) have somewhat different objectives, but safety of principal, growth of capital, and generation of retirement income certainly should be among them.

If you are ever sitting with your Financial Advisor or Planner, and the information you provide is being recorded as check marks on a form of some kind, ask the person to stop. Your "personal data" is going to be plugged into a computer program that will regurgitate a "sophisticated personal financial plan". You will then be presented with a "plan" that includes the same mix of products that are recommended to everyone else who uses that particular computer program. The package is meant to impress you. The language and the detail are designed to gain your trust. The smiling person at the desk across from you is going to convince you that this is a personalized plan, just for you.

You can get the same software and do the plan by yourself! (Not at all recommended.) What you want from this professional is: *__his or her experience and knowledge applied to your circumstances with a resultant plan that is simple, practical, manageable, and based on assumptions that you understand and agree are appropriate.__*

If the "advisor" can't do a basic plan (including asset allocation and income projections) and recommend any portfolio changes in a few face-to-face hours, he or she may be doing you a disservice. Commissioned Financial Professionals get paid for product sales only. Some "CFPs" get paid for the time spent in planning. **The presentation of the plan is not nearly as important as the plan that is presented!** Very few financial professionals will have the competence or experience to create a personalized investment plan from scratch!

The strategies employed to achieve the planned objectives can also be analyzed and compared with numbers that make sense. The equity portion of the portfolio (70%, for example) will be invested in individual Investment Grade Dividend Paying Stocks only, no exceptions. These stocks will be traded actively as profit targets are reached. The fixed income portion of the portfolio (30%) will be invested in various vehicles, including Municipal Bonds, Government and Corporate Debt Instruments, Preferred Stocks and Unit Trusts (a product that has excellent features for fixed income investing, but despite a pretty serious "mark-up", one that is not pushed real hard by "Financial Advisors"). The fixed income portion of the portfolio may be traded, but the primary objective is cash flow. (Unit Trusts are reviewed in Chapter Seven.)

Our model **(an equally weighted, diversified portfolio of only high quality, dividend paying, NYSE equities combined with a similarly diversified group of interest rate sensitive securities) has no indices to be compared with. It also has no inherent speculation within it. It is an action model, not a stagnant one! It** is forward sighted, proactive, and productive! What does all this mean?

It means that you need to come up with a method of performance evaluation that works regardless of what the popular averages do, especially since those averages have recently parted company with the realities of the market place. As you get into this for a few years or a few cyclical changes, you'll begin to smile when your friends talk with you about their market experiences and their "performance". You'll really know what you are doing (not to be confused with knowing what the market is doing, which is an impossibility) and whether or not you are meeting your goals. If portions of your portfolio are down in market value, you will understand why and will be able to deal with it. You'll just dazzle them with your brilliance, your discipline, and your sense of calm!

"Having a rough year in 'The Market' Steve?" was the question Financial Planner Joe raised with me the other day. "Not at all, Joe. In fact, the past year and a half has been gangbusters for trading and income generation!"

Strategy Relevant Data Gathering

Your strategy for achieving some of your portfolio objectives can be described as "Low Risk/ High Speed Stock Trading". You will buy only the highest quality stocks and only when they have fallen at least 20% from their highs of the past 12 months. You will then sell them as soon as you can make a net/net gain of around 10%, or more. You will also own fixed income securities for income production only, and all of the equities purchased will produce a dividend. How can we evaluate the performance of such a "personalized" strategy?

You need to evaluate, and to understand, the relative performance of each separate piece of your investment program: trading, income production, and working capital growth.

Annual Trading Summary

The first step is to construct an Annual Trading Summary. This is an extremely easy and functional tool to put together. Easy because it is simply a process of matching each "Sell" transaction with the appropriate "Buy" transaction(s) and assessing the amount of dollar gain, the percentage gain, and the holding period. Any decent spreadsheet program will do this for you, including all the calculations necessary for the preparation of your IRS Schedule "D" Form. (Have you noticed that the IRS only recognizes realized gains and losses? Interesting, don't you think?) Here are some guidelines for evaluating "Trading Performance".

Transactions should be more than 90% profitable AND you should make money on better than 90% of your selections. These are not the same thing, but you should be able to achieve both if you stick to the rules, many of which fall into the realm of "greed control". Nine out of every ten trades should be for a profit, and your trading activity should include all of the stocks in your portfolio over an eighteen to twenty four month period. (Actually these are conservative expectations, unless your selection criteria are inherently speculative!)

The average net/net gain should be about twice the one year CD rate that was in effect at the beginning of the year, but at least 10%. The average holding period should be less than nine months, but it will more than likely be less than six months. **The one-year CD rate is used as a benchmark because it represents what you could achieve with an absolutely risk free, for lack of a better word, product.**

If you take another look at the data presented in **Table Three**, you will see the type of information you need to record and the types of calculations that are to be made. In this illustration there are fifty-six "sell" transactions for an average (after commission) gain of a bit more than 10% and an average holding period of less than four months. There was just one loss transaction. You would be extremely pleased with those results, particularly if you remember what happened to this sector of the stock market that year.

Obviously, a conservative trading discipline can work even in the worst of times! But how many of your holdings didn't pan out? A process called "portfolio aging" (explained below) examines that important point. Trading is the key to the whole portfolio's ultimate success; so don't waste time kidding yourself. Some things are going to have to get sold at a loss eventually. Accurate aging information is a must, though; otherwise the proper amount of "patience" won't be applied.

Base Income

All of the securities in the portfolio contribute to what is called your "Base Income". **Base Income is defined as the income that results from dividends and interest on the securities held in the portfolio. It DOES NOT INCLUDE net Capital Gains.** This is because there is no guarantee that there will actually be any Capital Gains next year, although that is a very remote possibility with this trading method! In order to meet our long-term goals, it is imperative that our base income from operating the portfolio be greater than it was the previous year.

If you are true to your asset allocation model, the base income will grow quickly because 30% of all income (including capital gain income) is reinvested for more income production.

What if there are no Capital Gains? The worst-case scenario is that you now temporarily own a "Buy 'n Hold" portfolio! AND you still have an annually increasing cash flow! If you have a speculative, poorly diversified portfolio with no regular income, the worst-case scenario becomes a bit grim.

I know exactly what you just thought about, and you're absolutely correct! Here we have a simple, easy to manage solution to a very real (but not nearly as scary as we've been led to believe by the financial community) problem. Inflation! **Inflation is**, straight from "Webster's New World Dictionary": **"an increase in the amount of money and credit in relation to the supply of goods and services, [and] an excessive or persistent increase in the general price level as a result of this, causing a decline in purchasing power."** (Dismal science indeed, this is exciting!)

Financial Institutions, particularly our friends who sell Mutual Funds, invariably instruct you that investing in the stock market is the only way that you can possibly hope to "outpace" inflation, "the perfect hedge", they will spout from their infinite fountains of wisdom. Now I personally think that the impact of inflation (which varies from one economic sector to another) is significantly less for some people than it is for others due to countless personal life style variables, but inflation certainly does exist! And as much as I live and breathe "stock market" every day of my life, you might expect me to say that I agree with "The Street" on this one point. **But it's as absurd as any of the other reality cures that these manipulative super (sales) stars come up with! It just sells Mutual Funds; there is not one logical bone in this entire body of baloney!**

If my cost of living increases, if my "purchasing power" diminishes, by what stretch of the imagination is an increase in the Market Value of my Mutual Funds going to help...unless I sell them and spend the money? But that's not what they are telling you to do. "They" are telling you to buy more of the funds so that the value of your portfolio keeps up with inflation. I don't know about you, but most of the places I go to eat, play, view, party, vacation, ride, and so on, only accept money! They just don't care about the value of my stock portfolio. If inflation drives up the value of my home, it just increases my real estate taxes, not my income.

So how do you deal with the inflation "boogie man"? Right, by increasing the level of your annual income at a rate greater than the rate of inflation. Even the Labor Unions, with not nearly as many MBAs per square inch as Wall Street, have figured this one out! Ever heard of a "cost of living increase" going anywhere but into the recipients pay envelop? I don't think so.

Wanna' beat inflation? Just manage your portfolio so that your "Base Income" grows each year by more than the inflation rate. How? By managing your asset allocation properly. You're going to have to do this yourself, because none of your "Financial Advisor" friends have figured it out yet, and if their institutional superiors have, they're not telling anyone. Income growth just doesn't sell Mutual Funds!

What about the magical "Buy-and-Hold" portfolio? What kind of impact does inflation have on that icon? Let's say our growth in value has actually beaten the inflation rate. We still don't have any income to pay the bills, because income wasn't part of the "plan". We've got to sell now to restructure the portfolio to produce the income that we never thought about until we were forced into early retirement last week. Since we've never taken any profits, ever penny of profit is only 67% ours to spend and aren't we fortunate that interest rates are at their lowest levels in twenty years?

So I guess, we didn't really keep up with the inflation rate after all, did we?

Portfolio Aging

In a trading environment, reasonably rapid turnover is the key to success. Setting up a portfolio "inventory" sheet that lists the purchase dates of each of your equity holdings is an easy way to monitor your performance in this important area. As issues are sold they are removed and replaced by new purchases. Older holdings should be identified and watched closely for an exit point.

The "age" of the stocks in the portfolio should reflect the desire to trade frequently. The better (less greedy) you become, the more likely it is that the average age will be less than 6 months, which is an achievable and a reasonable target. The fact that a stock fails to become "tradable" quickly enough doesn't detract form either its value or its ability to produce income. It's just quite likely that you can replace it with a more volatile one!

"Shark Attack!" (Not a Golf Story.)

In retailing, there is an unethical marketing strategy called **"Bait and Switch"** which works something like this: an advertisement is placed for a popular product at a special sale price. When the shopper gets to the store, the advertised product is "sold out" and sales people try to "switch" the consumer's interest to other products.

In the financial world, certain "professionals" will use an approach that I would call **"Attack and Switch"**. Here, the sales person, leading either with his lofty designation (CPA, CFP, RIA) or his firm's big name and solid reputation, goes straight for the portfolio juggler vein: "Boy did your funds perform badly, ours were in the top 10%", "You shoulda' done better compared with the Dow". "Why don't you own an annuity?" "We've got a lot of work to do here." "My dad can beat up your dad."

A portfolio needs to be analyzed in light of the plan and objectives that were used in its development. Proper observations, after a brief review might sound like this: "Did you mean to construct such an aggressive (conservative) portfolio?" "What was your fixed/equity allocation model?" "Your income target?" "Are you planning on retiring soon?" etc.

Watch out for land sharks whose entire pitch is a criticism of the competition. Something you own (maybe everything)

should be just fine! Always aggressively question major changes into new securities of the same asset class.

The "Working Capital" Model

If we score good marks in Trading, Income Building, and Aging, it is reasonable to assume that our bottom line portfolio value will increase. And although this is entirely true (it will increase), the timing of the increase may be totally out of line with more conventional measures. This is because we are constantly seeking out new opportunities that are moving in what direction? You should have thought "down" immediately!

1987 provides an excellent illustration again. Wheelbarrows full of profits were made that year, and reinvested in equities that were dragged down (in market value only) during the last two months. Working Capital grew by 15% or more, but market value told another story. There were no bankruptcies and no dividend cuts. Unless you followed the typical Wall Street "sell low" advice, your "Market Value" rebounded nicely and Working Capital just kept "right on truckin'".

The Wall Street geniuses got you "back in" right before the next correction. Remember?

Since we are buying good companies down in price and selling good companies that have moved ahead in price by 10% or more, what is left in the portfolio at the end of the year, or at the end of any day of the year, for that matter? You are absolutely right. Stocks that are not quite camera ready because they are in cyclical downturns, or because they have temporarily fallen out of favor with Wall Street for some other reason. If you are trading properly, you will either have to develop the patience and fortitude to deal with this OR adopt a totally different (and much more useful) method of examining performance.

The events of 1987 provide wonderfully illustrative materials! From January through August, there was a 44% gain in the DJIA, which happened to contain only New York Stock Exchange

179

companies at the time. Within less than 4 months, all of that gain was erased plus a percent or two, and the DJIA ended the year with "negative" numbers! Still it really was a great year by "rational, objective based" portfolio analysis methods, if not by Wall Street's arbitrary, transaction creating index method!

Without going into boring detail, I'll summarize by saying that trading was phenomenal in 1987, through the end of August and after the middle of October. Base Income was also very high because interest rates were also, and there were many utility stocks in trading portfolios. We'll use these facts to illustrate a much more practical model for portfolio performance evaluation.

A "Working Capital" View Of Two Portfolios:

	Trading Portfolio	Buy and Hold Portfolio
Amount Invested	$100,000	$100,000
Trading Results	$15,000	-
Dividends	$3,000	800
Year-End Working Capital Value	$118,000	$100,800
Year-End Market Value	$115,640	$98,784
Highest 1987 Market Value	$130,000	$144,800

The "trading portfolio" is the equity portion of a program developed according to the guidelines described in this book. The other is the classic "Buy and Hold" equity portfolio with no trading targets or income discipline. Note that "Working Capital" value will only go down when money is withdrawn from the portfolio for any reason, and when actual trading losses occur. So long as the focus on Working Capital is maintained, illusory "paper" increases and decreases in value will not influence the asset allocation model (as it will your decision making). **You would really have to be a career**

masochist to use market value and weighted averages to evaluate the performance of a trader's diversified portfolio!

Now I realize that this approach is totally different than anything you've ever dealt with before, but in one fell swoop it surely eliminates all of those nagging ifs, ands, buts, that make standard "bottom line" "market value" analysis totally useless (to the investor). The Parker Brothers Monopoly Game could provide a useful illustration. The winner is always the person with the most money invested in income producing assets.

A Better Way

I created the "Working Capital" method of portfolio performance evaluation many years ago, when it became evident that a trading strategy was quite a bit different from most styles of investment management. In years of rapidly rising interest rates and, more recently, with the divergence of the popular averages from the realities of the broad market, this method sorts things out clearly. It shows you where you are and allows for meaningful comparisons with where you've been. As a kicker it allows for an instant and accurate appraisal of asset allocation!

"Working Capital" is defined as the actual Cost Basis of the securities in the portfolio as opposed to their current market value. This concept is also consistent with the retail store approach towards equity investing which was discussed earlier. Income of any kind, including realized capital gains, and deposits increase your working capital while withdrawals and realized capital losses alone decrease it. Current market value is not a factor. It only causes errors in judgment anyway.

Since you will constantly monitor the age of the securities in the portfolio the tendency to hang on too long to nonproductive assets is also avoided. Along with the ATH (All Time High Profit Level) selling decision discussed in Chapter Five, your portfolio will remain a lean and mean growth and income machine forever!

Don't you think Wall Street knows all this? OF COURSE THEY DO! But you absolutely will never hear about it from the marble tower dwellers. They thrive when you act emotionally, not when you behave rationally. Remember, they are there to nourish your greed and your fear. They want to deal with pigs and sheep. That's fine, so long as you understand the nature of "the beast" and act accordingly!

Working Capital Value

The total "Working Capital" will always be more than the Market Value of the portfolio, unless the bulk of the portfolio is invested in fixed income securities. (AND then only if interest rates have moved down since the time the Fixed Income securities were purchased.) This is both expected and accepted because it is easy to understand without having to sift through a dozen research reports that try to explain an array of "unknowable(s)" about the economy and the company's Management Team. However, the closer the "broad" market gets to truly high ground, the narrower the difference between working capital and market valuations. Is this clear? Working Capital doesn't change as a function of market value. It grows through the addition of cash from deposits, dividends, interest, and realized gains. It decreases when losses are realized and when cash is withdrawn from the portfolio. **The day-to-day changes in market value that Wall Street wants you to worship can now be thrown out into the street with the other garbage!** Maybe this hypothetical (?) conversation will help.

Good Year, Bad Year

So how do you respond to that "How are you doing in this market" question?

"Pretty well so far. Trading has been really good because of this wonderful market volatility. I've taken lots of quick, short-term profits that I've put back into new fixed income and equity positions. Most of my older holdings have come back well enough to escape gracefully!" "My Base Income hasn't been growing as quickly as I'd like lately because of lower interest rates, but I've actually been able to sell some fixed income stuff profitably as well. I expect to increase working capital by at least 10% this year, just like last year. Overall it's been another great year!"

Be prepared for a blank stare (in 2000 and 2001), an open mouth and a "what are you talking about? The Market averages have been down for nearly two years!"

To which you will respond: "Really, **I don't pay much attention to those figures, they have no correlation at all to the design and structure of my portfolio"**

Don't forget to smile while your friend makes one more attempt: "Oh, I see, when did you get out of the market? You sure were lucky!"

"Actually, it doesn't ever make any sense to be out of the market. My equity allocation has always been around 70% and it will stay there until I'm a bit closer to retirement. I consider myself an investor, not a speculator"

We are replacing our profitable investments (products we have sold at our store) with new ones that have potential for future profit (inventory on the shelves). Thus our current portfolio value will not "catch up" until new buying opportunities dry up. If you have nothing to buy, "smart cash" builds up (compounding at money market rates) while profit taking continues. In recent years (1998 through March 2000), there were always many more stocks going down than going up, so finding new investments was not a problem. Over the past 18 months or so (through July 2001), the environment has turned around completely. **Refer back to the "Never Violate the Rules Section of Chapter Three and memorize "The Investor's Creed"**

183

The Power of Trading

To use the "Working Capital Model", which was designed out of an appreciation for the power of trading, you have to find tools that are more useful than indices and averages to help you appreciate a little better just what is going on out there on a day-to-day basis. Two readily available numbers really zero in on what's going on in the real world.

As explained in some detail above, Issue Breadth Statistics are published daily and reveal the actual numbers of stocks moving up and down. Similarly, the number of stocks achieving new one-year highs or declining to new annual lows is also reported daily. This is certainly not as exciting as listening to and hyperventilating with every new ATH in the Dow Jones Industrial Average. But any seven year old could tell you that: when more stocks are going down than are going up for an extended period of time, or *vice versa*, "The Market" is not nearly as "hot" (or cold) as Wall Street would like you to believe.

The Working Capital model works well with meaningful numbers such as these!

Investment "Time"

If I were to buy an existing portfolio of securities (a Mutual Fund) on January 1st of any given year, it might be important to me to look at its value on December 31st. I could then compare my performance with other, similar entities as a form of managerial control. Is this practical or productive? It certainly is not if there have been any self-initiated changes made to the portfolio during the time period. Even for the majority of Mutual Funds, just comparing the simple year-to-year unit value (Net Asset Value) change with the change in an average or index, just doesn't compute! **If the manager of a mutual fund is not trading, just what are you paying him for! And, believe me, you are paying!**

Investment "Time" is a concept that Millionaire's understand and appreciate. It involves the application of patience and reasonableness to a living entity that has no start or end date! **Portfolios are dynamic. Their changes, all of their changes, cannot be quantified, catalogued, or crammed into some arbitrary time period (a calendar year) for analysis!**

An ex-client of mine knew all about trading! His program was progressing extremely well, with serious profits being generated on numerous trades. He seemed content and confident, until a visit to his Accountant toward the end of November. He was advised to sell all of his "losers" to offset as much of his profit as possible. The majority of stocks in his portfolio were less than three months old! Had he explained the portfolio management trading strategy to his Accountant? Did the Accountant appreciate the intrinsic value of the companies whose stock he would be selling? Why hadn't he said something before I had made the more recent purchases?

I asked him to call the broker to initiate the transactions because I could not take the responsibility and his Accountant did not have the power. Well sell them he did! We would just "buy them back" again in January! (Don't ever fall for that one; I shouldn't have to explain the fallacies!) He was pleased; I was confused. I think he was happier actually losing $10,000 in real money, than he would have been reducing his gain by $3,600 in paid taxes. Don't fall into this trap. Think how upset you'll be when you have nothing to take a loss on!

Every Investment Program requires time to produce the desired long-term effect. A shortsighted analysis, made too soon, inevitably causes errors, sometimes fatal ones, as in the case just cited. Individual investments require time to produce trading gains. A calendar year racetrack allows an average of just six months for each investment to produce. Some will; the others won't be given a chance.

Of "Bottom Lines"

At a small seminar a few years ago, we were debating whether or not this form of analysis (i.e., the Working Capital Model) was really the "break through" it appears to be on the surface. One person accepted the value of profits and of income and he could see how frequent trading "should" lead to excellent growth in values, long term. But he couldn't help but focus on the year-to-year value changes in "the bottom line". Any business, he pointed out, must focus on the bottom line!

Absolutely! But **businesses focus on bottom lines with names such as: profits, total sales, return on invested capital, inventory turnover, and the like.** They even compare such numbers with results in other years. This practice makes abundant sense, since growth in these important areas produces growth in the enterprise as a whole, and benefits all concerned! **Never do you hear them crow about how the value of the inventory has risen 20% or 30%.** If it did, the business could be in trouble! **In fact, growth in the value of inventory by a company, or within an industry is often mentioned in the media as the reason for falling stock prices.** And who spoon-feeds that information to the media? You got it, Wall Street! Too many heads spoilin' the brew!

Table Five is taken directly from an annual report prepared for a Profit Sharing Plan that has been using the approach described here since 1983. The total amount invested that year was $24,000.

Table Five: Working Capital Analysis

(Asset Allocation: Equities = 60%; Fixed Income = 40%)

	1999	1999	2000	2000
Beginning Working Capital =		**$309,691**		**$331,357**
Cash Withdrawals from Portfolio =		(2,790)		(2,954)
Dividends Received =	$6,137		$7,735	

		1999		2000
Interest Received =	$6,467		$8,056	
Total Base Income =		$12,604		$15,791
Net Capital Gains =		$11,852		$27,178
Ending Working Capital =		$331,357		$371,372
	1999	1999	2000	2000
Growth in Working Capital =	7.00%		12.08%	
Net Amount Invested Since1983 =		$61,752		$58,798
Total Gain in Working Capital =		$269,605		$312,574
Year End Portfolio Market Value =		$278,005		$305,140
Actual per cent Invested in Fixed Income =	40%		40%	
Actual per cent Invested in Equities =	60%		60%	
Average Annual Amount Invested =		$68,647		$68,278
Total % Gain in Working Capital =		392.74%		457.80%
Total "Spendable" Income =	$24,456		$42,969	
"Spendable" Income as a per cent of Beginning Working Capital		7.90%		12.97%

Using the Working Capital Model, a negative year would signify poor trading results, which ended up with serious net realized losses, coupled with a poor showing in the Base Income area. With a properly constructed portfolio, such a sad story will probably never be told. Working Capital analysis focuses on the purpose and design of the portfolio. Things move forward without regard for the vagaries of Market Value. In the portfolio presented here, what would a market value closer in total to Working Capital mean? It would point to a serious downturn in interest rates pushing up the paper value of fixed income securities, or, if not, to a manager who is not taking profits properly.

Note also how the Working Capital Model clearly shows the compounding power of a properly managed asset allocation! For those of you who are still fixated on bottom-line "Market Value" analysis, note how a 10% gain (in 2000, WOW, seriously!) translated into (or was the result of?) realized "spendable" income of roughly $43,000! Why is spendable income so important? Sounds like a final exam question to me!

Break Time: "MISSING THE BOAT", A Study In Discipline!

Managers learn quickly that they have limited resources at their disposal to help them achieve the interim goals and long term objectives of their organization or business. Most find that a well thought out plan, with a consistently applied set of operational procedures, helps to move the company forward through an ever-changing economic environment. There are no clear charts to follow, and no certainty about the future to guide decision-making. Decisions therefore, have to remain focused and cannot commit the organization to directional changes that could threaten the company's long-term viability.

Managing an investment portfolio is no different. The parallels are overwhelming! The message is clear: "adopt a sensible program and stay with it. If change appears necessary, move slowly and without risking the health of the portfolio. Never let emotions take a "leadership role" in the enterprise!

I can't help but think of a "genius" ex-client who (early in 2000) told me how I had "missed the boat" on "The Market" by sticking stubbornly to my high quality, profitable, and dividend paying company selection criteria. Another "ex" determined that the conservative investment style that we had used so successfully for many (nearly twenty!) years was simply "broken and useless". To the scrap heap it went, in favor of a new age guru and what he concluded was "new" and "hot", straight from his personal contacts in the media. "The future of investing," he called it!

No one is happy with single digit gains when their buddies (and their Accountants) have all become expert in producing exponential growth! "Income is for fools!" "By this time next year I'll be rich!" "Good Bye!" As in many other life situations though, some temporary and foolish pleasure can cause permanent and long-lasting pain!

At the end of every stock market "rainbow" is a black hole, in which you will find the charred remains of many a "Wall Street" speculator but, sadly, no evidence at all of the people who led "the Pigs" into the pit. I can't emphasize strongly enough how even "treading water" in quality investments and a balanced portfolio (during cyclical speculative fervor) always comes out ahead in the long run. The bubble always bursts! The carnage is always devastating! Missing a speculative ride on a hydroplane is far better than going down with the ship! "Boring investment portfolios may not get the media attention, but they always seem to come out of hard times undamaged, whole, and strangely more attractive than those flashy speculative upstarts!

Institutional Wall Street, its captive Media, the Financial Press, and the 20-year-old MBA "seers" thrive on delivering their "snake oil" to you, the "savvy" investor. They always have. Nothing ever changes! **The definition of "savvy", you ask? It is a person who swallows everything that the "Street Chefs" place on the table before him.**

Why would anyone be surprised at the demise of the NASDAQ? So many tales could be told to re-emphasize lessons that are only temporarily learned, like: Greed Rules! The Pigs Always Lose! **Will you be caught in the next speculative bubble? There absolutely will be one, you know.**

Administrations will change, and so will the direction of interest rates. Stock prices will move up and down, forever I hope and fully expect. The magnitude of the opportunity for profit is directly proportional to the magnitude of the change, in either direction.

Maybe! You just have to understand the rules. It's depressing when you appreciate just how many people either don't know that there are rules, or think that they can make up their own as they go along!

The NASDAQ "meltdown" just isn't an investment concern. (Nor is it a "Contrarian" opportunity!) It was simply the bursting of another, beautifully orchestrated Wall Street speculative bubble. Inevitable! Predictable! Justifiable! Wonderful! The Pigs (really do) Always Lose! But they will be replaced by a new generation of Pigs, sooner rather than later. Nothing ever changes.

Don't think for a minute that what you have learned here is applicable to a NASDAQ Market that is down more than 60%! It isn't. Remember the "junk bond" story? Junk is junk. Stick with value, and remember always that no one knows what the future will bring.

The aftermath of greed is so much fun for the value trader to observe. Ahhh, human nature! Remember Red Auerbach? I have this image of myself, sitting on a chaise at the beach, feet up, puffing on a victory cigar, sipping a Diet Pepsi, just watching those speculative boats slipping beneath the waves. Join me. It's so fun! (Sic)

But let's press on and learn some more about the "playing field" of the Investment Game. Can you guess what it is?

CHAPTER SIX: MANAGING THE IGNORANCE

A Basic Lack of Knowledge

Is it clear to you now that there isn't a whole lot of hard, scientific, factual wisdom out there? **Wall Street doesn't want you to know it, but ignorance is the playing field for the investment game.** One of the keys to success in the markets is to be aware of this. Instantly you will realize that 99% of what you hear and read about investing is irrelevant! (This book is the other 1%!) A consolidation of all the opinions, predictions, research reports, tips, news flashes, and whispers would be neutral! Because nobody really knows what is going to happen next. **No amount of "past", be it analyzed by a shoeshine boy, a group of little old ladies, or 100,000 "Yallies" equals "future'. And "future' is where you are going to be.**

To invest profitably, you must be able to distinguish between what is and is not "knowable". To invest profitably, you must stubbornly limit the number of inputs you allow into your decision making process. To invest profitably, you must keep your eyes focused on the road ahead, and avoid looking back. To invest profitably, you must never think in terms such as "coulda", "woulda", and "shoulda" yourself and you must also be able to tune out any input that includes such terms. (Sellers of investment products, for example, live in "couldaland"!) To invest profitably, watch the tape on CNBC with the volume turned off.

Advice Levels

There are really two levels of advice. **Level I advice is usually asked for by the investor and provided by some form of professional.** It is your responsibility to familiarize your "professionals" with your plan! It is your responsibility to synthesize such advice to see if it fits with your plan! **Level II advice is generally unsolicited and comes from entities that have an interest in making you take some form of action.** This includes the media, various types of "experts", and others who have developed panaceas for the vagaries and uncertainties of the investment markets. It is your responsibility to tune this out entirely. It will cause you to second-guess yourself and to apply hindsight to your plan!

Once you have established a plan, and a set of rules, strategies and procedures with which to implement that plan, you have to be extremely selective in the advice you seek or accept. If you have a trading portfolio and/or a portfolio that is allocated by formula between fixed income and equity securities, sources of advice and analysis must be limited to those who have some idea about what you are trying to accomplish!

Here are some basic guidelines: Avoid taking advice that is unsolicited and/or that is offered by individuals who have a commission interest in what they are recommending. Avoid taking investment advice from people who have not made their money investing. This eliminates most of the professionals you will hear from! Have a look at the personal balance sheet of any one who recommends directional changes. This should be a big help!

Finally, you have to avoid direct "Wall Street" advice like the plague! This is the day-to-day commentary that filters down through the media in the form of analysis, projections, interviews, commentary, insights, opinions, and predictions.

Surviving Within a World of Cross Purposes

The purpose of an investment program is to grow and to preserve wealth and/or to increase income for retirement. The plan is to follow a prescribed set of actions that can reasonably be expected to accomplish a reasonable set of predefined goals. It makes no sense at all to compare the results of such a program with the movement of anything, particularly things that are not constructed in a similar manner! It is also foolish to assign arbitrary time constraints to something that, by definition, has no beginning or end.

Somewhere along the narrow streets of lower Manhattan, the purpose of an investment program has become lost. It resides in a temporary cardboard and pallet shanty while, many stories up, Investment Companies prosper.

Boeing, Boeing

Way back in the dark ages of my investment career, I was on a business trip where I had the opportunity to spend some time with one of my employer's Separate Account Managers. (An Insurance Company Separate Account at that time was really just a Mutual Fund reserved for what I believe is still called either a "Defined Contribution" or a "Savings and Investment Plan". Today's popular 401(k) Plans would fall into this category.)

This person was responsible for billions of client investment dollars! "Why" I asked, "do you hold so much Boeing stock? The value is about three times the cost basis. Why not take some profit and buy something else, diversify or add to income?" "Because Steve" I was told matter-of-factly, "Boeing is one of our largest insurance customers and they like us to hold a large position in their stock!"

So what do you think would happen to Boeing's market price if they switched insurance companies? And what lesson is to be learned here? This isn't Price to Earnings or "current" ratios we're talking about. Nor is it sales projections, profitability or even "buy out" rumors. This is politics, greed, and manipulation, plain and simple. And who has more influence on market prices than such major Institutional Money Managers? Those of us who go out there and buy a few hundred shares of McDonalds for our IRA have no clue what is motivating the buy and sell strategies of these huge investors! They make major decisions, buying millions of shares of stock, just because their clients' think it would be a nice idea? No, manipulation and influence peddling is not a new thing, it's just gotten bigger and more dangerous!

Window Dressing

Once every quarter the media blithely reports how their Institutional bedfellows are rushing in to buy large quantities of the Quarter's most popular issues and separating themselves from issues that have "performed" poorly during the past three months. This is a "business as usual" scenario that has been a fact of life in the market ever since the first pension fund was given to an outside Money Manager for supervision.

The concept here has nothing to do with investing and everything to do with marketing! "Let's show our clients how smart we are by highlighting our brilliant stock selection capabilities in our quarterly reports. They'll see that we owned the "hot" stocks and had nothing to do with those "losers"! These "managers" are paying too much for some stocks and taking losses on others for no other reason than to fool their big clients!

The really sad thing is that it works so well! One reason is that the highly paid executives of big corporation will bend over backwards not to go through the expense and embarrassment of changing Investment Managers. They have to "look smart" to their bosses and to the company's Employee Benefits Committee.

It works equally well with **a Media that repeatedly fails to ruffle any feathers by analyzing things that would expose manipulation of this type,** and prefers to analyze and predict an unknowable future. They just don't have the "guts" to say, "hold on a minute, that makes absolutely no sense at all!"

And, yes, it mesmerizes you, and millions of other unsuspecting individual investment hopefuls, who rarely take the time to be suspicious of information they receive from the people who occupy high and influential places. **These are the experts, after all, and their credentials are so impressive!**

The Art of Looking Smart (IMF, 03/22/01)

"Wall Street has created a new Art Form! No matter what the cost, 'they' must appear to be smart. They didn't oversell speculative NASDAQ issues; they were ambushed by a recession that caused these companies to lose their value so abruptly. 'Let's blame Greenspan! He raised interest rates too fast and caused this economic downturn.'[Funny that they haven't rebounded with falling rates!] Totally untrue, but significantly more face saving than an admission of the manipulative tactics they routinely use to persuade you to make poor investment decisions! Did anyone ever say 'SELL' or 'DIVERSIFY' (on the way up)?"

"Could there be a conspiracy in here somewhere? Let's look at some reality. No one cried 'recession' until months after the NASDAQ fell on its dot-com face. While that market was crashing, the NYSE average held its ground and Quality Growth/Income portfolios rose by better than 20%! Has anyone looked inside the major players' trading accounts (Merrill, Morgan Stanley/Dean Witter, etc.) to see when they took their profits and moved to more conservative holdings? Is it really in the best interests of the investing public to allow new issues to be marketed from start to finish the way they are today? Ever wondered why the IPO market dries up during corrections?"

This is the environment of the individual investor. You better be scared! 90% of the movement of stocks in our markets is the result of "institutional" trading! And these guys are a whole lot more into politics and marketing than they are into investing! Hey, it's their job! This is how they feed their families and no one seems to care if they lie, cheat, and steal their way to those million dollar bonuses. So it becomes your job to protect yourself from believing that the numbers presented to you by these charlatans have any basis in reality! Trade! Take profits!

Interest Rates

Every portfolio will eventually contain securities whose primary purpose is to produce ("spendable") income. Nothing can keep these securities from fluctuating in market value with changes in the anticipated movement of interest rates, and this is the way it should be! *They are, after all, called interest rate sensitive securities!* **If you are managing your asset allocation model properly you will always have dollars available that can be used to take advantage of rising interest rates.**

One of the biggest "scams" in the investment world is the evaluation of price movements in fixed interest securities as though they were equity investments intended to produce growth in market value. They aren't, and you have to understand this.

Years ago, when interest rates moved into double digits, my elderly Aunt Alice accumulated a portfolio of GinnyMaes that delivered income at a rate of about 13%. As interest rates were raised higher and higher, the "market value" of these Federally Guaranteed securities fell, as they were expected to, but not by Alice!

This was a problem! Even though her income was greater than she needed for her total maintenance, she couldn't cope with the decline in value reflected on her monthly brokerage account statement! And she "knew" that interest rates would just keep on going up forever! Happy with the income, unhappy with the force of interest rate gravity! What a dilemma! **(Some people actually should keep their rate sensitive securities in "certificate form" stashed in a safe deposit box, so long as they are "registered"!)** Why? Because they won't be able to observe the fluctuations!

Incidentally, I've observed over the years that people become increasingly pessimistic as they age, and that they worry much more about the future than one would think! Watch out for this in your own thought processes and behavior. Reach out for a younger person's perspective if you sense a negative change in your attitude.

So Alice went to her local bank, sold the absolutely Government Guaranteed securities, and bought ("invested in" would be incorrect because...) some 8.5% Certificates of Deposit (CDs)! "No more erosion of my nest egg she boasted proudly." At least not until her income shortfall forced her to liquidate some of those wonderful CDs to meet expenses. Now why do you think that her banker (a Financial Advisor, of course) didn't suggest that she place her Ginny Mae certificates in her safe deposit box? Now that wouldn't do the bank much good, would it? **Wouldn't it be ironic if the bank took Alice's money and used it to invest in some wonderful 15% Ginny Maes?** Let's do the math. Here they've guaranteed Alice an 8.5% return and they also have to make enough to cover their inflated overhead of about 3%. With these self-liquidating government guaranteed securities, they could cover the entire "fixed overhead" on the CD and walk away with a guaranteed profit of 3.5%. **The only problem would be the banker's inability to sleep nights afterwards. Yeah, right!**

Stay away from any person, product, system, or computer program that represents itself as a cure or a solution for the terrible problem of changing interest rates. Avoid things with words like "hedge" and "derivative", etc. anywhere inside. If it sounds too good to be true, it probably is.

Rising interest rates are the investor's friend, because investors can take advantage of the higher yields by investing a portion of their cash flow either in new fixed income securities or in more of those that they already own. **Falling interest rates are also the investor's friend,** because they can realize capital gains when they sell some of their existing fixed income holdings that have gone up in price as a result of the lower interest rates. On the flip side, rising rates can be the speculator's worst enemy, especially when leveraging is involved!

The Use of Margin

Margin borrowing, or "leveraging", writing uncovered option contracts, "shorting" and the like are flawed investment strategies. They are inherently speculative because they are based on a presumption of knowledge. Of? That's right, the future. If I can borrow on my portfolio at 8%, and invest the proceeds at 15%, why wouldn't I do so? Because there are no guarantees out there (even of 5% in the stock market), and "Margin Calls" do happen! Options and shorting strategies require certain price movements to occur within a specific time period. The only person who will make money on this type of program is the "Financial Advisor" who sells you on the idea.

__But, does Wall Street try to stop the speculative addictions of its' clients? Please! "Let them take drugs" would be more like it!__

As speculative as margin borrowing is known to be, every Wall Street Institutions' Monthly Account Statements highlight precisely how much you are able to borrow! **I have a client who, at one time, was very impressed with the amount of his "BUYING POWER"**! Don't hide this number with some "euphemism"; spell it out!

Your investment portfolio becomes collateral for a loan, just like a gold watch at a Pawn Broker. **The brokerage firm is encouraging you to borrow, just as a stereotypical loan shark would!** Shouldn't there be a *__"WARNING: Margin Borrowing is Addictive, and Has Been Identified by the SEC General Office as a Major and Direct Cause of Financial Distress and Even Bankruptcy."__*

Wall Street must be a whole lot more politically connected than the tobacco companies ever dreamed of being, as hard as that is to believe! **Don't you expect better than this from an entity called a "Financial Institution"? You should! But you can't!** If you are on a fixed income from your portfolio, and you tell your

"Financial Advisor" to buy securities for you on margin, I'll bet you $10 that he doesn't say no!

Margin borrowing is for emergencies only, and with a limit below 20% of the portfolio value, if possible. Only the most well disciplined people should consider its use at all, and it should be "cleaned up" as soon as possible.

Rallies and Corrections

Technical analysis can be useful (maybe), but when it begins to take on "gospel" like qualities, it has gone way too far! By what stretch of the imagination does an arbitrary "up 20%" or "down 20%" in a weighted average identify market rallies and corrections? Why do the "technicians" get to label these events anyway, and without question? As I've pointed out before, there are easier to understand numbers that do it better, and what plays out as a correction in one area is likely to be a rally in another.

Popular Causes of "Corrections" Wall Street loves to have "technical" support for its explanations of what's going on in the financial markets. Higher Interest Rates are often cited; as are the economic downturns they call recessions. Just how important to the average guy do you think a quarter or two of declining GNP (Gross National Product) really is? **Here's a sure fire way to identify the next meaningful recession (IMF, 03/22/01):**

"When unemployment goes up month after month. When prices actually go down! When a parking place can be found at the Mall within a hundred yards of the entrance you really wanted to use. When you can walk into any restaurant in town, particularly the most expensive ones, on a Friday or Saturday night, without a reservation, and get immediate seating. When there are no rush hour traffic jams on weekdays or "volume only" problems on Sunday afternoons. When professional sports events are being played with a growing percentage of empty seats. AND the acid test, when you can walk onto any public golf course on a weekend without a tee time and wait less than two hours to play."

"When all of this happens, we have recession. Until then, only hype. Only a manipulation of your fear in the same manner as your greed was used against you last year…"

In spite of all the hype and headlines, both events (rallies and corrections) are your close financial friends! And both can be easily identified by non-MIT PhDs just by paying attention to the numbers discussed above (Breadth Statistics, and New Twelve Month Highs vs. New Twelve Month Lows). A "rally" is going on when significantly more stocks are going up in price than are going down, and for an extended period of time! A "correction" is going on when significantly more stocks are hitting new "lows" than new "highs".

The Media wants you to love rallies and to hate corrections. Rallies are "good" they spout, and corrections are "bad". Nope! Both are simply facts of investment life, which are going to be with us always! If you are investing properly, you are gleefully taking profits during rallies and just as happily taking advantage of investment opportunities during corrections! Flip back to "The Investor's Creed in Chapter Three. **The only people who are unhappy with corrections are those (buy 'n holders or greedy pigs) who didn't take their profits during the last rally!** There is a little known investment truth between the lines here that I hope you will recognize and come to appreciate. **The ancient "Buy and Hold" strategy is, by its very nature, speculative because of the presumption of knowledge that lurks inside!**

Patience Rules

It's easy to get greedy during extended rallies, and frightened during corrections that don't seem to want to end! Underline what you've read earlier about setting reasonable targets. Try to think of the "profit taking" cash you are accumulating as "smart cash" that has done its job and is now in search of new investment opportunities.

At the same time, the daily diminishing size of your "Buy List" is making you look ever harder for new opportunities. Don't fall into the trap of buying marginal issues that just barely meet your quality standards. Be patient! You'll be kicking yourself later if you don't have enough cash to pick up a falling GE, Merck, or Kimberly Clark!

Remember that **Institutional Wall Street is powerful enough (and greedy enough) to cause both rallies and corrections.** One causes irrational buying; the other brings on panic selling. How can they possibly lose?

Let's make it at least a possibility. There's a specimen "Letter to Your Congressman" in Chapter Seven. Should there be a rule in place at brokerage firms something like this: a) a firm can only collect a commission on a profitable "sell" transaction, unless b) all purchases of the security were signed off on by the client as "unsolicited", and/or the firm has a signed "no, I don't wish to take my profits" letter from the client in its files. (**Most investors either don't even notice, or choose to ignore, the "unsolicited" notification that the firms sneak onto their confirmation notices. This means that the transaction was the investor's idea, not the broker's.**)

Or possibly a rule like this: c) a firm may not collect a commission on a security that is purchased for a client at a price that is at or above the twelve month high price for that security, as of the previous trading day, unless and until the client makes a net/net profit on the sale of that security.

How Do You Spell C-o-r-r-e-c-t-i-o-n? (IMF, 07/10/01)

"If you don't LOVE "corrections", you need to rethink and redesign your investment strategy! Pretty bold, you say? Just what is a correction, anyway? It is absolutely NOT a 20% drop in some index or average. That would be much too easy. It's also NOT something that can be predicted with any degree of accuracy. (I purposely did not say certainty, a term used improperly and disrespectfully on Wall Street!)"

"Corrections ARE the "buy low" element in the classic investment formula! They happen to individual securities, groups of similar securities, industry groups, etc. They generally do not impact all securities at the same time. They are absolutely not something to be afraid of! They have always happened and they always will happen. You Do Not Want That to Change! (By the way. Never buy any product or service that "protects" you from corrections!)"

"Corrections ARE the result of forces at work in the investment world, some good, some bad. If you feel that "Profit Taking" is the "Dark Side" of investing, you're confused. It is the *raison d'être* of investing, the creator of realized financial objectives!"

"Over the course of time, the vast majority of securities that go up in price will 'correct'. How much and when are unknowable and depend mostly on Wall Streets' interpretation of what's going on in the economy. If you set reasonable profit goals, you will have sold a successful investment before it "corrects". Wall Street will never tell you to take profits! It will rarely tell you to buy a security that has fallen in price! Go back and read that again! Beware of anyone who tells you what "we think". (I just threw that in to make you think!)"

"Wall Street has convinced you that it can predict the future, identify good investments with superior research, or even that it can give you enough information to make wise investments on your own. It can't and you can't! There is more to investing than minimum commissions and on-line trading. Research is a self-serving sales pitch. Corrections happen when good people are manipulated into making poor decisions, moving money from quality to speculation, creating poorly diversified portfolios that are destined to collapse."

"Investing has become an art of filtering information to avoid the media hype that leads only to mistakes. Quarterly results are not the long-term goals you should be concerned with! Wall Street is transaction driven. It doesn't matter what you do, as long as you do something! You need to get yourself a plan, and you don't have to be a rocket scientist to figure it out."

"Correction is spelled O-p-p-o-r-t-u-n-i-t-y, or Y-a-r-d S-a-l-e, or B-u-y N-o-w! How do you get the money to take advantage of such opportunities? Suffice it to say that I've taken profits on more than 100 different stocks already this year, many several times!"

"Good News" / "Bad News"

"The market went down today because there are just too many people employed. Times are just too good! This economy is just too strong and someday this is going to cause prices to go up. When that happens, inflation could become a problem and the FED will have to raise interest rates to slow things down!" Sound familiar? How about: **"the market jumped up today, rejoicing over the increase in first time jobless claims during the latest reporting month!"**

This topsy-turvey kind of thinking is not going away anytime soon! Don't let it be a problem for you, because what it accomplishes is really just what you should want it to after reading through this book! A market that moves quickly in both directions, not predictably, but certainly in a manner that can be managed profitably!

CHAPTER SEVEN: MISCELLANY

Every project, those that are fun and those that are not, eventually comes to the point where one can lean back, view what has been accomplished, and say with conviction "DONE"! And then there's investing! Actually, I believe that you now have enough information to move forward productively. If questions remain, there is a "forum" you can use to raise them. The methods and procedures described to you are easy to use, logical, and founded on basic, and sound principles of two disciplines: Management and Investing. Don't toss it aside because it isn't mainstream, recognized, or put forth by the normal Media or Financial Institution Gurus.

Several additional subjects either didn't "fit" the flow of any of the book's Chapters or deserve their own post-training presentation. Not the least of these is a section on how to go about changing your portfolio from what it is to what you now know that it should be!

Breaking The Code of Silence ("No Load" Mutual Funds)

The Automobile Industry has always been one of the most important in America. Millions of new and used cars are sold (and leased) every year. In the old days, "What's good for General Motors is good for the country" was an economic axiom! What I could never understand though (and still can't) was how any of the car dealerships ever managed to make a buck when they were selling cars "below invoice"! How many cars do you have to sell at cost or below before you make a profit? Why are all these dealers beating the doors down to obtain additional franchises? I guess they make it up in volume! I've known many car dealers, one retired, but none of them would "spill the beans"! **If you accept all this automotive propaganda as the truth, you are a prime candidate for this "certified pre-owned" good as new Lexus, AND for "No Load" Mutual Funds!**

Here's the real deal, as reported by my friend in low places, Deep Pockets:

"Mutual Funds. This area is one of the most confusing that investors have to deal with. The interesting part is that people believe what they want to believe and it is often difficult to help them. Let's start with the most basic and most important concept. FREE DOESN'T EXIST ON WALL STREET! Please look in the mirror and repeat that ten times each day. When you truly understand this you are on your way to avoiding disappointments on the 'STREET OF DREAMS'."

"OK! You're thinking: he's wrong, he's wrong, what about no-load funds? Wanna' buy a bridge or go on a snipe hunt? For once, just for once, read the prospectus! The managers of the most popular no-load funds are paid millions. The companies that sponsor them make millions. The offices that house the headquarters of these funds are marble covered palaces! Where does all of this money come from? THE INVESTORS! Truly believing that no-load funds are cost free to the investor is like buying an EZ-Pass tag and telling your friends that the Governor lets you use the New Jersey Turnpike and the Garden State Parkway for free! You know it's not true but it makes you feel better if they believe it."

"No-Load funds have many ways to charge investors. 12-b (1) marketing fees, fund expenses, and trading costs to mention a few. These don't include the hidden costs of the trip to Europe that the management team made on the Concord to uncover investment opportunities in France. The 12-b (1) fees and fund expenses are stated in the prospectus. You may have to dig to find the trading expenses (commissions) hidden toward the back somewhere, but they are in there. Investment performance less all of these fees and expenses is what remains to be returned to the investors. It is not uncommon for a no-load fund to have 12-b (1) fees of 1%, add on fund expenses of 1.5%, and 1% in trading costs. There it is, a no load fund that costs 3.5%. Got it? We will talk about loaded funds later."

*   *   *   **

You have noticed, I'm sure, that prospectus material is totally incomprehensible. By the same token, many firms monthly account statements are unnecessarily confusing. This is partially because they are created by Staff Departments, within the institutions, which have absolutely no contact with clients. **In the case of the prospectus, it allows the real costs and risks of a security to be buried under an impenetrable cloak of "legalese", which is, more often than not, misunderstood by even the best Securities Attorneys.** The reason is simple. If you knew all the risks, if you appreciated all of the costs, would you buy? Of course not!

Statements are subtly designed to create transactions; particularly the more "sophisticated" ones. They may also contain a lot of inaccuracies that can cause you to make poor decisions.

I had a wealthy client with more than two million dollars in Municipal Bonds. Over the years, Municipal Unit Trusts and Closed End Municipal Funds began to yield much more than individual bonds and the portfolio was adjusted to reflect this change. The brokerage firm's statements included the Closed End Funds under the "Equities" category and the Unit Trusts were listed as "Mutual Funds". "What have you done to my portfolio?" was the message on my answering machine one Saturday morning.

All was explained to the client's satisfaction, but from that point on I was forced to accept lower yields in individual bonds to the detriment of the long-term growth of the portfolio! The client didn't want to have to "think about it"!

The Real Scoop on Annuities

Securities Firms, Banks, and Insurance Companies have always been "The Big Three" of the financial institutions that reside on "Wall Street". At one time, it wasn't too difficult to distinguish between them because their businesses and their products were quite different. Securities firms sold stocks and bonds; Banks provided safekeeping, check clearing, and financing services, and the Insurance Industry sold Life Insurance policies and Annuity Contracts. It was a simpler world, and one less prone to the conflicts of interest that exist in and about the modern "Wall Street".

Today, Securities Firms own Banks and sell Insurance Company products. Banks sell Mutual Funds and Insurance. Not to be out done, the Insurance Industry provides banking and securities products as well. Actually, it is difficult to distinguish one institution from another! In and of itself, size is not a bad thing. It increases power and influence to about the same extent as it decreases speed and efficiency. But problems occur when Senior Managements get too "close" to one another and important distinctions between products begin to get overlooked, perhaps innocently, perhaps as part of a devious multi-industry strategy.

The "G" Word

One of the time honored distinguishing features of the Life Insurance Industry was its ability to "guarantee" certain payments and benefits under the insurance policies and annuity contracts that it sold to people for their protection and retirement income needs, respectively. They were not investment products although they certainly were sold with an emphasis on the savings discipline they encouraged in purchasers. The "guarantee" feature was unique and sacred. Like bank savings accounts and federal government securities, risk of loss was not supposed to be a factor. Modern day "Variable Products" sold by the industry have blown away this valuable feature of both insurance and annuities. The sales pitch emphasizes the prospect of gains in the stock market instead of the safety and security that used to be the product's and the industry's trademark. Wall Street "sells" what the speculating public wants to "buy", and the speculators are always looking for shortcuts to fortune. Pick your path carefully; the bridge is out!

What Is An Annuity?

An "annuity" is a series of payments, typically of the same amount, made over a specific period of time. (No attempt will be made to explain the endless variety of annuity contract types you can purchase, but suffice it to say that any departure from a "straight life annuity" reduces the payout because of the "additional life contingency" it adds to the contract.) A "Life Annuity" pays a fixed amount to one annuitant until his or her death. Any leftover funds belong to the Insurance Company; the Insurance Company pays any shortfall. A simple concept, actuarially pure, easy to deal with and no room for surprises! (Until the government inappropriately stepped in to say that the actuarial tables were discriminatory.) From that day forward, it was decreed; men are contractually bound to live as long as women, and women are no longer allowed to live longer than men!

The Most Important Concept that you will never be told about by your Financial Planner or Advisor! The Insurance Company becomes the sole heir to all of the assets held in your annuity contract.

As the industry strengthened and learned its way around the State Insurance Departments, it was able to lobby for the addition of an "investment element" that could be added to or made a part of the Annuity Contract. The wisdom of this change is, at the very least, questionable. The marketing of the "variable" annuity product line, if not criminally fraudulent, is, at best, reprehensible! For the most part, annuitants are still being "sold" a guaranteed retirement benefit. The risk involved is not explained, or dismissed out of hand as "totally unlikely, given the upward march of the averages over the past decade". If a client does figure out that a portion of his or her retirement plan is now invested in (any kind of) a Mutual Fund. "No matter," they are glibly advised, "this is a great fund with a spectacular track record. It will most likely bump up your income to the level you need to pay your bills!"

Risk? What risk? (Sadly, the vast majority of annuity salespersons actually believe their own sales pitches!) As far as securities salesmen are concerned, "RISK" is just a "board game" they played in college!

Who Needs an Annuity?

Please don't take offense, but annuities were developed for the protection of the indigent. Today they've been chromed, spit-polished, and supercharged, and are promoted as an "outstanding investment opportunity" demanding to be part of any well-constructed portfolio! Guess what, they still are just a great retirement income protection tool for the poor. The "poverty level bar" has risen though, and this is how to determine if you need an annuity or not. **IT ACTUALLY IS JUST THIS SIMPLE!**

The "real" annuity concept: both income and principal are disbursed to the annuitant until the fund is used up. Theoretically, an annuity is a systematized process in which a certain sum of money is liquidated in a manner such that the last contractual payment (bringing the fund balance to zero) is made on the first day of the month in which the annuitant dies. Obviously, this is not a precisely calculable event!

Annuitants are quoted a "rate of return" that is significantly higher than that which is actually being received by the company, (or are led to believe that the amount they will receive is the actual earnings on their deposit). It's always significantly higher than they could get from any other "guaranteed fixed income investment". The key concept is that absolutely nothing is passed on to the heirs when the annuitant dies.

Is this for you? Forget all the sales talk, the key numbers are easy to develop and to analyze. Most important is your personal expense estimate. How much am I going to need to live on when I retire? Be conservative (that means to use numbers higher than you really expect). Let's pretend that the number you decide upon is $50,000.

The second number is your personal estimate of the amount of "guaranteed" income you expect to receive from all sources, include Social Security, Pensions, etc. but ___absolutely do not include anything that your investment assets might produce.___ (Incidentally, Social Security payments, your Pension, or that wonderful Lottery Check are samples of annuities.) Again, be conservative, keeping your estimate a bit lower than what you actually expect. Let's say that this number works out to be $24,000.

That's it! Now all you have to do is to determine if your investment portfolio can possibly generate $26,000 per year. For the purposes of this analysis, the current market value of your portfolio is used, so go get the old E-Bonds out of the safe deposit box and determine the value of everything that is marketable...but don't run off and sell anything yet. At today's low market interest rates (which is all that the insurance/annuity company can actually earn) you would need about $370,000 to get the job done, with abundant safety.

If you don't have quite that much but can anticipate a "windfall" (an inheritance within less than five years or so) that would get you to that level, or if you are not in particularly good health, an annuity is the last thing you should be shopping for! Family considerations not withstanding, you should be able to invest the money conservatively, generate adequate income and have an estate left over for your heirs!

If you have a larger estate than needed to produce enough cash flow for retirement, you can still create and manage a portfolio with some of the assets invested for (that's right) growth! Annuities are **just not "the right stuff"** for a person of means.

The Ransom Concept

No self-respecting "Financial Advisor or Planner" would ever think of talking you out of buying an annuity! **They are the "mother of all commissions" in his product bag!** The salesman can get as much as 8% of the amount you turn over to the insurance company as a commission. Yup! It's even better for them than a Mutual Fund.

But, of course, there's more. Once they have found you, they'll never let you go, not without severe penalties that can last for up to eight years, one for every percent the company has already laid out to the salesman. You'd be better off investing the money yourself and taking your grand kids to Maui. Investors hate penalties as much as they hate commissions, so they allow themselves to be held for ransom rather than get out of what invariably turns out to be a bad deal.

Be careful though, if you decide to make a change, I understand that they now have a very convincing sales pitch. They'll allow you to switch for lesser charges, if you agree to buy another annuity. Institutional creativity never ceases to amaze me.

Yeah, There's Even More!

The market for Annuity "Products" has become huge, and there are now thousands of "Institutions" involved in selling them, with or without their Mutual Fund add-ons. Why? The commissions are huge for the salesmen and the Management Fees are huge for the Mutual Fund sponsors. So what's the problem? Isn't this competition good for the consumer? Aren't Insurance Premiums lower and annuity payouts higher than ever before?

Here's a better question: why have there been more insurance/annuity company failures in the few years since the introduction of "variable products" than in the entire history of the industry before that time? This one's easy to answer, but it will take a few paragraphs to explain how the Annuity "Guarantees" are calculated. There are three basic "assumptions" involved:

1. **Mortality:** Mortality rates are scientifically calculated and maintained in table form by professional actuaries. The new, Federally created, "Unisex" humans have a "known" life expectancy, and all companies use the same tables in their premium and annuity payment calculations. Males will get a lower payment than they should, and women will get more than they would have in years past. (No doubt about which sex is smarter. Maybe some day that won't be legal either!) **Not much room for manipulation here.** Question: If non-smokers pay lower life insurance premiums, shouldn't smokers get higher annuity payments? Maybe if they sue…

2. **Interest:** The actuary then determines a rate of return that the company is absolutely sure it can earn on the Fixed Income Securities in its "general account". A range of very conservative rates is allowed because of the extremely long-term nature of these contracts, maybe three or four percent, even less. This becomes the guaranteed contract rate. It is anticipated that any excess will be distributed to contract holders as dividends. **A conservative company will use a lower interest rate assumption than an aggressive company, thus creating an opportunity for price differences.**

3. **Expenses:** This is the big one, hot for manipulation! The actuary has to guess a number to include in the estimate of expenses related to this particular product. I'm not sure how well controlled this is by the State Insurance Departments, but **this is where an aggressive company can really make out by low-balling their number and**

arriving at an unrealistically high annuity payout figure.

Failures happen when earnings are less than assumed or expenses are higher than anticipated. In the meantime, owners and executives get rich until it all unwinds and the Insurance Company's Insurance Company is called in to pick up the pieces. The "con" can go on for a long time, so long as new money comes in that can be used to make payouts. It could be years. **So how smart do you think it really is to go after that "highest of all annuity payments". You just may be a lot healthier than the company you are counting on! It depends where you are in the _"Ponzi Scheme"._** (A Ponzi scheme is an investment scheme in which returns are paid to earlier investors, entirely out of money paid into the scheme by newer investors.)

And now they've added another variable to make assumptions about, the stock market! Had enough? Fortunately, you now have enough information to go out there and assure that you will not need to deal with this in your future. If you have deferred annuities, escape.

Don't laugh this off. There have been half a dozen Insurance/Annuity Company failures in recent years. **STAY AWAY FROM THE LOWEST INSURANCE PREMIUMS AND THE HIGHEST ANNUITY PAYMENTS AND STICK WITH LONG-TERM COMPANIES!** Minimize your risk. The best tool for that, most of the time, is your brain.

Unit Trusts and Closed End Funds

Unless you have a huge portfolio, you will no doubt become discouraged when it comes time to "fill up" the fixed income side of your portfolio. Preferred stocks are easy, but buying odd lots of Corporate, Government, and Municipal Securities isn't really the best way to go. You will wind up paying higher than normal markups for securities with less than wonderful liquidity, and lower yields than you might be aware of. Two Investment Products that fill the gap nicely are Unit Trusts and Closed End Bond Funds. You should use both of these security types in your investment portfolio.

Unit Trusts are put together by Wall Street Brokerage firms and are then turned over to an Institutional "Trustee" for supervision. They are not "managed" in the manner we have described here, nor are they "hedged" in any (impossible) way against the vagaries of interest rate movements. The securities within the trust are not traded, except under emergency (a serious financial problem for a particular bond issue) or "clean-up" (liquidation of a small remaining portion of an issue) conditions. Here's how they work:

Millions of dollars worth of Corporate, Municipal, or Government Securities are purchased and used to create very large, diversified portfolios. Once the portfolio is created, it is placed with a Trustee where it is held "in Trust for the benefit of its owners". No new securities are ever added to the portfolio and it is expected that the trust will self-liquidate over a known period of time. The Brokerage firm sells "Units of Ownership" in the trust to its clients at a serious mark up, but not nearly as much as an individually constructed portfolio of the same quality would have cost. The trustee's job becomes one of collecting the interest and principal payments from the bond issuers, and sending checks out to the Unit Holders. Yes, the trustee gets paid for the service it provides, but a very small amount. **Naturally, the Institution will use one of its own divisions as the Trustee.**

Unit Holders receive interest and a portion of principal every month. Occasionally, a bond within the trust may be "paid off" by the issuer to such an extent that the trustee will liquidate the remaining portion of that particular issue (or the trust itself). Thus, a regular monthly cash flow from a high quality, diversified portfolio is assured. **There are a few minor annoyances to contend with (monthly adjustments to your "cost basis" for example), but unit trusts are an easy way to get a large portion**

of the fixed income job done at yields that really are very competitive. Don't lose sight of this important fact: it is the yield that is important, only the yield. Generally, investors should plan on holding Unit Trusts to the very end, but profits should certainly be taken if the opportunity presents itself. Mark ups are not a factor as they are with individual bonds because the Trustee "fixes" a "net asset value" per unit each evening.

Closed End Funds are totally and completely different from the "open end" variety that you see listed in the newspapers. They are particularly useful: a) in developing a monthly income generating Municipal Bond Portfolio, and b) in developing a start up diversified equity portfolio of under $20,000. Closed End Funds are put together by Brokerage Firms in a manner similar to that used for Unit Trusts, but no Trustee is needed. Every Closed End Fund will specify a "type" of portfolio direction and it will be managed in line with this stated investment approach.

Here are some Equity Closed End Fund Names: "Blue Chip Value", "Duff & Phelps Utilities", and "Petroleum & Resources". Some Municipals: "Dreyfus Strategic", Muniyield New York Insured, and Nuveen Investment Quality. **Yes, there are Closed End Funds with Corporate and Government Bond portfolios, mixed portfolios, and so on, ad nauseum. But, in spite of their excellent yields, they don't seem to react "properly" in response to changing interest rates and Capital Gains opportunities are much rarer than they are with the equity and municipal closed ends.**

A specific sum of money is used to construct the fund and no new money is ever added directly by the issuing firm. A "net asset value" is determined and the initial issue of shares is sold to the public just like any other new equity issue would be, but without all the hype, publicity and speculation. These securities are just plain boring to Wall Street, which is not necessarily a bad thing. They bring stable income to a portfolio with an excellent prospect for capital gains!

Closed End Funds trade on the exchanges just like common stocks. The only way additional shares can be issued is through an offering to existing shareholders. Thus, you control the level to which your interest in the fund can be "diluted" by additional shares. Unlike an open-end fund, they can trade at their net asset value, above it, or below it, depending on the market demand/supply relationship. The S & P Stock guide makes it easy to determine if the market price is above or below the Fund's "net asset value".

REITs (Real Estate Investment Trusts) are Closed End Funds that operate just like the other varieties mentioned above. Historically, there have been some notable failures (Rockefeller Center Properties, for example), but they are generally excellent income generators with excellent Capital Gain producing volatility in response to perceived interest rate movements.

A "Shell Game" Called "Bond Swaps" (by: "Deep Pockets")

"The 'bond swap' is as old as Wall Street. What a scam this one is! People desperately try to avoid taxes, losing thousands as Wall Street Con Artists literally steal their money."

"A bond is an IOU from the issuer to an investor/lender; a contract to pay interest for a given period, at a stated rate, until a certain date in the future. Then, at maturity, the principle is returned to the lender. The contractual interest rate is fixed, but it is 'adjusted' by the market place by selling at a 'premium' or a 'discount' from face value. A bond's credit worthiness and the number of years until maturity are the primary forces influencing the rate. Agencies such as Moody's and Standard and Poor's do all of the research to determine the rating (credit worthiness, or risk level) of the bond."

"At tax time, the scam goes like this: Harry the broker knows that Mr. Jones hates to pay taxes, especially capital gains taxes on his stock portfolio. The bond market is a 'bid' and 'asked' market where trades are not done through an exchange, and the amount of 'mark up' is nowhere to be seen by the customer! Mr. Jones is encouraged to sell his bonds at a loss, and to buy 'SIMILAR' bonds to replace them. This way he will maintain the income stream yet still book a 'PAPER' loss on the bond sale."

"WRONG! The broker marks the Jones' bonds down four points or $40 per bond, keeping $12 per $1,000 for himself and surrendering the remainder to the brokerage firm. The Firm then marks the bond up four points and sells it to someone else, someone who could also be doing a 'swap'. The replacement bond that Mr. Jones buys has been similarly marked up four points. So, without knowing it, Mr. Jones is out of pocket a total of $80 per bond, or a $1,600 invisible commission on his $20,000 bond swap.

[Broker Harry has been provided with lists of potential 'bond swap' pairs, prepared for all 'Financial Advisors' by the firm's research department. Brokers are encouraged to push their clients into these transactions. Why don't the institutions produce lists of "swaps for profit"? They know their customers all too well, don't they!]

"To cover his tracks, the broker replaces the sold bond position with either a lower quality (riskier) bond, or one with a significantly extended maturity date. The total prices match up, and everyone is happy. Mr. Jones has no idea that he has been ripped off! He has generated a nice commission for his broker while exchanging his bonds for others of lesser total quality! This is something like the 'Three Card Monty' games that sucker tourists on the side walks of New York. Played lately?"

Your Government Really Does Love You: The IRA Bonanza

There has always been a great deal of speculation concerning the rationale for the Government's "gift" of the IRA (Individual Retirement Account) to the American taxpayer. Without even attempting to explain the history of the IRA, its rules, requirements, and fine points, **let's just focus on why it should be taken advantage of by absolutely everyone!**

Don't let the diminutive (but ever increasing) size of the annual contribution turn you off to the concept: **you are allowed to put away a sum of money every year to accumulate on a "tax-deferred basis"!** In a relatively short period of time, the total annual income generated by a well-constructed IRA portfolio will certainly exceed the annual contribution by a wide margin. Don't bother to waste a minute of time whining about the prospect of paying taxes upon withdrawal at retirement. The way Social Security has become a political football, there's an excellent chance that the tax rules will change in your favor anyway!

In the overall scheme of things, a $2,000 contribution boils down to less than forty dollars a week! I doubt that anyone who is reading these words can't afford that. At the moment, most individuals are entitled to the further benefit of deducting the contribution from their taxable income. That's the same as getting a "matching" contribution of up to $300 from Uncle Sam!

Your Accountant, in his infinite (lack of) wisdom, will advise you not to contribute if the contribution is not deductible. Big mistake! Why put the two grand some place else, where the income is immediately taxable, when you can do this instead? If its not deductible, good record keeping will assure you that it won't be deductible upon withdrawal.

Some very important "don'ts" need to be addressed.

At the top of the list is: **DON'T EVER SPECULATE WITH THIS MONEY.** Many people make the mistake of thinking of each annual contribution as an opportunity to make a big "hit" to get things rolling. This rarely works, and results in a portfolio filled with mistakes, generating no income and unlikely to ever fulfill it's potential. Speculating is always a waste of time and money.

Construct the IRA as you would any other portfolio, starting with an income generating Closed End Mutual Fund. Continue to add more of these funds until the portfolio "Working Capital" reaches $20,000. Then begin to move into individual equities. If this is the "only" portfolio, normal diversification rules apply. If it's part of a larger "Investment Plan", it becomes the perfect arena for trading high quality equities!

DON'T SPREAD THE MONEY AROUND. The larger the "pot" becomes, the easier it is to manage. Take every opportunity to "roll-over" other "qualified" money into one primary IRA portfolio. ("Qualified" is a term used to identify money that is not subject to the income tax, yet.)My IRA, for example, contains a roll-over, all my annual contributions, and my SEP IRA (a vehicle reserved for the self employed.) Some "newer" IRA types (ROTH, Education, and Healthcare) must be maintained separately. Refer back to the first "don't".

DON'T WAIT UNTIL APRIL 15TH TO MAKE LAST YEAR'S CONTRIBUTION. Why would you defer the moment when you start to earn tax-deferred income? Your Accountant again? To obtain the maximum benefit, try to get the money working on January 2nd, every year.

Finally, **DON'T THINK OF THE IRA ITSELF AS AN "INVESTMENT",** or as something you need to go out and "buy". It isn't an investment. It is a special "account" into which one places money that will be used to purchase various securities. Securities are investments. Financial Institutions, particularly

219

Banks, will try to "sell" you an IRA. It's just their way of fooling you into a CD, a Money Market Fund, or a Mutual Fund.

Zero Coupon Bonds, Why Not?

So what do you really "know" about "Zero Coupon" Bonds? A bond is a super formalized, legally enforceable, IOU. In effect, you are lending your money to someone and they are promising to pay you a specified rate of interest for a definite period of time. The principal is then paid out as well. Generally, they represent the "debt" of Corporations, Federal Agencies, and Municipalities. Of course there are variations, but remember the KISS principle and follow along.

Zero Coupon Bonds are "Investment Products" and are marketed by the Financial Community in all different shapes and sizes, and with a slew of fancy acronyms like "STRIPS", "TIGERS", etc. First the Financial Institution purchases large quantities of the Treasury, Municipal, or Corporate securities in the market place, staking their claim to the stream of interest payments that they will receive from the issuer. Then, they flip through an interest rate projection table, or use a simple computer program, to calculate how long it would take to double or triple the value of the securities at various rates that are somewhat below the rate they will "specify" in the product they sell to consumers.

The sales pitch sounds wonderful: "Our new series of ZAPPP Zero Coupon Education Assurance Bonds will triple in value in eighteen years, just in time for little Johnny's first college tuition payment." So in 18 years, your $15,000 investment has become $45,000. Very Impressive, until you flip through the present value tables and calculate the actual rate of return. For example, at 7%, a dollar triples in about 16 years, not 18. The higher the rate, the less time it takes. Additionally, Uncle Sam is not willing to wait eighteen years to collect his share of the interest so you will actually experience "Negative Cash Flow" during the holding period of the product.

None of us really knows where interest rates will be at any time in the future, but it's pretty easy to determine whether the present level is "historically" high or low. If you were really foolish, for example, you could rush out right now (August 2001) and "lock in" the lowest interest rates in years. Your Financial Advisor would just love to accommodate you! Sure you're locking in a low rate with fixed income vehicles that pay out the interest regularly. But, at least with them, you have the opportunity to re-allocate and to re-invest the income in the event rates move in either direction!

The plot thickens when you realize that the seller (broker, Financial Planner) has a bit of control over your actual rate of return. The lower the internal rate he gets you to accept, the higher his commission! **GOTCHA'!** By the way, when you buy bonds, you don't get the pleasure of seeing the amount of commission; there's no requirement to disclose them so you can bet that no one will!

Furthermore (Remember Rule One: There are no freebies on Wall Street.), the vendor of these ZAPPP Zeros is not at all concerned with your grandson Johnny's future. They are buying the bonds cheap (or underwriting them, for a really exciting "double dip"), putting a mark-up into their calculations, and giving you an interest rate well below what they are receiving. They are tripling their money years before you are. You don't think that they are taking advantage of your "love" for your family, do you? Not our trusted friends on Wall Street!

Talk about Greed, Manipulation, and Conflict of Interest! Let's throw in Malpractice, if there is such a thing for investment professionals. I've seen these things in portfolios of people who are at or near retirement and in need of income. And then there's the utter idiocy of Zero Coupon Municipal Bonds! People actually bought them, proving once again that Wall Street can sell absolutely anything to anyone. How do you think they did with those Zero Coupon foreign bonds?

Psst! If you purchased any "Zeros" in the past (when interest rates were higher) you have a chance to redeem yourself by selling them at a considerable profit. **Just Do It! But don't think for a minute that it was a wise decision to buy them two or three years ago! There are no freebies on Wall Street.**

The "Ransom Concept": Part Two (by: "Deep Pockets")

"**LOADED FUNDS: A DIRTY LITTLE SECRET.** Mutual funds marketed by the wire houses have a sales charge: front end (A shares), or back end (B & C shares). What does this mean to the investor? Which type should one buy? Which class is best for ME? Lets take a look!"

"'A' shares are seldom marketed by brokers. However they are very popular with insurance agents who are licensed (series 6) to sell Mutual Funds. Bottom line, investors are encouraged to pay a five percent sales charge up front. Even though you invest $10,000, only $9,500 gets into the fund. Where does the other $500.00 go? You guessed it right into the pocket of the salesman. Never do this! It is the most expensive way to buy a fund. Insurance salesmen on balance are in the business for only a very short time, so why not bag you big time right up front? By the way all of those fees we talked about with "NO LOAD" funds still apply! In normal markets, it will take almost two years just to cover all of these costs."

"'B' shares have no up front sales charges but tie you in for up to six years. Leave the fund group for a more attractive opportunity or out of frustration and you will get bagged up to six percent in year one, declining to one percent in year six. Brokers like this class because they still get the four percent commission and tie you into them for the next six years."

"'C' shares are the most efficient class in the loaded fund arena. You get tied in for only one year and there is no up front sales charge. Many brokers balk at this fund class because the commission is only one percent. Be careful! A few of the most greedy funds charge a one percent sales charge on 'C' shares."

"In all three classes the funds "SHARE" a portion of the performance with the firm that sold the fund in the first place (trailer commissions). This arrangement kicks back anywhere from ½ of 1 percent to 1 percent of your money to the brokerage firm for as long as you hold the fund. 'C' shares pay the largest trailer commission and are the top choice of all the wire houses. **CHECK THE PROSPECTUS!** **It's all buried there in a confusing format so that you won't read it!**"

Penny Stocks

Go to any decent library (Internet or neighborhood) and research First Jersey Securities. The only people who make money in "penny stocks", commodities, and "naked" options are the brokers who sell them. Just don't go there, I DON'T CARE HOW GOOD YOU THINK IT SOUNDS! I just spent more of your time than these ideas are worth.

Changing Strategies the Right Way

Years ago I had a wealthy client who enjoyed traveling to exotic places around the world attending investment seminars. Every few months, I would receive a call asking if I was familiar with the incredible success one guru or another had had with his new approach to investing. "I want you to go out to Dallas and speak with this guy so that you can redesign my portfolio to be more in step with this new strategy", Al would say. For years, I was able to poke enough holes in each new miracle cure to avoid what I knew was eventually going to happen.

One year, I was invited down to Florida to play golf with Al, his broker, and the latest investment Guru. I had just figured out that my travel expenses to manage Al's portfolio exceeded the income that his account generated, so I attempted to stop the "wheel spinning" for both us. I explained the finances of our relationship, and suggested that he come to New Jersey with his entourage to meet at my office. I didn't expect him to come and he didn't disappoint me. His new manager would only accept cash deposits…

*   *   *   *   *

Major change in a securities portfolio should be evolutionary, not revolutionary. Some of what you've learned here just might be interesting enough for you to consider altering your direction or asset allocation in any number of ways. **Make certain you are making an intellectual and not an emotional adjustment!** In other words, don't sell your present holdings out of "hate" for their current "performance". High Quality "technology" companies are just as beaten up right now as the No Quality variety. Be patient.

A shift in strategy must be given both "implementation" time, and "development" time. In most instances, there is plenty of time to get things coordinated, unless you are already in, or near, retirement. In that case, take two aspirin and call a portfolio doctor in the morning.

"Implementation" is the process of changing the asset allocation and/or the securities within the portfolio. "Development" is the management of the transitional (and changed) portfolio in accordance with the new rules and guidelines. Here are some "first step" ideas, assuming that you have established a reasonable plan:

: Organize all of your portfolios in one easy to access brokerage firm that provides detailed and comprehensible statements and annual summary information. Combine IRAs, SEP IRAs, etc., to minimize the number of separate pieces of paper you have to deal with. [I've taken over portfolios that contained nearly one hundred different Mutual Funds!] Simplify your life, and your record keeping!

: Cease all automatic reinvestment programs of any kind whatever, including the repurchase of additional mutual fund shares. All income should be directed to your primary personal or IRA brokerage account. Then you will be able to use the cash flow to implement change.

: Identify securities where reasonable profits can be realized. If some are securities you've owned since puberty, sell a portion each year unless the value is more than 50% of the total portfolio. Then reduce it to that level immediately. Determine the cost basis of all securities.

: Get ready to sell all securities that don't fit your Quality guidelines, at or near break-even. The ATH decision can be used later with the others.

: Sell those Zero Coupon Bonds (yes, even Municipals). If they are not in a profit position, they certainly should be.

: Inappropriate annuity holdings should be looked at closely. Treat any "Mutual Fund" element like you would any other fund, looking for a profitable exit point. You should be able to exit the variable portion without penalty. If not, use the annual "no penalty" withdrawal provision (Yes, every annuity has an annual "no penalty" withdrawal provision.) until the penalty falls into the 1% or 2% range, depending on the abundance or scarcity of new opportunities.

"Conflict of Interest", an Organization Chart

The Organization Chart that follows is based on that of a real live Wall Street Institution's "Securities" Subsidiary. That almost says it all, doesn't it? One Institution owning, influencing, and controlling another, multiplying the levels of conflict of interest! This is commonplace on Wall Street, where the "Hydra" reaches out to touch and to manipulate transactions in every possible way. It is common for Institutions to share "Directors who are familiar with the intricacies and traditions of the business". These Institutions have become the biggest seat of financial power in the world! They are in it together, the new and improved "untouchables".

The question becomes: "Is there any other entity big enough, strong enough, rich enough, or with enough independence and integrity to control the Institutions of Wall Street"? The answer is: No!

The "Wall Street" Institution
Organized Conflict of Interest

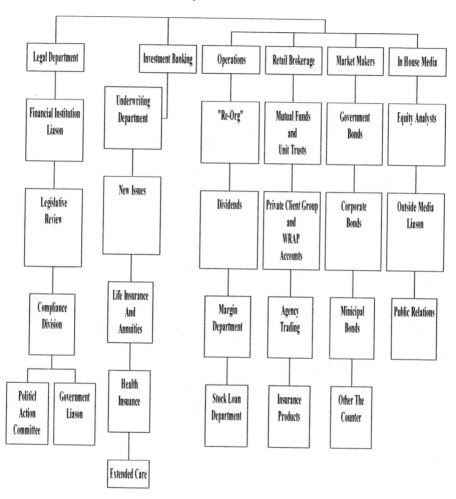

"Conflict of Interest", Part II (by "Deep Pockets")

"We talked earlier about the dubious reasons that analysts at brokerage firms recommend stocks. Remember, almost all buys and no sells? There is another group that we need to keep our eyes on, those who promote [and endorse] the products and services of others."

"Media talk show hosts plug the products and services of others when the sponsors of their shows pay to advertise on the programs. Doesn't much matter what the merits are, if your have the cash to buy advertising they will push the product. The third party endorsement is a powerful marketing tool. Some of these media hosts in recent years actually got into the act themselves, selling their own scams and duping people out of millions. One of the most infamous 'cons' involved investing in Real Estate."

"One talk show host that I knew personally pushed a broad array of investment products and services. Everything from annuities, CMO's, Investment Management, to Mutual Funds, Precious Metals, and Discount Brokerage were pushed weekly. Some of the endorsements conflicted. I couldn't understand the logic behind some of the ideas. One day I received a copy of the host's outside speaking engagement schedule and it all made sense. The host was speaking at seminars sponsored by providers of the very products and services touted on the show. Thousands of dollars were paid to the host to speak at the seminars, again endorsing the 'PRODUCT OF THE DAY'. **Read between the lines, or is it 'read between the lies'!"**

Five Minutes of Politics

Corporations are "legal persons" that the government can "steal" from with far more impunity than they can from you or I! The problem is that corporations can't vote to protect themselves like we normal persons can. Sure they can throw their money at some corrupt legislators, but in the final analysis, they are leaned on hard to be good citizens in their communities and to pay, and pay, and pay some more!

Beating up the corporations started early in the past century in response to many abuses of size and power, no doubt. But things have changed now, and corporations are "owned" by you and me to such an extent that we (the voters) should throw our weight around! My pet project is to repeal the corporate income tax, in a way that the windfall could only be used to increase employment and non-managerial compensation, and to pay dividends to shareholders, period. Corporate dividends would be taxable to the recipient, but all forms of Capital Gains taxes would be repealed.

Why such a drastic change? Because these laws were originally intended (as we are prone to do quite unconstitutionally in this country) to tax the rich and famous, not the poor guy that puts a few bucks in his IRA every year. Times have changed. We are the corporations! Corporate profits would increase because huge sums would no longer be wasted on frivolous expenses.

Teams of Accountants are employed by corporations of all sizes to make sure that money is spent in the most "tax-beneficial" manner! Think of the waste involved. A whole new class of confusing, debenture-type, Preferred Stocks were just created for this reason alone. If you own a small corporation, a lot of your time has to be spent on this non-productive exercise.

There would be more jobs and more spending money for everyone. The impact on Federal Tax revenues would be minimal because you and I would spend more, and that would create even more jobs, etc.

Want a good tax, just for the rich? 10% of any executive compensation package over $3 million per year (including stock options and the value of any other perks received from the corporation) goes directly into the Social Security Trust Fund. Another 10% goes directly into the shareholder dividend payment. Finally, 5% goes into a "new" Federal Health Care Expense reimbursement program. I can't think of any good reason why these overpaid "executives" should be paid even half as much as a proven Professional Athlete! At least the athletes provide great entertainment to everyone, and are (for the most part) a good example for the "youth of America". They tend to "give back" more anyway! Sure, they could be subject to the same tax above, let's say, $5 million per year.

Own any UPS? How do you feel about the company President or CEO building a 45,000 square foot home? Even if he's not doing it with any company money (doubtful), he just has to be overpaid! This is your money! **Management should be rewarded for its accomplishments, but so should the owners...YOU!**

Did you read about that record $18,000,000 home purchase in New Jersey recently? Wouldn't you like to know what that one is costing the shareholders!

<u>One Security and Exchange Commission Requirement (of the many that were intended to help you, the investor) really needs to be "rethunk"!</u> How many billions of dollars do you think corporations are required to waste each year sending Quarterly and Annual Reports, and Proxy materials to shareholders? I must throw away a thousand pounds of beautiful glossies each year, unopened, unread and unwanted. I get the stuff for companies I've sold off years ago! Why not one simple postcard, just once, asking a shareholder if any of this is wanted? Or, better yet a simple note on those required confirmation notices that would point to a "Wall Street" website where a person could go to "reach out and touch someone" to either get, or get rid of, this type of information. The data is available electronically to anyone who wants it.

<u>Finally, there's the complex issue of the Wall Street Institutional "Hydra" and its many interlocking interests that are so obviously in conflict.</u> It would take an awful lot to stop the bleeding completely, but something really needs to be done. Caveats, warnings, and fine print should never be a blurb of speed speech at the end of a commercial message and you shouldn't have to be a lawyer to understand a prospectus document. Syndicates shouldn't be able to retail what they underwrite, and the true compensation of all parties must be disclosed to securities purchasers in all transactions. The broker compensation system needs a total overhaul if it can ever be expected not to encourage fraud, and this is really just the tip of the iceberg.

A Herculean task indeed, but an important one! Then, **if we can get something accomplished in this area, we can roll up our sleeves and go after the Federal Bureaucracy**, and the ridiculous "pork-barrel" spending that gets INTO OUR EXPENDITURE BUDGET! There's enough waste there to give us all a zero tax rate for a few years!

Try something like this:

To The Honorable: (Insert your State Senator's name), State of: (Insert)

Something has to be done to stop Wall Street from misrepresenting its products, services, and compensation methods to the public. We demand an investigation of the interrelationships between the Major Institutions, their directors, and the Media that speaks for them."

It's time for meaningful, non-partisan change in other areas as well:

1. **Repeal the corporate income tax, in a way that the windfall could only be used to increase employment and non-managerial wages, and to pay dividends to shareholders, period. Corporate dividends would be taxable to the recipient, but all forms of Capital Gains taxes would be repealed.** Here's a good "sweetener", just for the rich? 10% of any executive compensation package over $5 million per year (including stock options) goes directly into the Social Security Trust Fund.

231

2. **[Be creative; insert your idea here.]**

3. **Revamp corporate reporting requirements to shareholders, recognizing our movement into the computer age!** How many billions of dollars are corporations required to waste each year sending Quarterly Reports, Annual Reports, and Proxy materials to shareholders? Most are thrown away, unopened, unread and unwanted. Why not one simple postcard, just once, asking a shareholder if any of this is wanted? Or, better yet a simple note on those required confirmation notices that would point to a "Wall Street" website where a person could go to "reach out and touch someone" to get this type of information.

4. **[Anything else bothering you? Remember, it's your money!** How about those prospectus documents that are impossible to read, or those Wall Street Analysts that lead you over a major speculative cliff every few years?]

We need better numbers to rely on, more responsible reporting that we can trust and an end to the manipulation and greed promotion that emanates daily from Wall Street. We demand change; we demand it now! We can handle the truth!

Yours Respectfully,

*   *   *   *

Current Events: A Partial Case Study

We've talked about Asset Allocation, Diversification, Stock Trading, and Objective Based Performance Analysis. One would reasonably expect that, after nearly seven years of experience with a program of the type explained in detail above, a person would have some idea of what the program was all about, and what should be expected from it. Well maybe!

Lives do change, and people bring new friends and relatives into their "inner circle" to help them with decisions that affect their finances. Here's a look at a developing situation, that I hope will help each of you better understand why it is so important for you to get every one "up to speed" with regard to your plan.

Late in 1994, I began to manage a portfolio for an unemployed late-30's widow, with five young children. The portfolio "Market Value" at inception was $480,000. A Stock Broker relative had constructed the portfolio, and the 30% that was in securities was predominately in "Proprietary Products" that were liquidated profitably over a period of a few years. The client would not be able to work, and it was estimated that $1,600 per month would be withdrawn for expenses. The "job" was to make the monthly income available and to grow the portfolio to the extent possible. The amount to be withdrawn was less than half of what I expected the portfolio to generate.

A 35% Equity, 65% Fixed Income, Asset Allocation was agreed upon, with the Fixed Income portion invested fairly equally in: Tax Free Bonds, Miscellaneous Government Securities, Treasury Bills, Corporate Bonds, and Preferred Stocks. Enough Cash to make a minimum of five monthly withdrawals was purposely held aside. The plan had been worked out between the client, a non-broker relative, and myself.

The plan has worked extremely (even incredibly) well, in spite of the fact that the average monthly withdrawal was increased in the second month, never to be heard about again! The average monthly withdrawal to date has been $4,150, but it would have been almost exactly $3,000 without a $100,000 loan that was made to another relative three years ago! In total, the client spent roughly $383,000 in just under seven years. What's left?

As of July 31st, the client still had Working Capital of $386,000! This translates into a positive monthly cash flow of more than $3,100 net of all expenses ever! Nearly 8% positive cash flow over that seven-year period with no speculations, and less than 40% invested in equities. The July 31st Market Value was at an "All Time High" Profit Level ($343,000), and it had achieved similar new "highs' seven of the last nine months. Market Value for the year 2001 was up over 7%.

Most people would be "dancin' in the streets", pointing an "I told you so" finger at everyone they know. We're talking right now, in the midst of what "Wall Street" has declared to be the worst year since The Flood! ***Enter the new relative/advisor.*** "I've looked at all the reports, and I can't understand: a) why you haven't shown the year to year Market Value figures since inception, and b) why you haven't sold the securities that are worth less now than when you bought them? **One of us is clueless!**

Should I send him a "free" copy of the book?

Too Frequently Asked Questions

Financial Professionals are asked too many questions because so little is "known" about the investment process by so many. Ironically, it's easier to explain things to people who actually appreciate how little they do know, than it is to "un-teach" someone who is convinced that they "know about investing". The size of the wallet, the price of the car, the expanse of the castle, and the tonnage of the yacht "meaneth naught"! **As most of you now appreciate, the more you appreciate how little you actually can "know", the more you are likely to be successful at investing!**

Here are a few questions that have not yet been dealt with and that deserve a few minutes of your time.

Is Socially Conscious Investing Productive?

If you were a billionaire, and an associate asked you to back him in a plan to do some strip mining near Yellowstone Park, withholding your capital could be beneficial to the environment. But small investors can have little, if any, impact by avoiding a Philip Morris, an IBM, or a Phelps Dodge in their investment portfolios. When you buy a stock, the money goes to the previous owner (theoretically), never to the company whose actions or politics you disagree with.

Companies that are that big and influential themselves have such a huge "float" (shares outstanding) that your efforts, and those of the various boutique Mutual Funds (Remember that I told you that Wall Street will sell you anything you ask for?) that are available to you, just aren't going to accomplish anything. **The best way to effect social change of any kind is with your vote!**

The same is true of proxy materials that you receive. Don't waste your time.

Does Technical Analysis Work, and For Whom?

It really depends on what you are trying to accomplish. This type of analysis is probably useful to figure out what might have happened in the past but it's too often given mystical gospel-like qualities that are purely Wall Street salesmanship. The future is totally unpredictable no matter how authoritative the data may appear to be.

Technical Analysis may, perhaps, provide insights and explanations sometimes. Predictions, NOT!

How Do You Feel About "Precious Metals"?

Much of my adolescence was spent wondering why some members of my family became so interested in collecting stamps and coins. But they weren't in it as "an investment" or as a "hedge against inflation" or anything else. They appreciated the beauty, the history, and the art. There was also a "competitive" thing to amassing a "best in show" caliber collection. It was a hobby/business, since some "trading" certainly did take place. In fact, I've seen a pretty lucrative financing business develop as a method of adding to one's collections.

If it's entertainment, fine. As a portfolio holding in bullion, certificates, coins, futures and/or any other machination of any kind, just forget about it. It meets absolutely Zero of the "Big Three" investment principles. Read the prospectus. This is one instance where your mattress is significantly less risky.

The only workable "hedge" against inflation is a portfolio managed in a way that increases your annual income.

Why Haven't You Discussed the "Core Portfolio"?

It seems to me that the concept of the "Core" Portfolio was developed by the Financial Community when it became fairly obvious that the archaic "Buy and Hold" strategy had outlived it's usefulness. It's pretty much the same thing, except that it names specific stocks that you absolutely must own if you expect to keep up with inflation, the market, the Joneses. Pick a reason.

It seems to me that it is really the result of an analysis of which stocks are the most popular at the moment, translated into a frontal attack on the wallets of investors who are urged to "hold on to these 'sure fire' mega performers" (at least until we suggest that you replace them with some other new hot number). It accomplishes two important things, possibly three: a) It creates a broader market frenzy for the "core" issues, and a resultant increase in price, just because, b) It encourages a high priced purchase transaction, and possibly a sale or two to provide the cash, and c) It just sounds so knowledgeable. So much more so than the old "buy a diversified group of solid blue chips, re-invest the dividends, and grow with the pace of the economy"!

Neither approach is recommended, for reasons that I feel are powerfully summed up in "The Investor's Creed", a fitting and proper way to say "DONE"!

"THE INVESTOR'S CREED"

"My intention is to be fully invested in accordance with my planned equity/fixed income asset allocation. On the other hand, every security I own is for sale, and every security I own generates some form of cash flow that cannot be reinvested immediately. I am happy when my cash position is nearly 0% because all of my money is then working as hard as it possibly can to meet my objectives. But, I am ecstatic when my cash position approaches 100% because that means I've sold everything at a profit, and that I am in a position to take advantage of any new investment opportunities (that fit my guidelines) as soon as I become aware of them."

It's Time to Make The Donuts

It's in your hands now. You have the training, the concepts, and the tools to get started in a whole new form of investing. I have no doubt that this method will work for you, if you apply the patience and discipline that are needed for it to happen! I sincerely hope that you succeed.

If you want to "jump start" your new investment program, I will be happy to provide a $14.95 "Starter Kit" that includes:

1. A combined (and current) Selection Universe and Stock Worksheet, Including the current day's "buy" list.

2. A Daily Order Log Format, and

3. Updated "Statistics that Matter".

Here's to your investment success!

"GO IN PEACE AND PROSPER"

ABOUT THE AUTHOR

Steven R. Selengut, MBA, RIA, has been in the Investment Management Business for twenty-two years through his New Jersey based Investment Management firm, Sanco Services, Inc., an International company he owns and manages. His career as an investor started in 1970, at age twenty-five, when he was given the responsibility to manage a $60,000 portfolio that had been held in trust for him for many years. He developed an Asset Allocation Model then (decades before the concept became popular) that he still uses today, and a trading approach to investing that made him wealthy early in life.

During his twelve-year career in the Financial Services Industry, and through conversations with several professional portfolio managers with hundreds of millions of dollars under their control, Mr. Selengut obtained an appreciation of the complete Wall Street (political, social, and economic) environment. Using this understanding of the "playing field" Mr. Selengut was able to retire before his 34th birthday to pursue a new career as a private investment manager. When he left his full time management position in the Pension Investment Department of a major life insurance company, he had no clients, just an idea and some new investment concepts! He was able to start fresh, build a new home, and keep both children in private schools strictly on the income produced by his investment portfolio!

Building an investment management business on your own, without major corporate sponsorship, or several huge clients to pay the freight, was no easy undertaking. The concept of individually managed, totally unique, investment portfolios with an annual fee, and commissions to an uninterested third party was totally new in 1979! Mr. Selengut developed a loyal following of dedicated clients, many of whom have been with him for most of his career! (Two clients retained the brand new Sanco Services, Inc. in 1979. Both remain Sanco clients today!)

* * *

The Wall Street Transcript has interviewed Mr. Selengut several times in recent years. More information about his Investment Management style and business can be found at www.sancoservices.com or by calling 1-800-245-0494.